IMAGES
of America

SCREVEN AND JENKINS COUNTIES

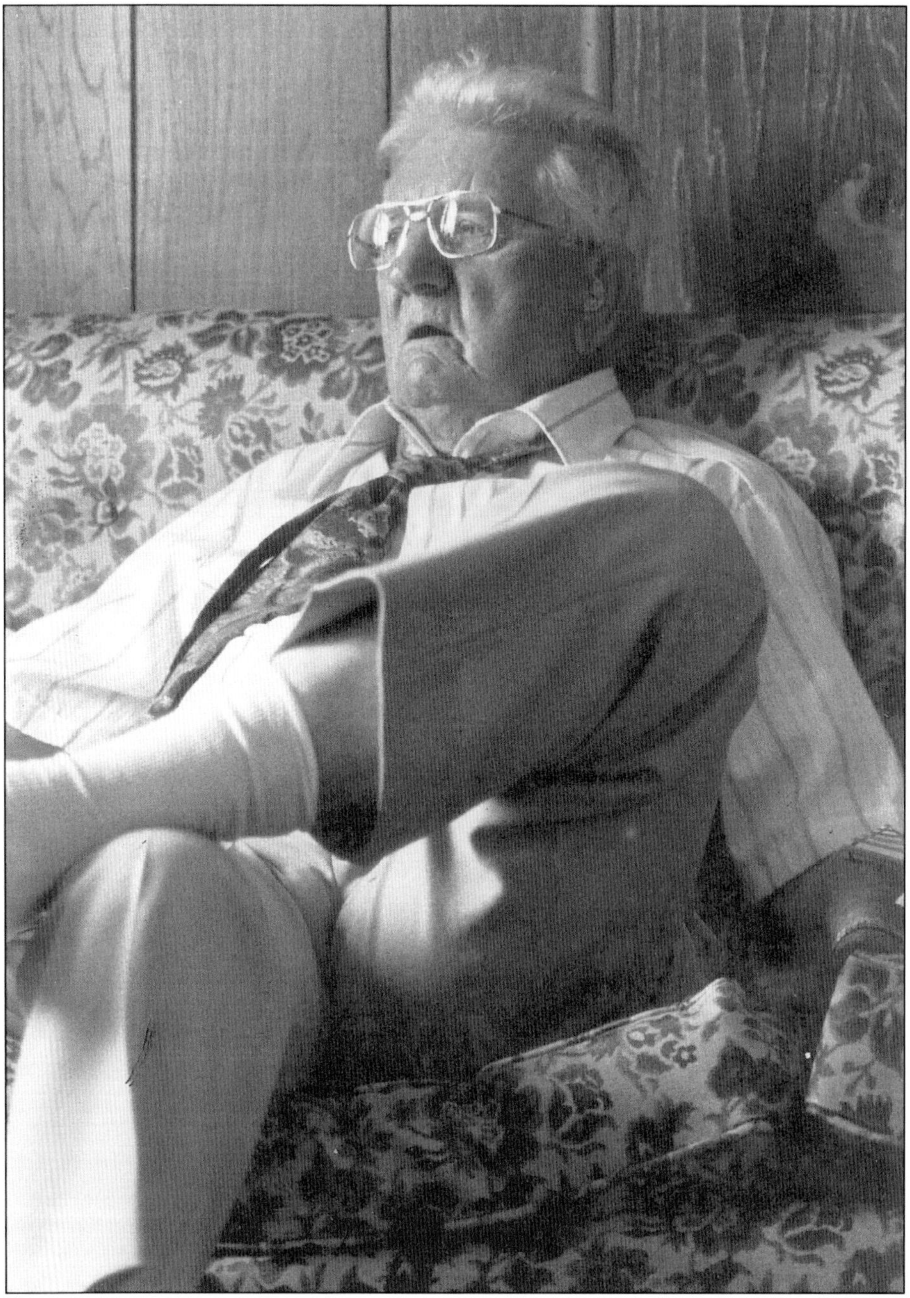

This history is dedicated to the memory of J. Brantley Lee, the author's grandfather and lifelong resident of Rocky Ford—Screven County's first seat of government. J. Brantley Lee enjoyed an 87-year love affair with his native county and made certain to pass on her story to his family, his friends, and anybody else who would listen. Thank you for the stories, dear man. Without the prompting you began when I was in the cradle, I never would have learned the importance of things past.

IMAGES
of America

SCREVEN AND JENKINS COUNTIES

Angela Lee-Ford

ARCADIA
PUBLISHING

ISBN 978-0-7385-0300-4

Published by Arcadia Publishing
Charleston, South Carolina

Printed in the United States of America

Library of Congress Catalog Card Number: Applied For

For all general information contact Arcadia Publishing at:
Telephone 843-853-2070
Fax 843-853-0044
E-mail sales@arcadiapublishing.com
For customer service and orders:
Toll-Free 1-888-313-2665

Visit us on the Internet at www.arcadiapublishing.com

Contents

ACKNOWLEDGMENTS

Many people contributed to this history of Screven and Jenkins counties: storytellers who shared their tales with me over the years, historical enthusiasts who helped me to locate pictures and other documents, and numerous "just plain folks" who encouraged me to complete the task. Thank you to all. I hope you enjoy the fruits of OUR labor.

My eternal gratitude goes to Screven County's historian at large, the late Dixon Hollingsworth. Without his volumes of research and writing on Screven County's early years, this author would still be working diligently to unearth many of the historical facts contained herein.

Special thanks go to Sandra Lively and the staff at the Screven/Jenkins County Regional Library in Sylvania. Their excellent local history collection proved invaluable to me as I spent hour after hour pouring over page after page. Some excellent photographs in that collection rounded out my research quite nicely.

Bob Hammond at the Burke County Museum lent a most appreciated helpful hand. My editors, Jim Dunn and Katie White, were patient and interested cheerleaders throughout.

Perhaps the most help has come from my family. Without their moral support and genuine interest, the project may have never been completed. My parents, Weyman and Emily Lee, both Screven County natives, kept me on track and pointed me in the right direction. My aunts, Frances Lee Hankinson and Tina Bazemore Callaway, have provided the impetus I needed to keep on keeping on in this quest to set down some facts about our native Screven.

And last but certainly not least, I must say thank you to my husband, Tim Ford, who has encouraged me at every step and spent many an evening enjoying the pleasure of his own company while his wife and helpmate waded through the past.

Introduction

The white man first came to the Screven/Jenkins County area some time in the 1700s. Indeed, until about 1750, only a few intrepid traders dared appear in the area, then Yuchi Land, where American Indians rambled freely throughout the wilderness between the Savannah and Ogeechee rivers and both sides of Brier Creek.

Georgia's first white residents lived in Savannah County—that and Frederica were Georgia's two colonial subdivisions. The land still legally belonged to the Yuchis, but most of the American Indians had moved to western Georgia, leaving behind hundreds of square miles of vacant land that the white man believed was his to conquer.

The white man's claim was strengthened in 1758 when Georgia was divided into eight parishes, and Church of England religious rites were established. The area known as Screven County was divided between two parishes, St. Matthew's (now Effingham County) and St. George's (today's Burke County). The boundary between the two parishes ran "up the Savannah River to Beaver Dam and southwest to the mouth of Horse Creek on the Great Ogeechee River."

The area became the white man's land in 1763, when the Indians ceded the land between the Savannah and Ogeechee rivers. Some 45 years later, December 14, 1793, marked the creation of Screven County as it is today. The Georgia legislature ordered that the new county should include land that was then a part of the lower portion of Burke County and the upper part of Effingham.

In the early days, probably no more than a handful of settlers came to Screven. In fact, Georgia's 1775 population was scanty too, totaling 2,380 white inhabitants and 1,066 African Americans.

Although the new county apparently failed to draw a colony or group of people like the Salzburgers in Effingham or the Scotch-Irish at Queensboro in Burke, a respectable number of settlers did come, mainly from South Carolina, North Carolina, Virginia, and Pennsylvania. A small German settlement sprang up in 1752. Dr. Johann Christoph Bornemann, the city of Gottingen's surgeon and an associate at the University of Gottingen, immigrated to Georgia to spend the rest of his life analyzing botanical studies in the New World.

Bornemann and his family settled on the banks of the Savannah River and called their American home New Goettingen (It was located just north of today's Burton's Ferry Bridge on U.S. Highway 301.). The Bornemann family included the doctor's wife, Carolina Magdalena Bornemann; the couple's infant son, Benjamin Wilhelm Bornemann; Mrs. Bornemann's parents, Johann Heinrich Greve and Louisa Margaretha Greve; and a servant girl. They arrived with several wagon-loads of belongings, including scientific instruments and a large library.

Eventually, other German settlers joined the Bornemanns in the New Goettingen area, but the settlement failed to survive as a village or community. It was, however, the birthplace of Screven County's first white child. Henrietta Bornemann was born January 12, 1755.

Two years later, in 1757, Mr. Bornemann died, and his wife married a neighbor, a fellow German named John Caspar Greiner. Their descendants can be found in Screven County today, spelling the surname as Griner.

Eventually, new settlers with English and Scotch-Irish names began arriving in the area. Most came from the Carolinas and Virginia, and some came from Maryland and Pennsylvania. They were third-generation Americans, who slowly populated the bottomlands along the Savannah River, Brier Creek, and the Ogeechee River, avoiding Screven's sandy country, which they called the "Pine Barrens." Among these early settlers were Nathaniel Miller, John Conyers, Caleb Howell, John Green, and Thomas Burton. William Clifton of Clifton's Ferry, near today's Scarboro, was a Georgia royal government officer in the late 1700s.

These and other Screven Countians were quick to answer the call when the American Revolution brought war clouds to the area. At Georgia's First Secession Convention, held July 4, 1775, at Tondee's Tavern in Savannah, Phillip Howell represented Screven. Caleb Howell, first lieutenant, signed a battalion of troops agreement to assist the Continental Army.

Screven Countians saw war firsthand on March 3, 1779, when British regulars and American forces locked horns in the Brier Creek Swamp, near its confluence with the Savannah River. Overall a disgraceful defeat for American forces, the Battle of Brier Creek spurred gallantry among left-wing Continentals and Georgians commanded by General Elbert and Colonel McIntosh. Those troops fought so vigorously that British reserves were summoned. Elbert fought until no road for retreat remained, then surrendered himself and the last of his men.

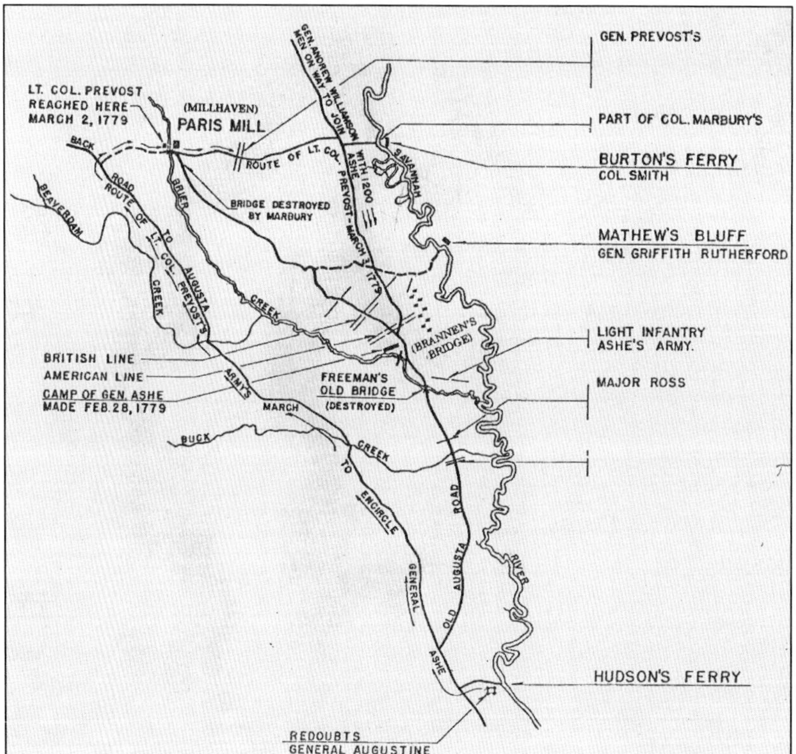

British regulars and American forces locked horns in Screven County's Brier Creek swamp on March 3, 1779.

The end of the Revolution saw numerous settlers arrive in the land that would become known as Screven County. More free land became available under a 1784 Georgia land law, and this included property in Burke and Effingham Counties.

So by the time President George Washington visited Screven in 1791, the population had increased considerably. Fair roads had been built. Freight traveled regularly on the Savannah and Ogeechee Rivers. Two stages ran through the area. One connected Savannah and Augusta, and the other followed the Ogeechee River and connected Savannah with the highly developed middle-Georgia area.

Washington arrived in the Screven area on May 16th, stopping for lunch at Garnett's Inn (located where the road to Hudson's Ferry crossed the stage road). He spent the night at Pearce's Inn, where his hosts for supper were Mr. and Mrs. Joshua Pearce. The next morning, May 17th, he stopped for breakfast at Skinner's house before continuing his journey into Burke County.

Two years later, in December of 1793, the Screven area became a Georgia county in its own right. Originally spelled Scriven County, it was named for General James Screven, a Revolutionary fighter killed at Midway.

Among the new county's active leaders were Benjamin Lanier, Lewis Lanier, Solomon Gross, Mund Gross, Caleb Howell, Phillip Howell, Daniel Howell, Stephens Mills, James H. Rutherford, Job Herrington, James Caswell, Isaac Perry, Seaborn Goodall, Clement Lanier, Lemuel Lanier, Robert Stafford, James Oliver, William Coursey,

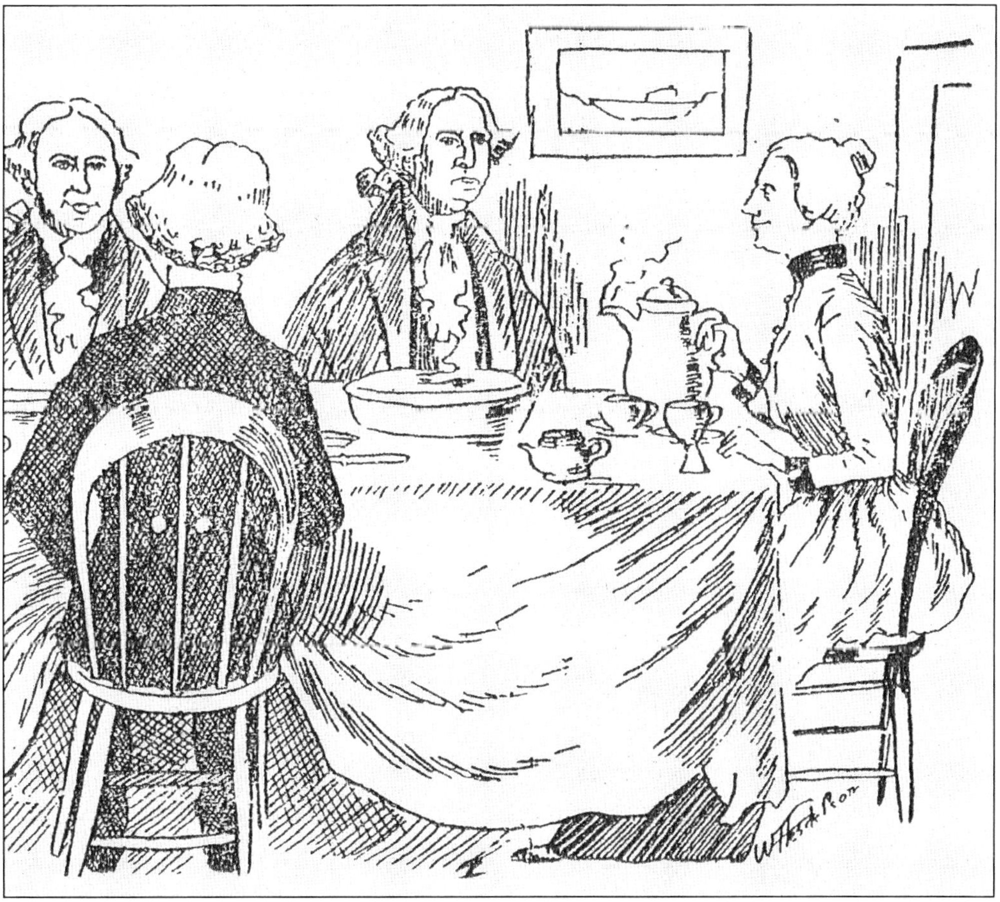

President George Washington enjoyed supper in Screven County in 1791 as the guest of Mr. and Mrs. Joshua Pearce.

William Skinner, P.R. Smith, Wheeler Gresham, William Blair, Daniel Bonnell, Enoch Godfrey, and James F. Lovett.

Three commissioners—Paul Bevil, William Skinner, and Jon Lott Sr.—were charged with locating the most central, convenient place in the county for courts and elections. The act also provided that "until the courthouse shall be erected the elections and courts for said county shall be held at the house of Benjamin Lanier."

So the first county seat of Screven was located at Rocky Ford, near Mile Branch, where Lanier lived. Benjamin Lanier, Lemuel Lanier, Valentine Hollingsworth, Francis Jones, Thomas Mills, Anthony Bonnell, Abraham Mincey, Robert Dickson, and Michael Dickson were among several North Carolinians who received grants in the Rocky Ford area between 1765 and 1770.

The new county was organized immediately. In an election on January 20, 1794, William Coursey was named sheriff; Thomas Hylton, clerk of the superior court; Robert Williams, clerk of the inferior court; Robert Stafford, surveyor; Lemuel Lanier, register of probate; and William Brigar, coroner.

No public buildings were constructed, and no schools were established. No civic improvements were implemented, and no taxes were collected. Citizens saw no need for taxes, other than to maintain a militia to protect the people from American Indian tribes or roaming bands of outlaws. The county's busiest officials were the clerk of superior court and the county surveyor, as unclaimed state lands were being settled rapidly.

The Benjamin Lanier home was the scene for Screven County's courts and elections until 1797, when county officials finally took formal action to locate the county seat and erect public buildings there. Legislation set duties for another set of commissioners and provided that "the seat of the public buildings in the county of Scriven, so far as relates to the courthouse and jail, shall be in the center of said county, or such other place as may be adjudged most convenient for the citizens thereof by James Rutherford, Francis Jones, Martin Martin, Anthony Bonnell, Sr., and Stephen Pearce, or a majority of them." The site for the courthouse and jail was to include no less than 5 acres and no more than 50.

And that is how the groundwork was laid for two prospering counties that would play vital roles in the development of Georgia. In the years to follow, residents of Jenkins and Screven Counties continued to build upon that solid foundation to establish a community that would stand tall through the centuries.

Their story is an interesting one filled with both joy and sadness, along with a lot of hard work. It is a story that we will share in the pages that follow. It begins with the curse, continues with the lonesome song of a train whistle, and leads to the 21st century. In between, we will find quite a story . . .

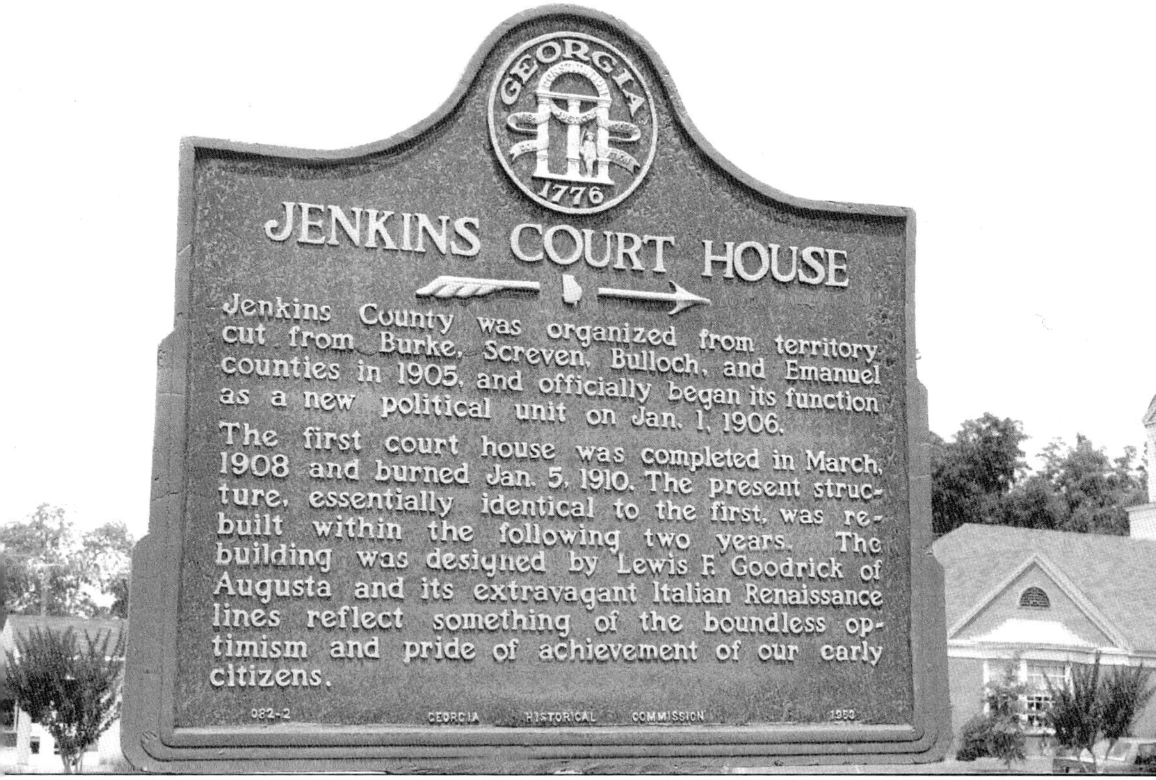
GEORGIA
1776
JENKINS COURT HOUSE
Jenkins County was organized from territory cut from Burke, Screven, Bulloch, and Emanuel counties in 1905, and officially began its function as a new political unit on Jan. 1, 1906.
The first court house was completed in March, 1908 and burned Jan. 5, 1910. The present structure, essentially identical to the first, was rebuilt within the following two years. The building was designed by Lewis F. Goodrick of Augusta and its extravagant Italian Renaissance lines reflect something of the boundless optimism and pride of achievement of our early citizens.
082-2
GEORGIA HISTORICAL COMMISSION

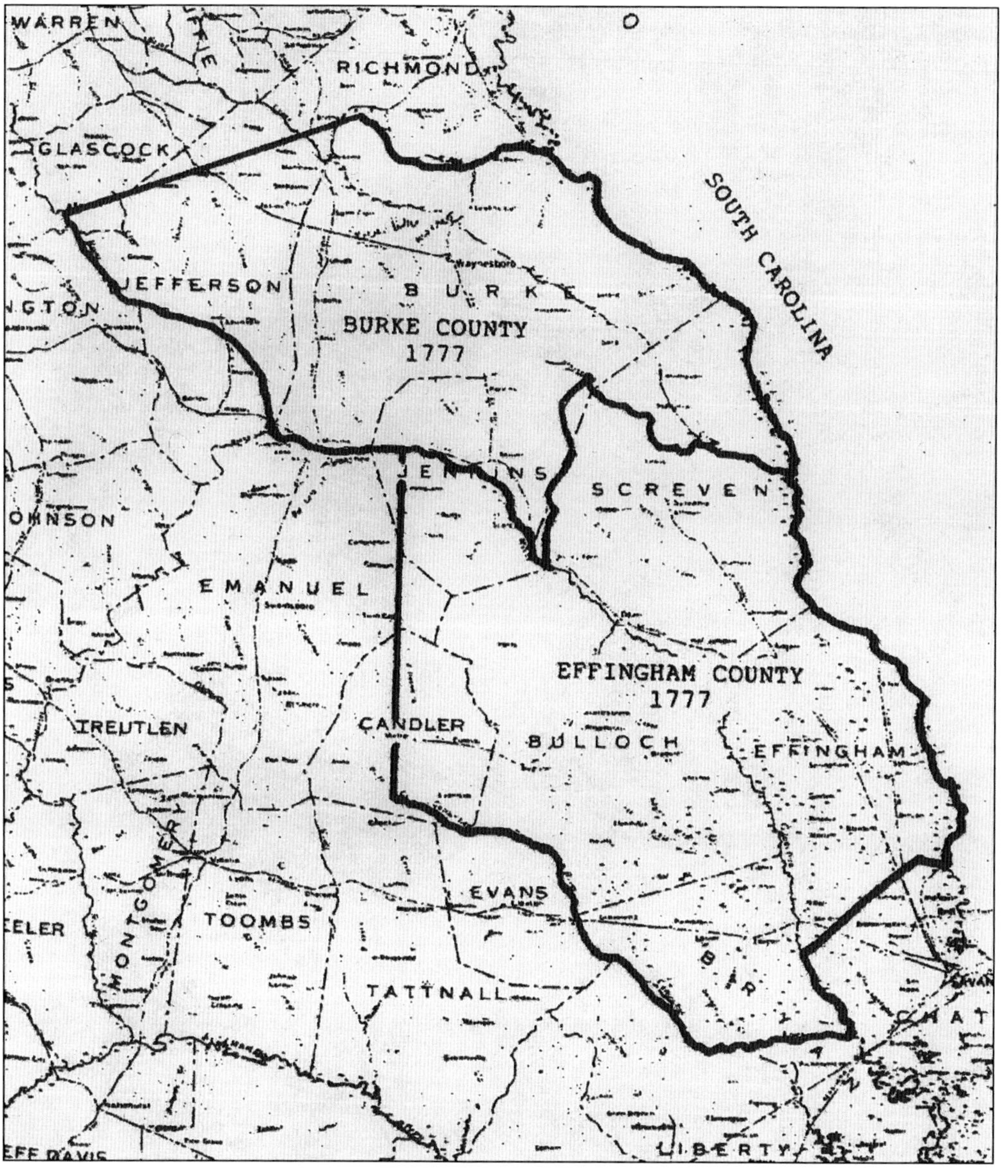
WARREN
RICHMOND
GLASCOCK
SOUTH CAROLINA
JEFFERSON
BURKE
BURKE COUNTY
1777
JENKINS
SCREVEN
JOHNSON
EMANUEL
EFFINGHAM COUNTY
1777
TREUTLEN
CANDLER
BULLOCH
EFFINGHAM
MONTGOMERY
EVANS
TOOMBS
TATTNALL
LIBERTY

One

A Legendary People

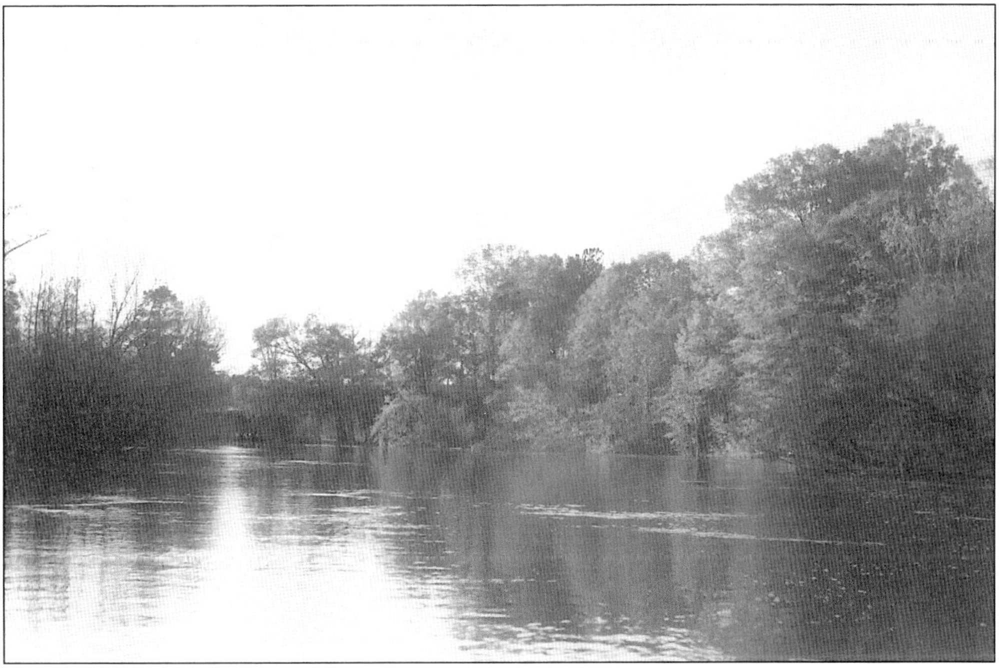

Screven County's story began along the banks of the Ogeechee River, where the area's earliest settlers carved homesteads from the wilderness. Benjamin Lanier, one of those early settlers who made his home near Mile Branch in what is now Rocky Ford, became a leading force in the new county's establishment. And so, when Screven County was officially formed in 1793, the legislation designated that Lanier's house would be the county seat until a permanent, more central location for the courthouse and other public buildings could be found. And so it was until Jacksonborough was designated the county seat in 1797.

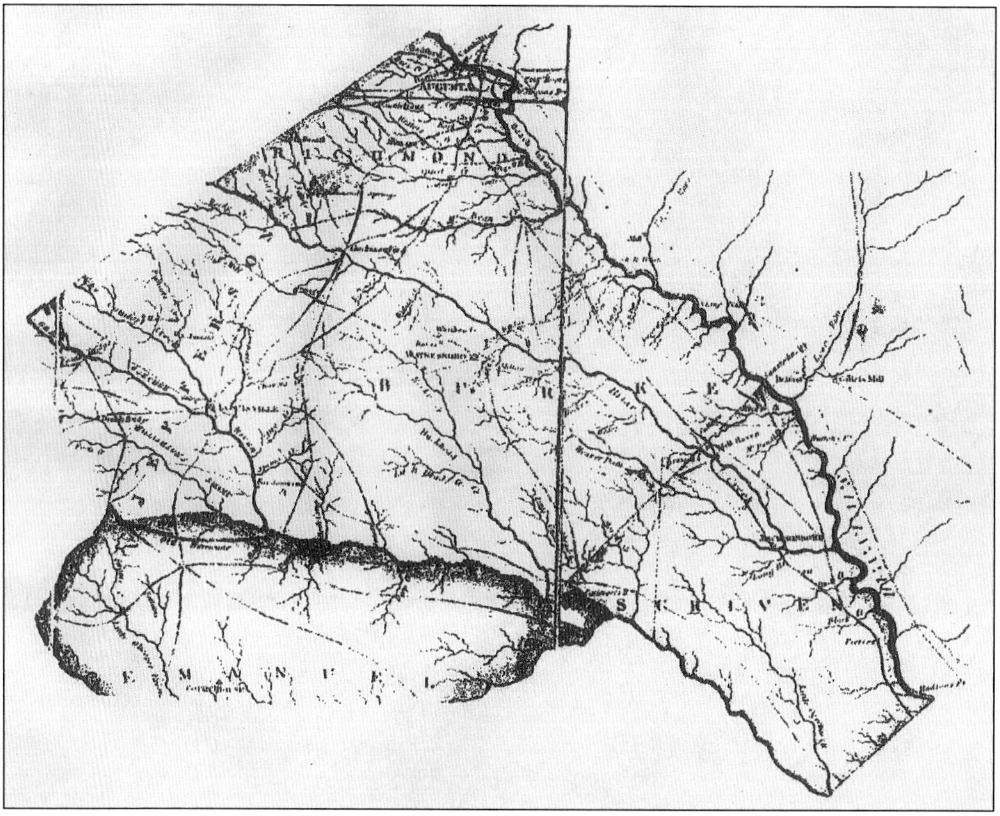

Commissioners officially designated the county seat on February 1, 1797. The location was Jacksonborough, a site almost, but not quite, in the center of the county. Nevertheless, a courthouse and jail were built on the 50-acre plat on Beaver Dam Creek, property conveyed by Solomon Gross. The Dell-Goodall House, shown on page 18, was built in 1815 and was one of the first houses to go up in the new town, which was named for Revolutionary War general and Georgia governor James Jackson.

The town was subdivided into lots 105-feet wide and 460-feet deep, which were sold to settlers who built crude houses, due to the fact that manufactured lumber was scarce. Several town lots were reserved for special purposes, such as public buildings, churches, and schools. Jacksonborough was incorporated on December 29, 1823. Shortly thereafter, townspeople organized a Masonic lodge, Farmers Lodge No. 33 of Jacksonborough, and Jacksonborough Methodist Episcopal Church was established. In 1830 and 1831, Screven citizens staged a lottery to raise funds for Screven County Academy. The school reportedly was located at Bascom, a few miles from the county seat.

This was a town with a rowdy reputation. Nineteenth-century publications even called it "a town of bad character." One chronicler reported that after a night of brawling among the town's ruffians, children frequently collected eyeballs in teacups.

Early county records were kept in leather-bound books. A cover for an 1821 record book still exists and is shown above. Note Seaborn Goodall's name, neatly inscribed.

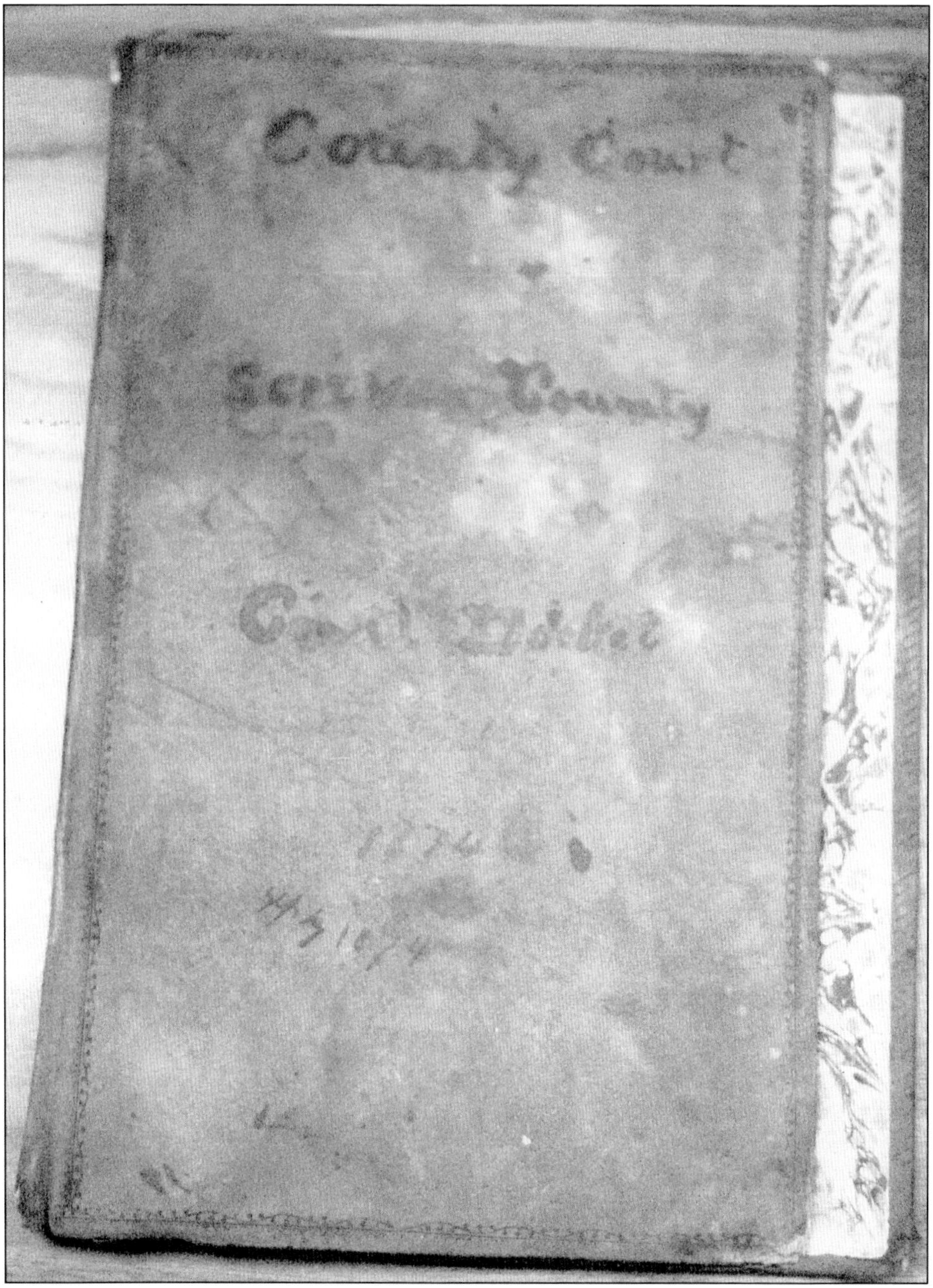

On the reverse side of the early 19th-century record book is another inscription for the year 1874. Apparently, early Screven Countians recycled materials regularly.

In 1832, county officials allowed a contract for the construction of a new courthouse. Charles W. Cluskey prepared the plans. Daniel Nelson built the structure at a cost of $3,200. A virgin pine building with a brick superstructure, the Screven County Courthouse was styled after the Burke County Courthouse in Waynesborough. By the early 1800s, Screven County's population had grown, but it still totaled little more than 1,500. Jacksonborough was the only village of note.

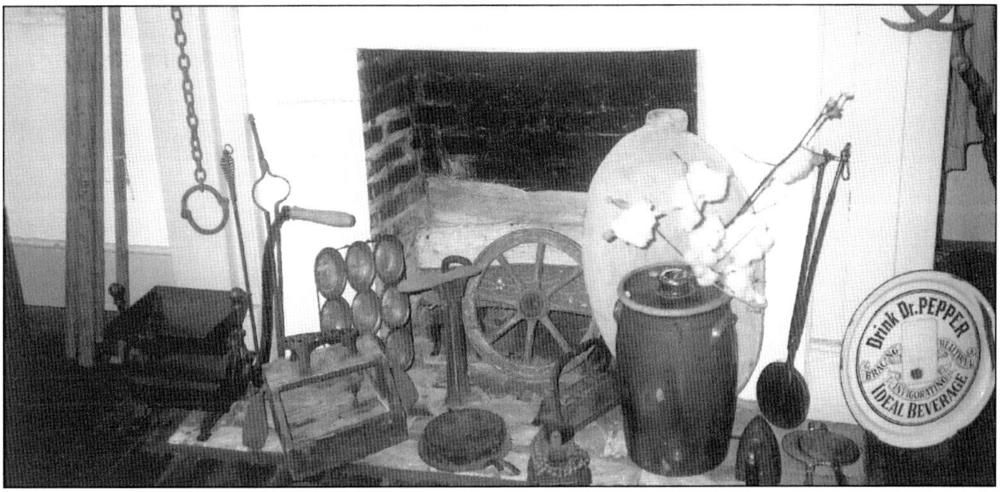

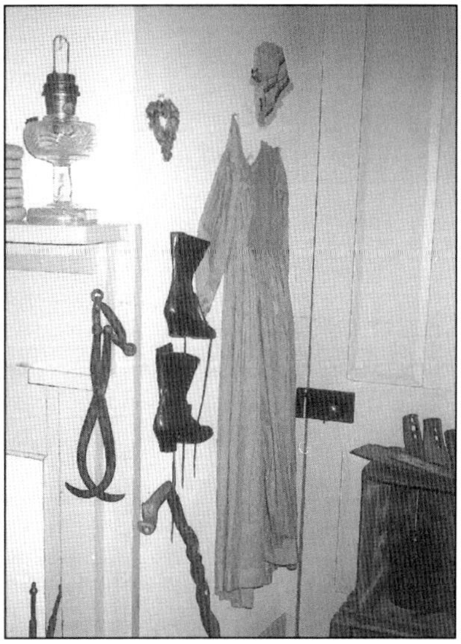

Most county residents were farmers, who did their own work with the use of what few tools were available. Homesteads were scattered throughout the county, with several miles between the clearings. The average family lived in a two-room log house with a lean-to attached for additional space, shived shingle roofs, and, often, clay floors. A nearby stream usually provided the family's water supply. A few acres of cleared ground, protected by rail fencing, surrounded the homestead and provided nighttime shelter for a few cows, hogs, sheep, goats, and chickens that roamed the pine woods by day. Daily life was a series of chores. Welcome breaks came when the settlers gathered at the meetinghouse for log rollings, house raisings, corn shuckings, cane grindings, quiltings, and the occasional breakdown featuring the fiddle or guitar.

Few roads were available to link residents to the outside world or each other. The Savannah River Road, Middleground Road (which ran through Jacksonborough, from Waynesborough to Springfield), and Ogeechee River Road traversed Screven lengthwise. Several roads led from Jacksonborough, into the county, and on to other counties. Paris Mill Road passed Paris Mill (near Millhaven) into Burke County and joined with Summerall Ferry Road at Stoney Bluff. Stoopto Road ran west into what became the Ogeechee settlement. Clifton's Ferry was located near the present site of Scarborough. Additional roads led to Burton's Ferry, via Bryan's Bridge (a covered structure) on Brier Creek, and Hudson's Ferry on the Savannah River. Transportation came in several forms—wagon, cart, chaise, stagecoach, and horseback.

In the early days, industry was an oddity in and around Jacksonborough and Screven County. The county's economic picture began to change once the 19th century dawned, and many water-powered mills were built throughout the area. Then Eli Whitney invented the cotton gin in 1803, and cotton production soared almost overnight, with the sale price climbing 30–40¢ per pound. Like the rest of the South, Screven County rapidly expanded its cotton cultivation. Slaves by the thousands were purchased to cultivate the white gold. New settlers flocked to the region. Large slave owners became wealthy, but those who were less fortunate remained in poverty. The difference in living standards became so wide that class distinction became common. The various groups of people were called aristocrats, "po' white trash," or slaves.

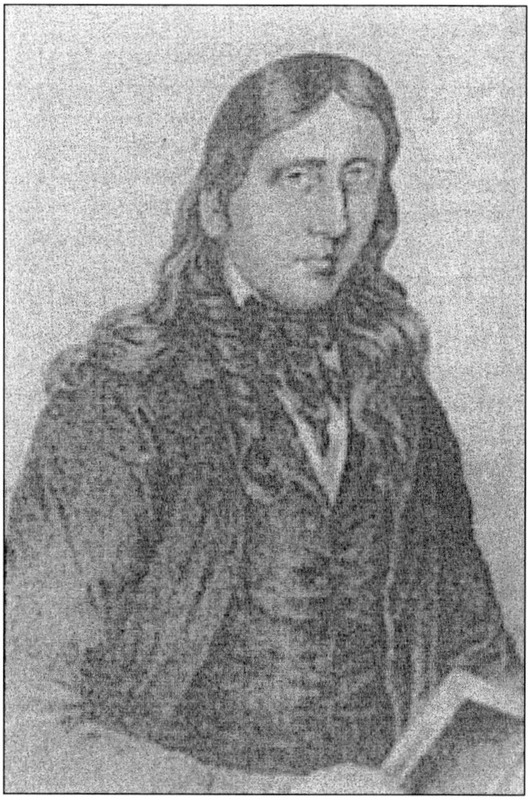

During this transitional period, Screven County attracted a visitor who left an indelible impression on its people—the Reverend Lorenzo Dow. A Methodist preacher from Connecticut, Dow was a well-known world traveler and eccentric, with a raging and passionate soul, who was, in equal measures, persecuted, prosecuted, feted, and lionized. He impressed town residents each of the several times he visited Jacksonborough, but his last visit was the most memorable, when rowdies stopped a meeting the itinerant preacher attempted to hold in the town. The preacher further riled the group when he followed them into one of several whiskey stores and tried to clean out the place.

Legend claims that, had he not been rescued by townsman Seaborn Goodall, the minister probably would have been hurt or killed. Goodall, a Methodist and a Mason, carried the preacher to his home, pictured at right, and let him spend the night there. The next morning, Dow encountered the ruffians a second time. This time they waited with an ample supply of eggs and ripe tomatoes, which they used strategically to pummel the traveling minister out of Jacksonborough. The Connecticut preacher retreated with dignity, but when he reached the Beaver Dam Creek Bridge that led south from the town, he stopped long enough to leave his tormentors with a curse none would ever forget. Dramatically shaking the dust from his feet, he raised his face and stretched his arms heavenward and asked God to destroy the town as he had Sodom, with one exception. He said the Goodall House should be spared because its owner had befriended him. Within 30 years, Jacksonborough was rapidly decaying. Vacant stores were crumbling to the ground. The courthouse and jail had been removed. And 40 years later, the town was gone—except for the Goodall house, which actually still stands to this day.

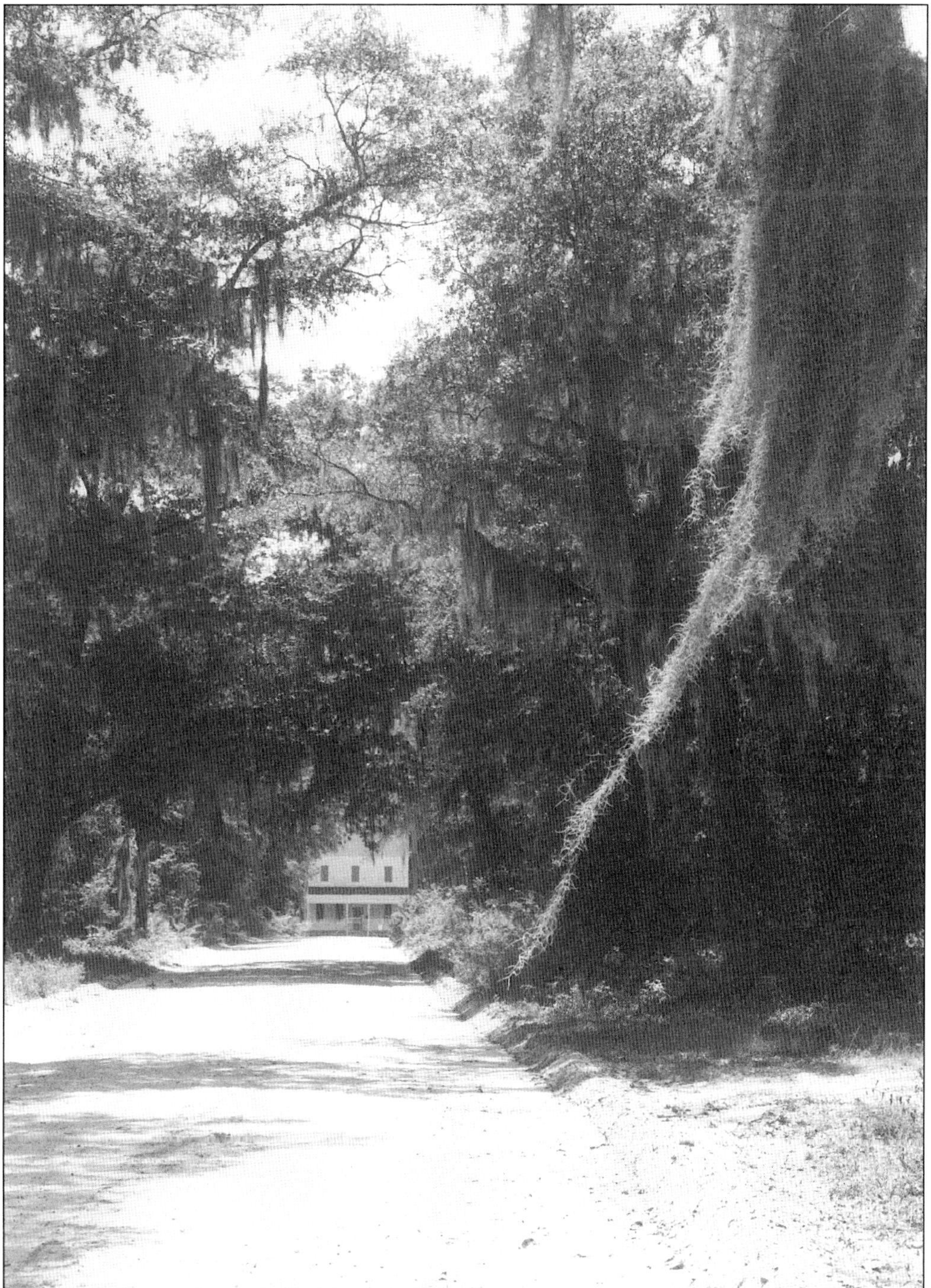

The Dell-Goodall House, the home of Seaborn Goodall who befriended Lorenzo Dow, was the only Jacksonborough structure not cursed by the angry preacher. Today, it marks the site of the long dead town.

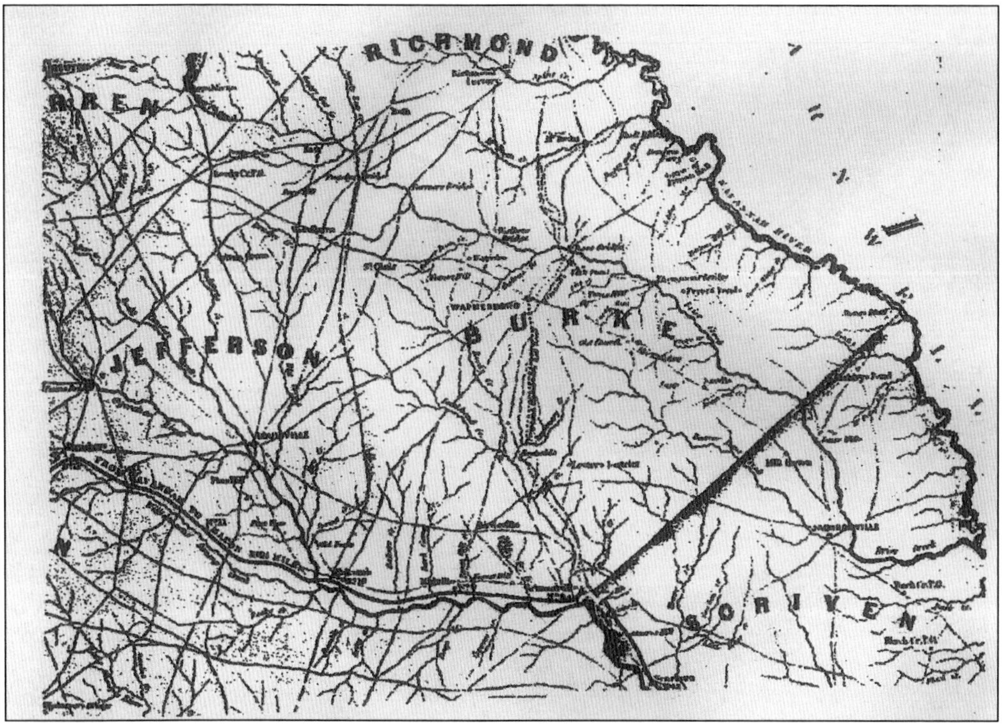

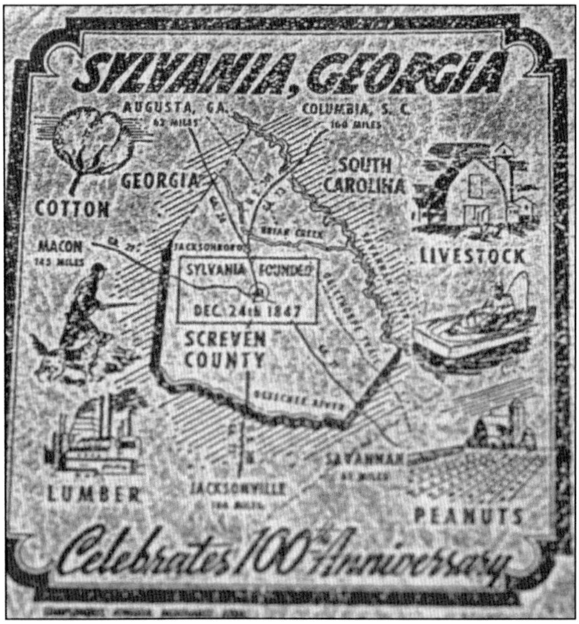

By 1847, Screven County's seat of government functioned in a new town called Sylvania, located just a few miles from Jacksonborough. The new town, located exactly in the center of the county, was created by legislation approved on December 24, 1847. On January 3, 1848, the commission purchased 50 acres of land from Charles Church. A plat showing 36 city blocks was prepared, and the parcels were sold at a public sale for a total of $972,750. Curtis Humphries built a courthouse for $1,575. James P. Bazemore built the jail for $400. No houses existed, but the town evidently sprang up quickly, because on August 10, 1848, a U.S. Post Office was established. Edward B. Gross was the first postmaster. In 1947, the town celebrated its 100th centennial.

Two

RIDING THE RAILS

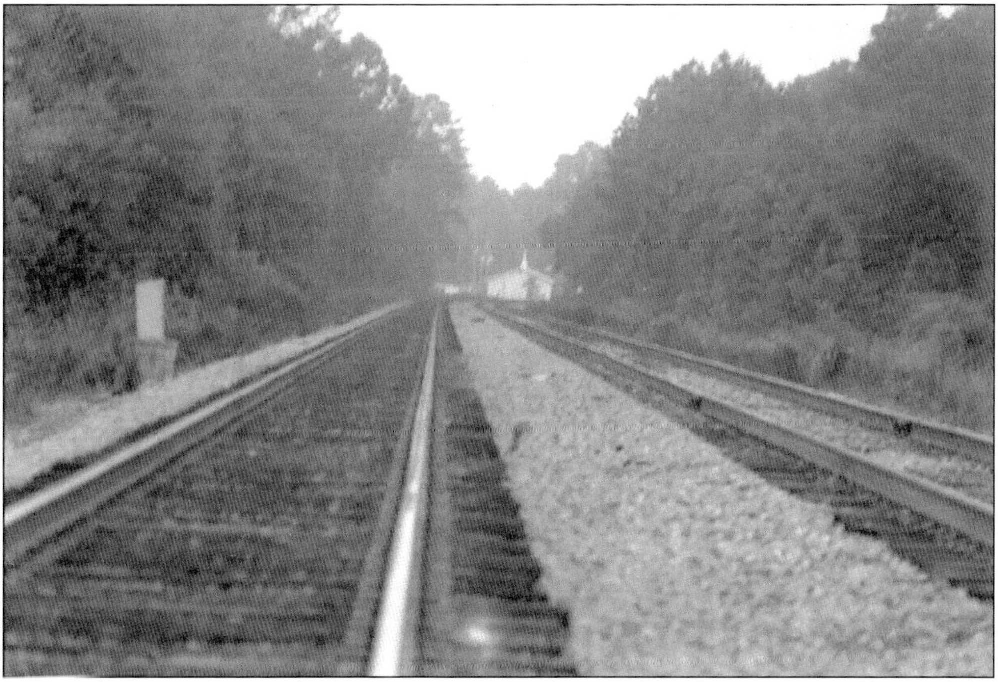

Screven County's economic life moved full-steam ahead when the Central Georgia Railroad came chugging through the piney woods. Construction began at Savannah in 1838 and followed the Ogeechee River through Screven. By 1843, the line was completed across middle Georgia to Macon, and the Central's rails stretched some 191 miles. It was the longest railroad in the world managed by one company. The period was an exciting one for Screven Countians and railroad officials alike. The annual report of Central's chief engineer, dated October 31, 1838, at Savannah, offers a glimpse of the excitement for those of us born too late to experience it for ourselves: "The iron (rail) is laid and the road completed 46 miles (Oliver is 45.9 miles from Savannah). Our Engines now run daily with the Macon Mail and Passengers to that point."

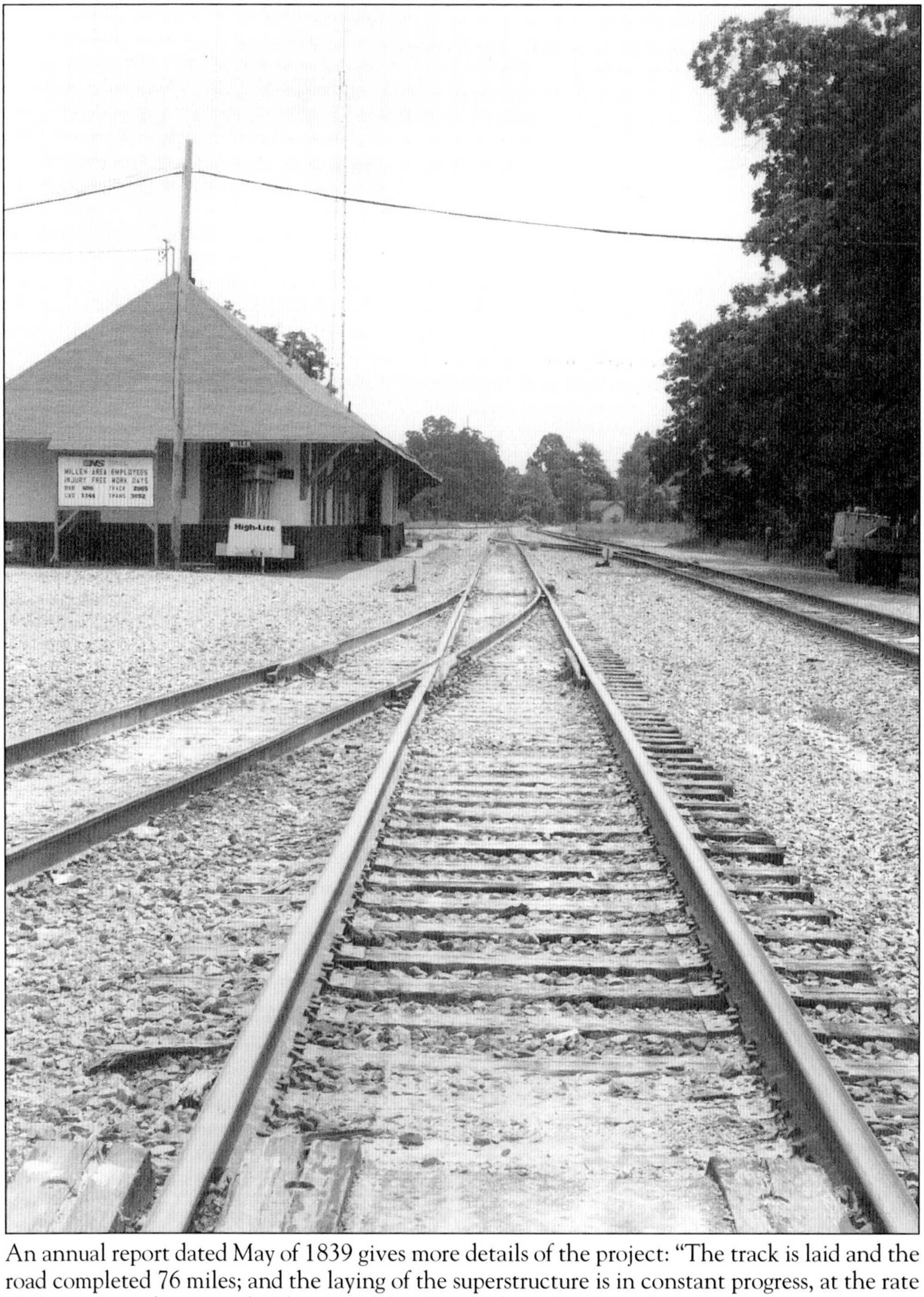

An annual report dated May of 1839 gives more details of the project: "The track is laid and the road completed 76 miles; and the laying of the superstructure is in constant progress, at the rate of about one mile per week. The site of the 80 mile depot has been designated, and preparations are now making to erect a large storehouse for the receipt and forwarding of produce and merchandise." That 80-mile depot became Millen, then a Screven County village just west of Adam Brinson's plantation. The 34 miles of rail line, from Mile Post 46 (later Oliver) to the 80 Mile Post (later Millen), were all within Screven County's boundaries.

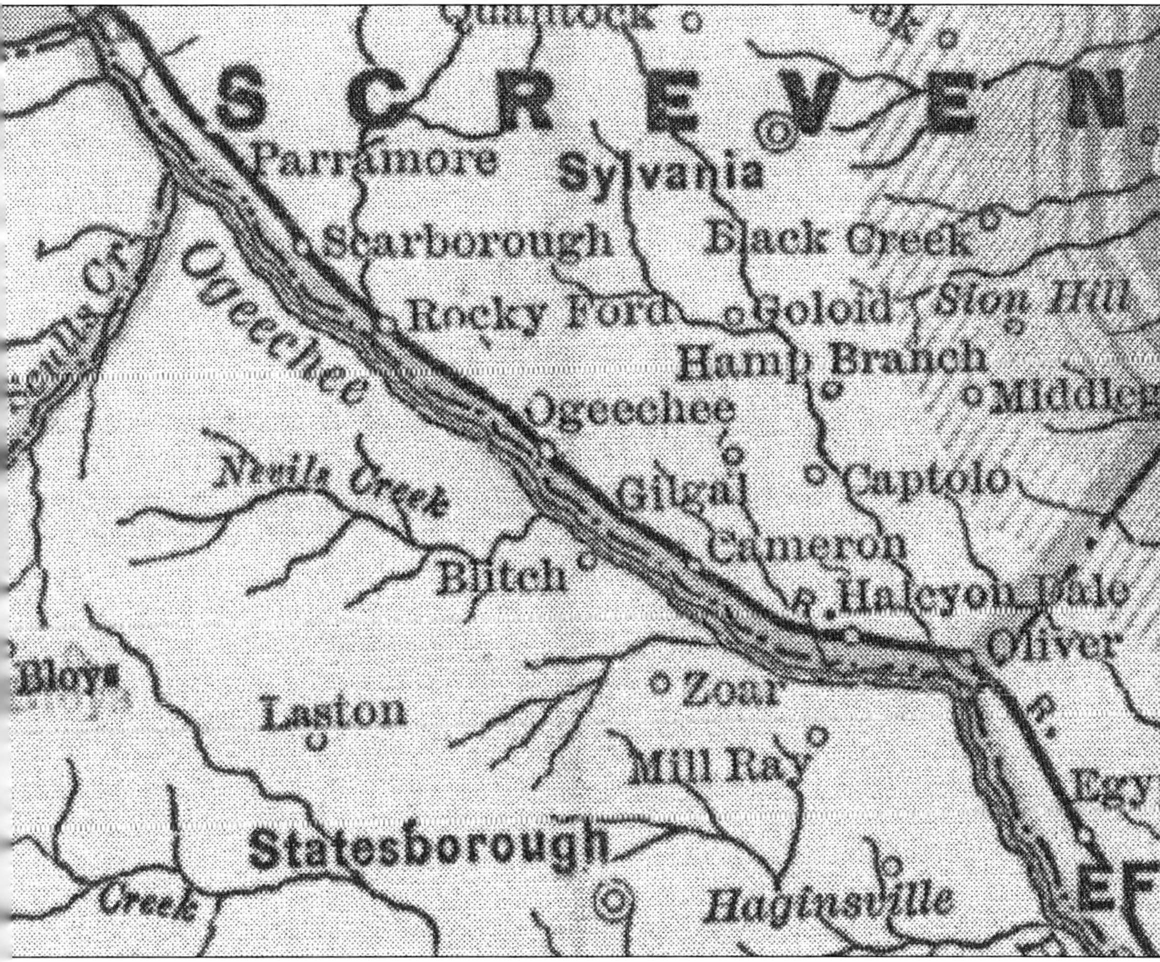

Contemporary Central of Georgia records give a detailed description of the railroad's course through Screven. Fields and plantations that were crossed are identified by names still known in the area nearly 160 years later. This map of the period gives a detailed view.

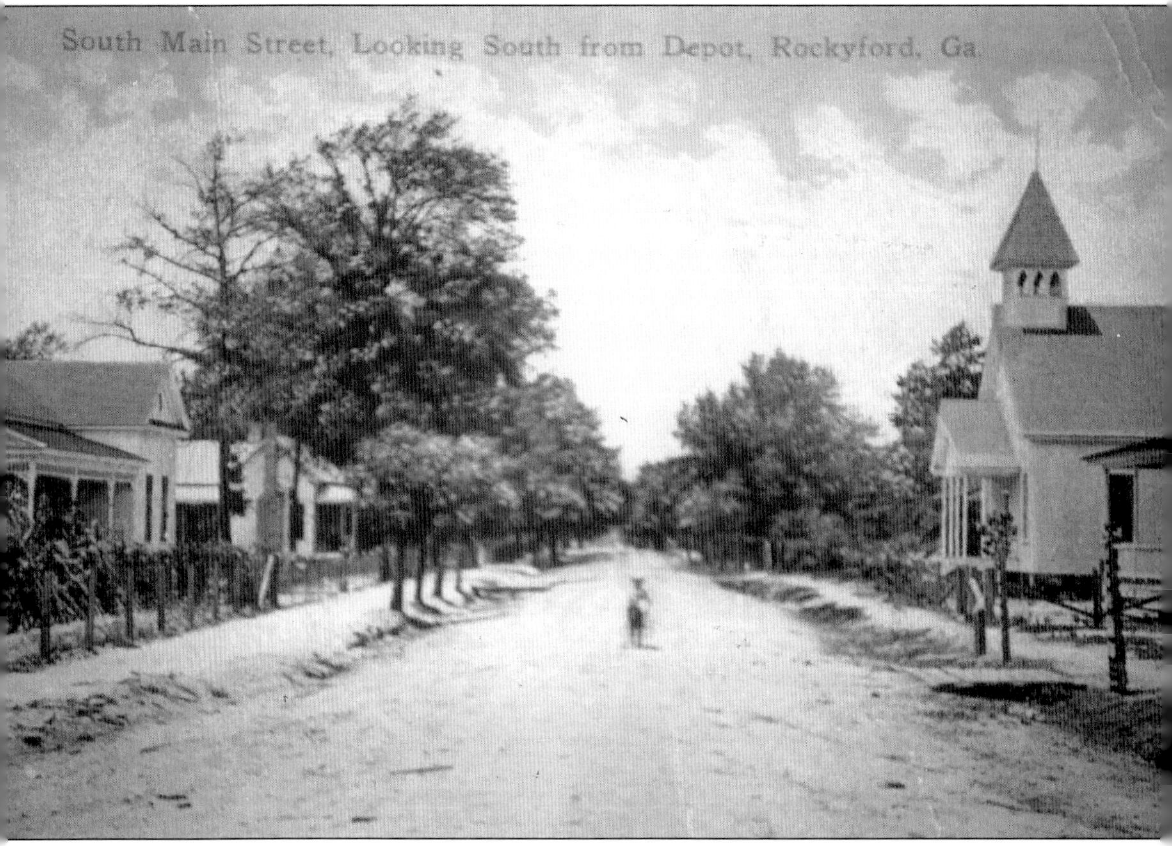

From Effingham County, the rail line crossed Louis Lanier's property near present-day Oliver. No such community existed then, but west of the Lanier property was George Oliver's land. The Oliver station was probably built there. Other landmarks included a church at the junction of the Louisville Road (now Georgia Highway 17) and a road going towards today's Newington. West of George Oliver's lands, the Central Railroad proceeded through Richard Phillips's property, Silas Morton's land, and John Jackson's tract, crossing Jackson's Branch and the Morton's Ferry Road on the Ogeechee, near Mile Post 48 $^{1}/_{2}$.

Near Mile Post 50, later Halcyondale, the rail line crossed cotton fields owned by Willis Young and Hardy Everett, then Archer's Mill Branch, and proceeded westward through "Red Bug Bay," near Hezekiah Evans's cotton fields. Next on the route were the properties of Charles Evans, John Morgan, George and Sarah Cooper, Ransom Rogers, and Miles Hunter. Near the present site of Dover, the line crossed Penelope Kent's cotton fields and Williams's Mill Branch. Farther on, it traversed the properties of Robert Williams, George and Mary Burns, and James Young, crossing Young's branch near the present site of Ogeechee Station. The westward route then crossed S. Young's cotton fields and ran through "Barber's Fields," then the fields of James Dixon, James and Jesse Lee, and Simeon and James Burke, before it reached "Cail's corn fields" (owned by Ruth Cail) and continued across David Burke's fields. The rail line then crossed the lands of George Newton, Benjamin Phillips and Joseph Daughtry, Mile Branch near Rocky Ford, and Horse Creek a little farther on. Mills Brinson's cotton fields were crossed just before the railroad climbed Paramour Hill and crossed Okane Branch, then Dry Branch Creek, and on through the property of Thomas Clifton and Roland Roberts, and then on and across part of Adam Brinson's plantation, to the present location of Millen, near Screven County's western boundary.

Engines and cars followed the track builders, so service to and from Savannah was provided without delay. In the early days of the railway, there were no stations along the line, so railroad

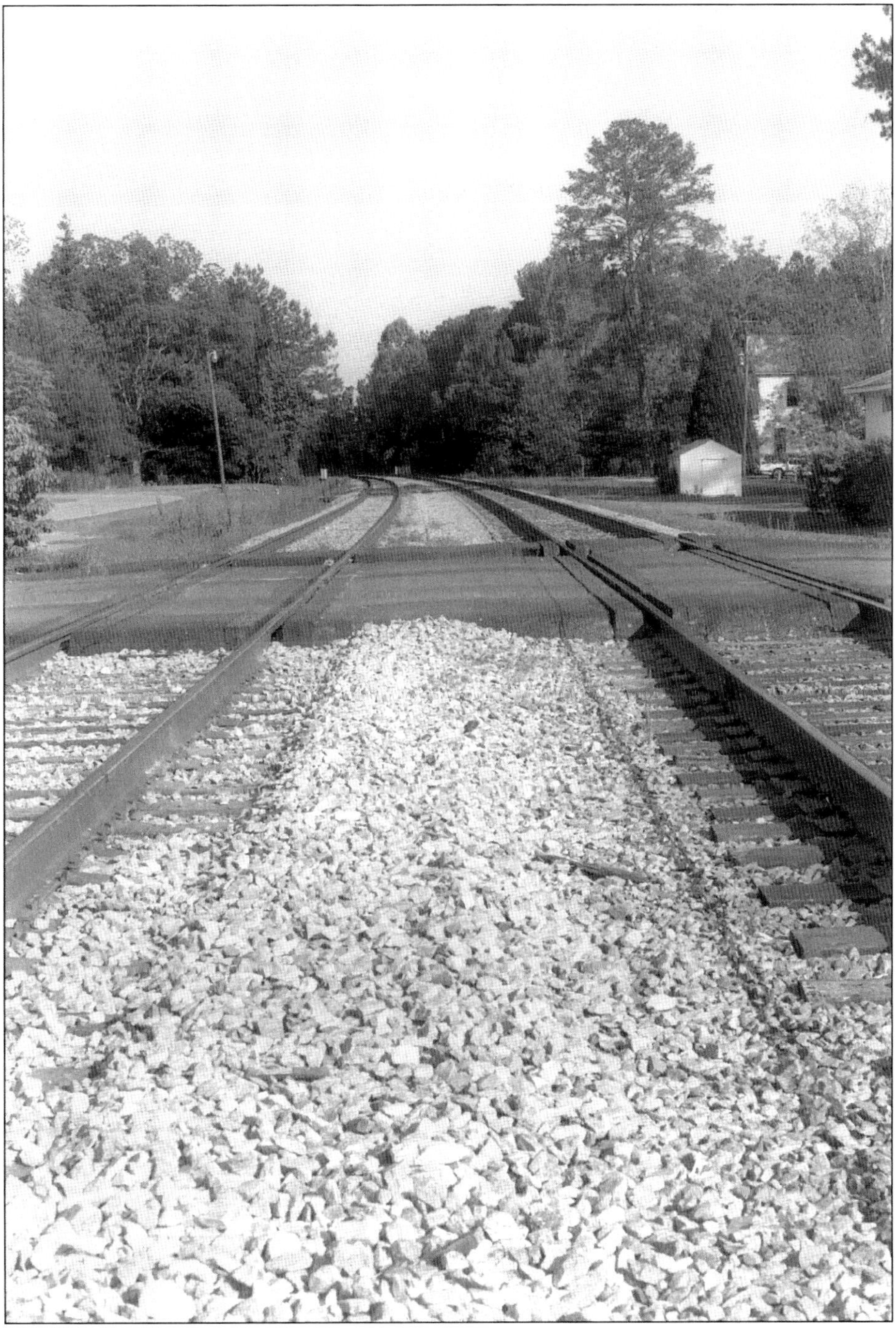

officials set up a service stop at least every 10 miles. Oliver, 45.9 miles from Savannah, was Service Stop No. 4 1/2; Halcyondale, 50 miles up the line, was No. 5; Cameron, 54.6 miles away from the Savannah station, was No. 5 1/2; Dover, 57.3 miles from the railroad's headquarters, was No. 6; Ogeechee, at the 61.5-mile point, was No. 6 1/2; Rocky Ford, located at the 66.4 mile marker, was No. 7; Scarborough was No. 7 1/2; and Millen, the 80-mile junction, was No. 8.

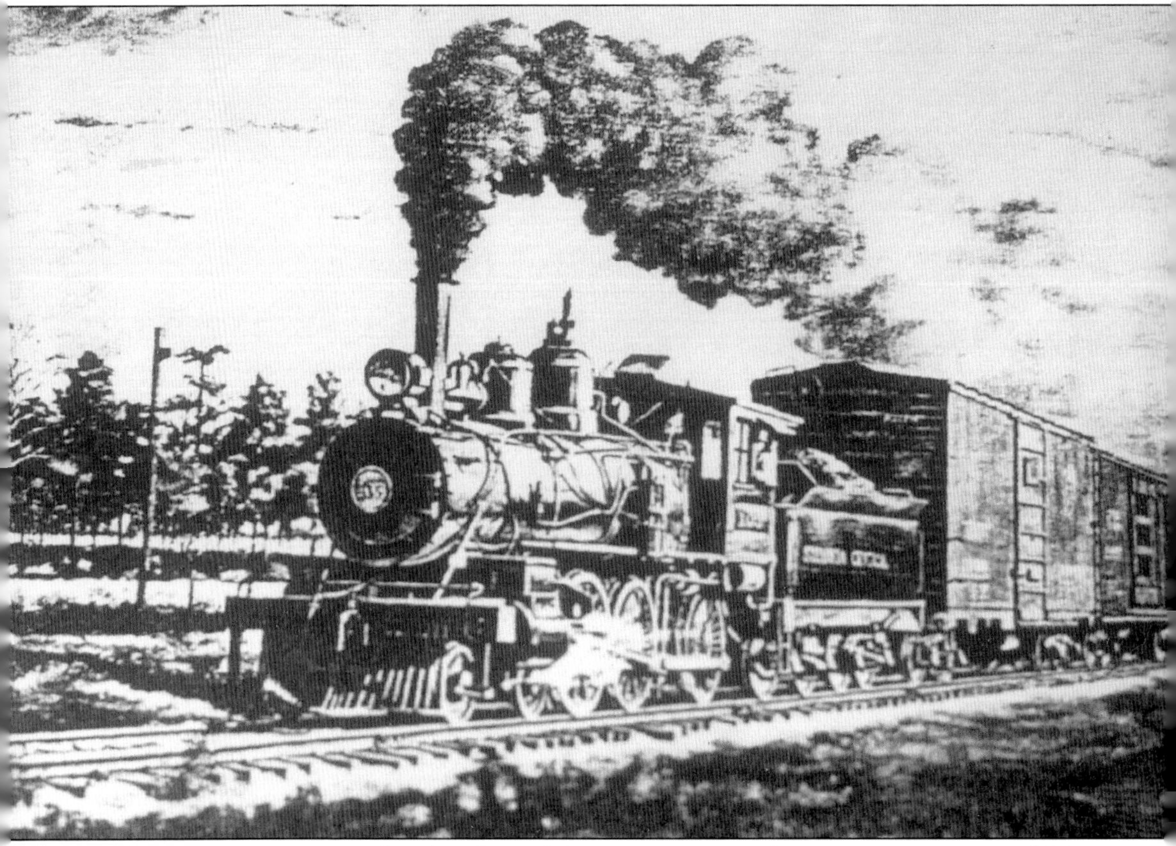

As a new century neared, railroad travel became a more and more important part of life in Screven County. Under a charter issued June 28, 1883, the Sylvania Railroad Company built and operated a small railroad line known under various names during its 75 years of operation. It is remembered as the Sylvania Central. The railroad connected Sylvania, which had no rails at the time, to the Central-of-Georgia track at Rocky Ford. A "mixed train daily" shuttled passengers and freight back and forth between Sylvania and Rocky Ford, its rail connection with the outside world. In 1947, the Sylvania Central was featured in Lucius Beebe's book, *Mixed Train Daily*. Its train appeared in full-color on the book's dust jacket and on the inside. Beebe called the Central "the archetype and paradigm" of short-line railroads. The Sylvania Central train made its last stop on March 27, 1954. Rail transportation between Screven and Bulloch counties became more expedient when E.E. Foy erected a railroad trestle across the Ogeechee River, near Rocky Ford, and purchased a small train engine to haul his mill products to the Central Railroad, to then be shipped to market. In the early 1900s, George M. Brinson, a Stillmore businessman, built several small railroads, including the *Wadley Southern* and the *Brewton and Pineora*. In 1906, he began building a line northward from Sylvania known simply as the Brinson Railroad. Brinson's railroad reached the present site of Newington in 1909. He also extended the line to Millhaven when he purchased the Savannah Valley Railroad, formed by combining several existing logging roads. Consequently, Screven County gained two new Screven County towns that were created in 1909—Newington and Hiltonia. George Brinson soon lost control of his railroad, but by 1917, it extended from Savannah to Camak, near Augusta, and was called the Savannah & Atlanta, or S&A, Railroad. It provided Sylvania with rail service until it was discontinued as a through line. In 1962, it became a spur line of the Central of Georgia. The Perkins Family of Burke County built an extensive rail system that served the company's sawmills in Burke and Screven.

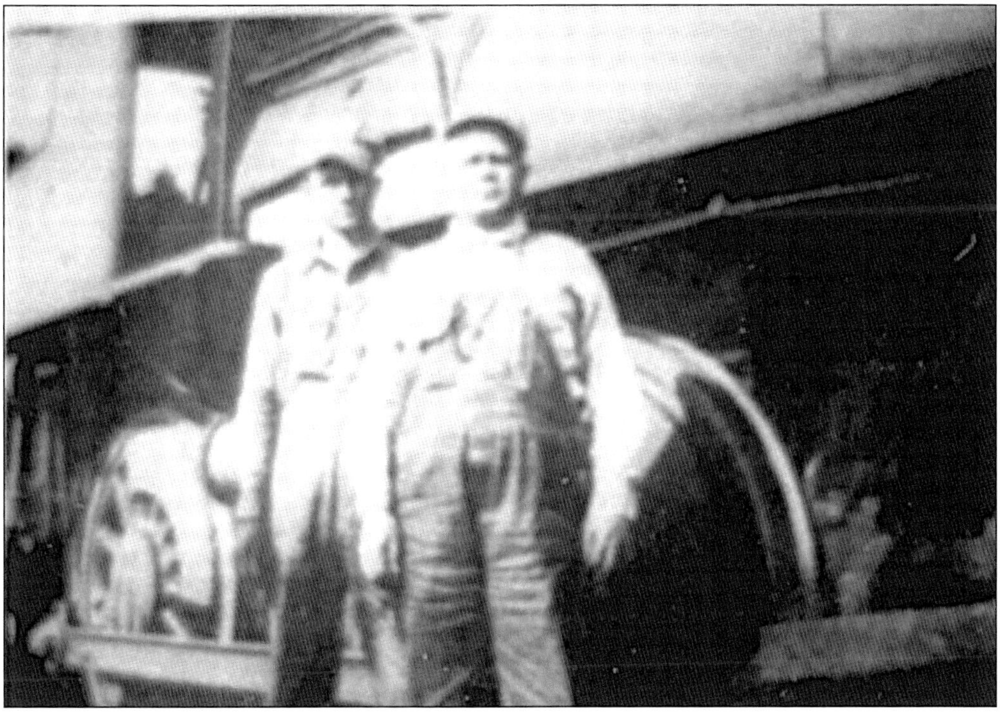

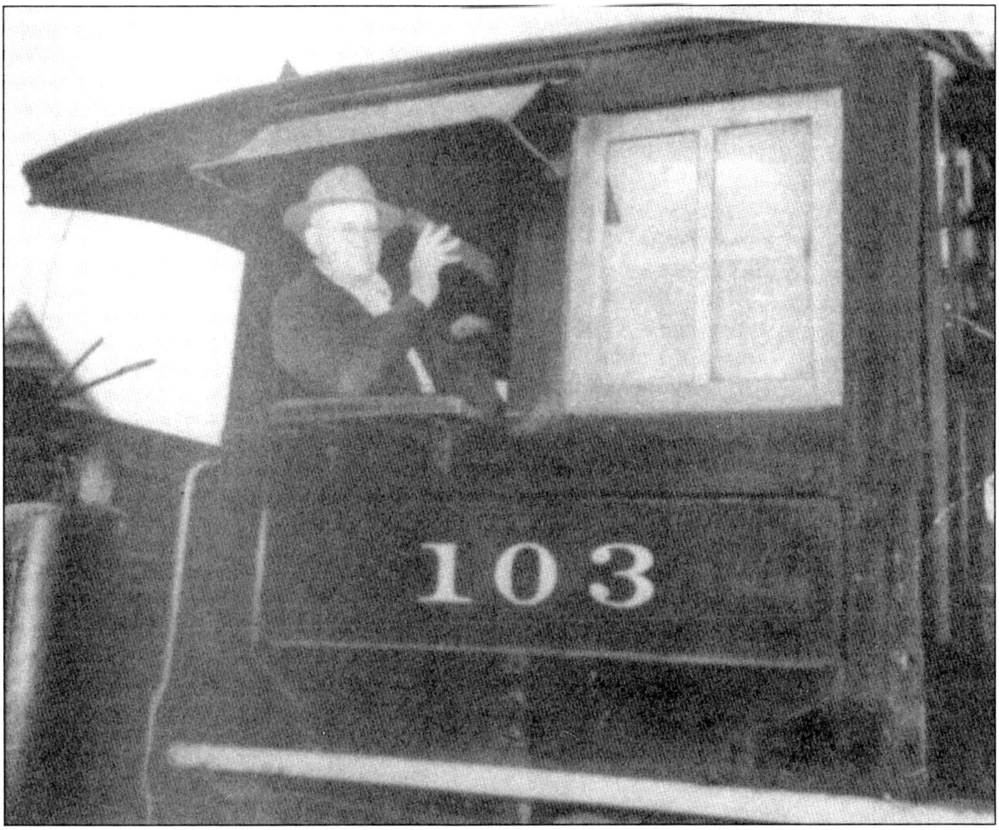
103

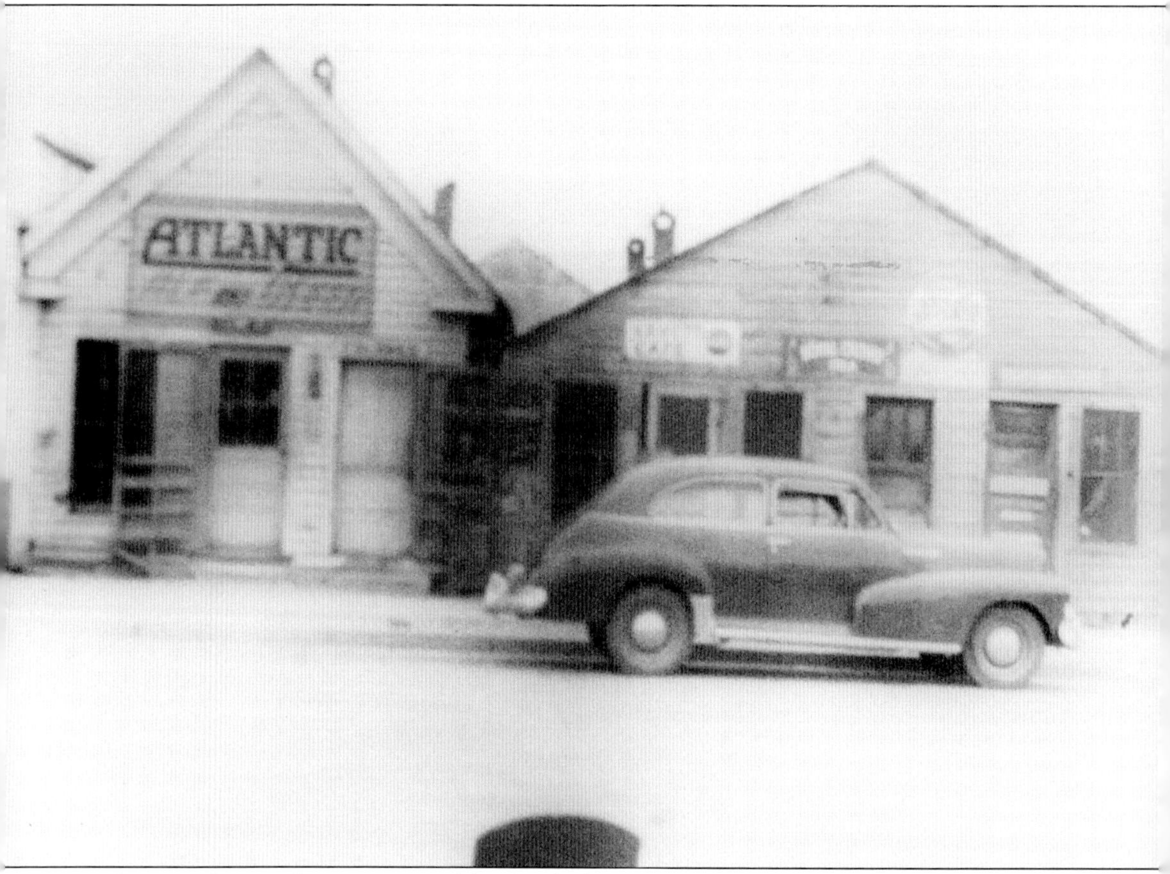

Screven County began to grow like few had ever imagined. Business was good, towns were springing up and growing like wildfire, and an exciting period dawned in the land between the Savannah and Ogeechee Rivers. Sylvania gained much from Jacksonborough, whose residents were rapidly moving there. On February 20, 1854, the general assembly passed an act incorporating the town of Sylvania, providing for the election of commissioners and other necessary officers, and conferring upon them special powers to run the city government. Those first city commissioners were Dominick J. Dillon, Winsley Hobby, Daniel E. Roberts, William Williams, and Charles Church. Sylvania was by far the busiest town in Screven County, which boasted 569 dwellings, 3,174 free people, one free colored person, and 3,673 slaves. The county's real estate was worth $1,260,577, and personal property was valued at $1,101,900. Downtown Sylvania became a disaster area when fire destroyed the business district on January 8, 1897. At the time, the business district was, for the most part, a row of wooden stores on the east side of the wooden courthouse. The only brick building in the downtown area was a small structure the county fathers had built on the south side of the courthouse to provide offices for the clerk of court and the judge of ordinary. At about 10 p.m. that night, someone spotted a flicker of flame in the livery stable loft. Two hours later, Sylvania was a town of smoldering ashes. At least 15 businesses and professional offices were destroyed by the flames, in addition to the two-story courthouse. Fireproof vaults in the brick building saved the county's official records. To prevent another disaster, the city council approved an ordinance prohibiting construction of wooden buildings on the business square.

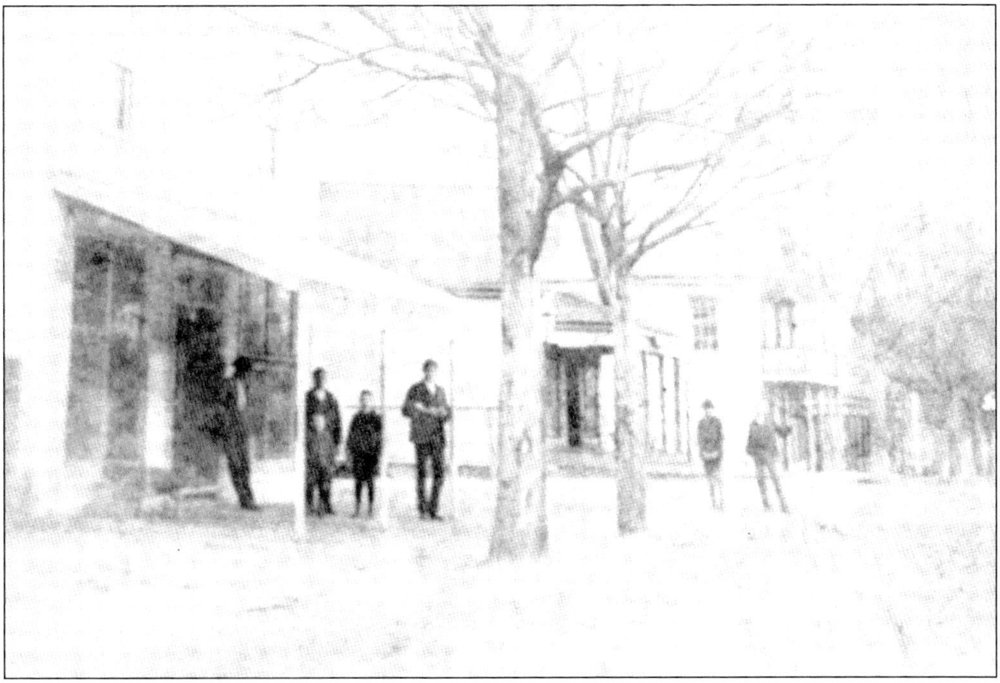

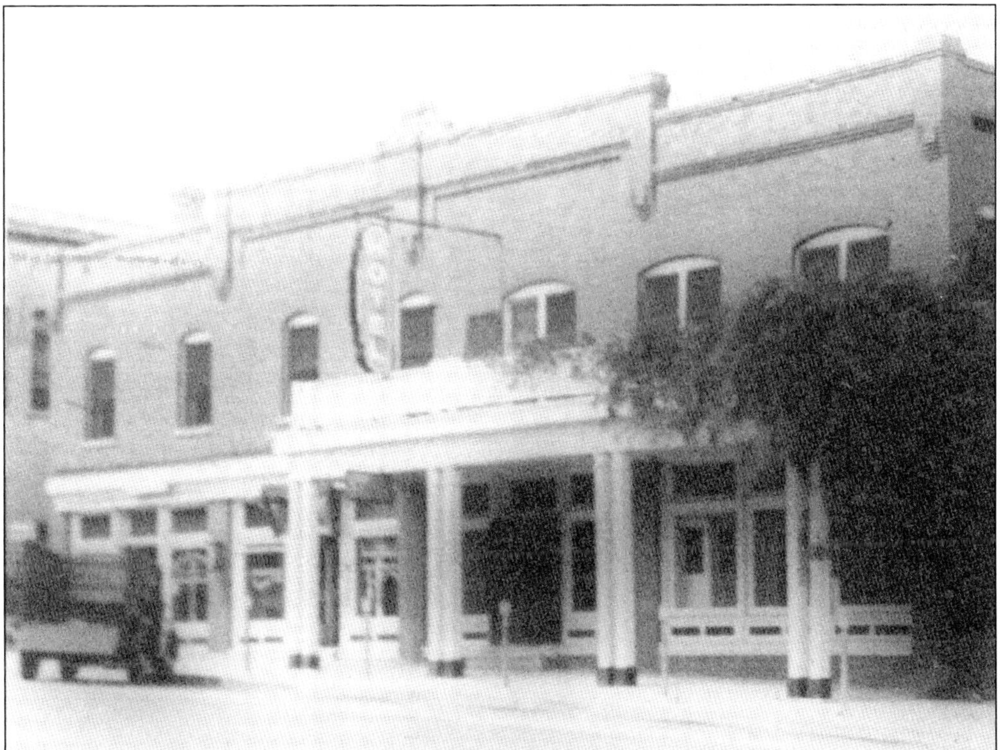

The 1897 fire brought a significant change to Sylvania's business district. Wooden structures were replaced with brick ones.

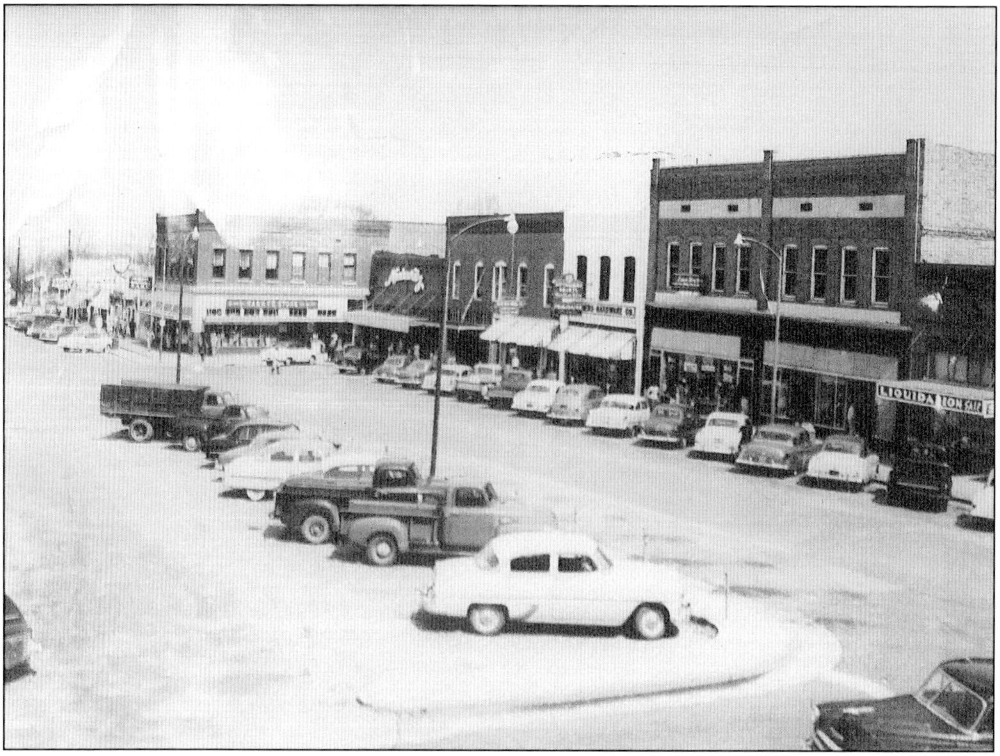

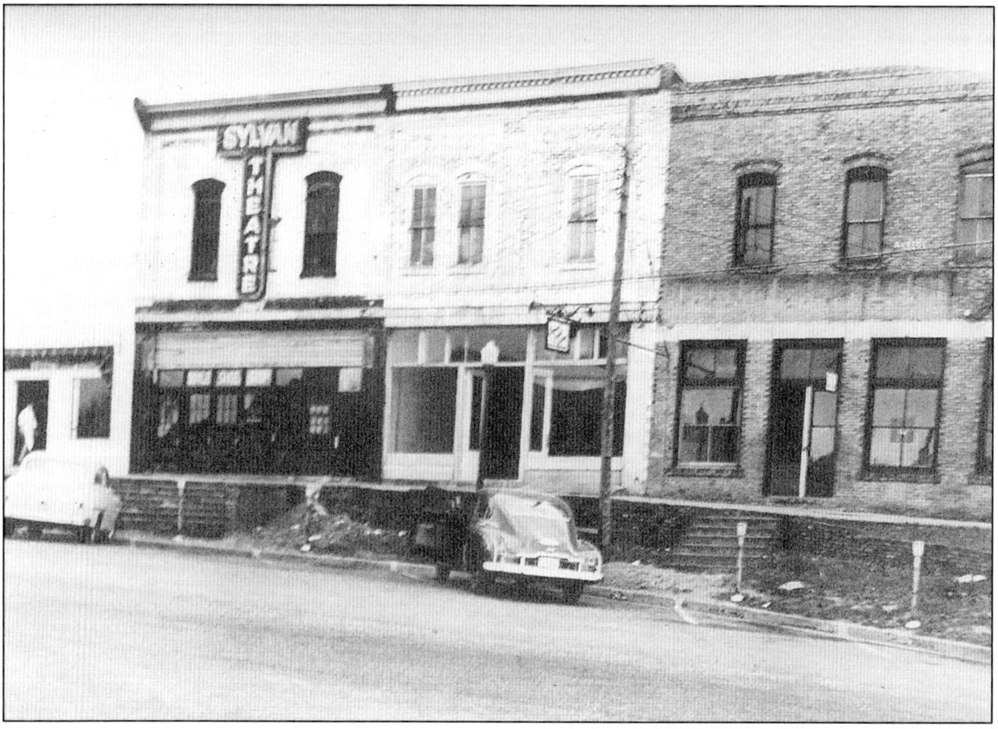
SYLVAN
THEATRE

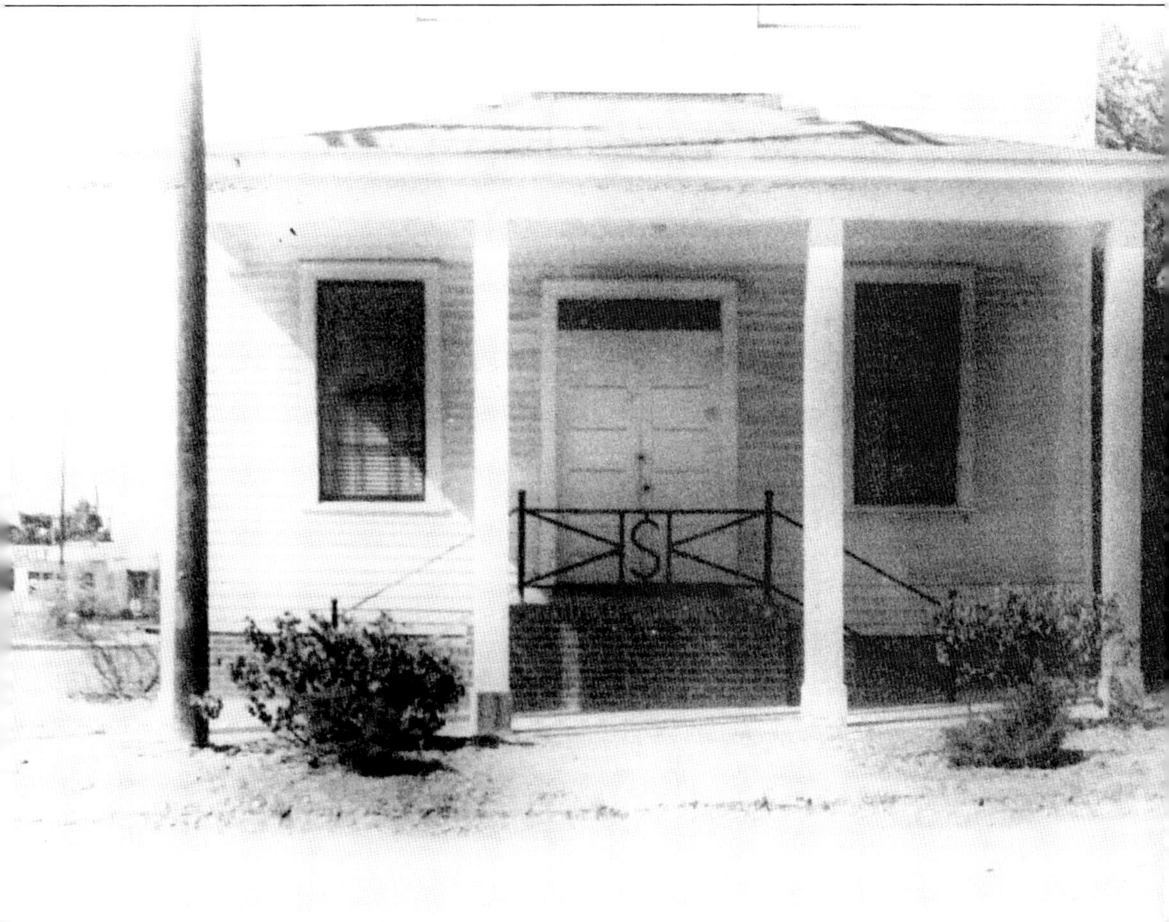

The downtown buildings that replaced the burned structures were made of sturdy, strong, long-lasting brick. The focus of Sylvania became its central shopping area, featuring brick structures that still stand today. Another development was the establishment of a library, above, to serve all the residents of the counties.

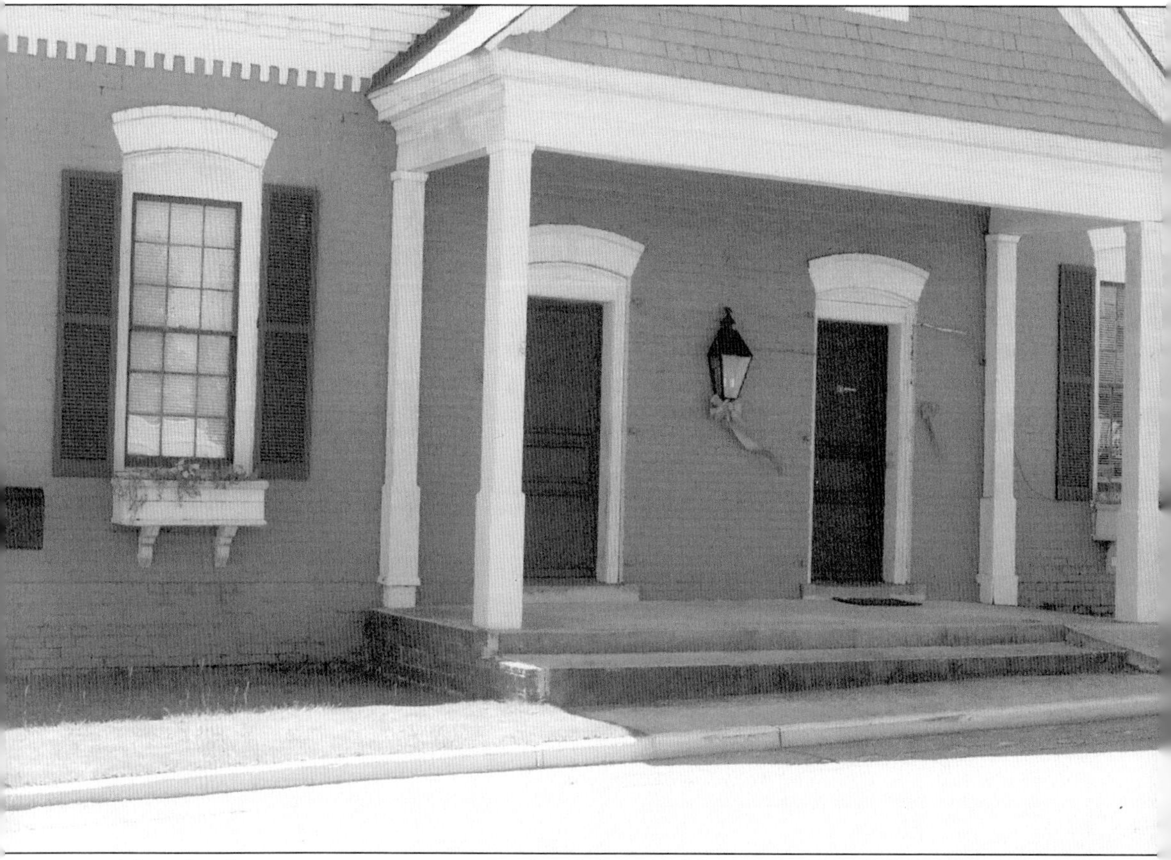

After the fire, county commissioners decided to build a monumental courthouse made of brick (shown at right). On April 20, 1897, the contract was awarded to Algenron Blair, who submitted the low bid of $16,190. By eliminating a clock in the tower and changing a few other specifications, the figure was trimmed to $15,000. Blair, who was 23 years old, successfully completed his first contract and went on to enjoy a long, successful career in the construction business. His ties with Screven County remained strong. While building the Screven courthouse, he courted a local girl, Caroline Livingston Singellton, and married her in 1898. The small structure shown above is still standing and was located behind the courthouse. It was the only part of the complex left after the fire.

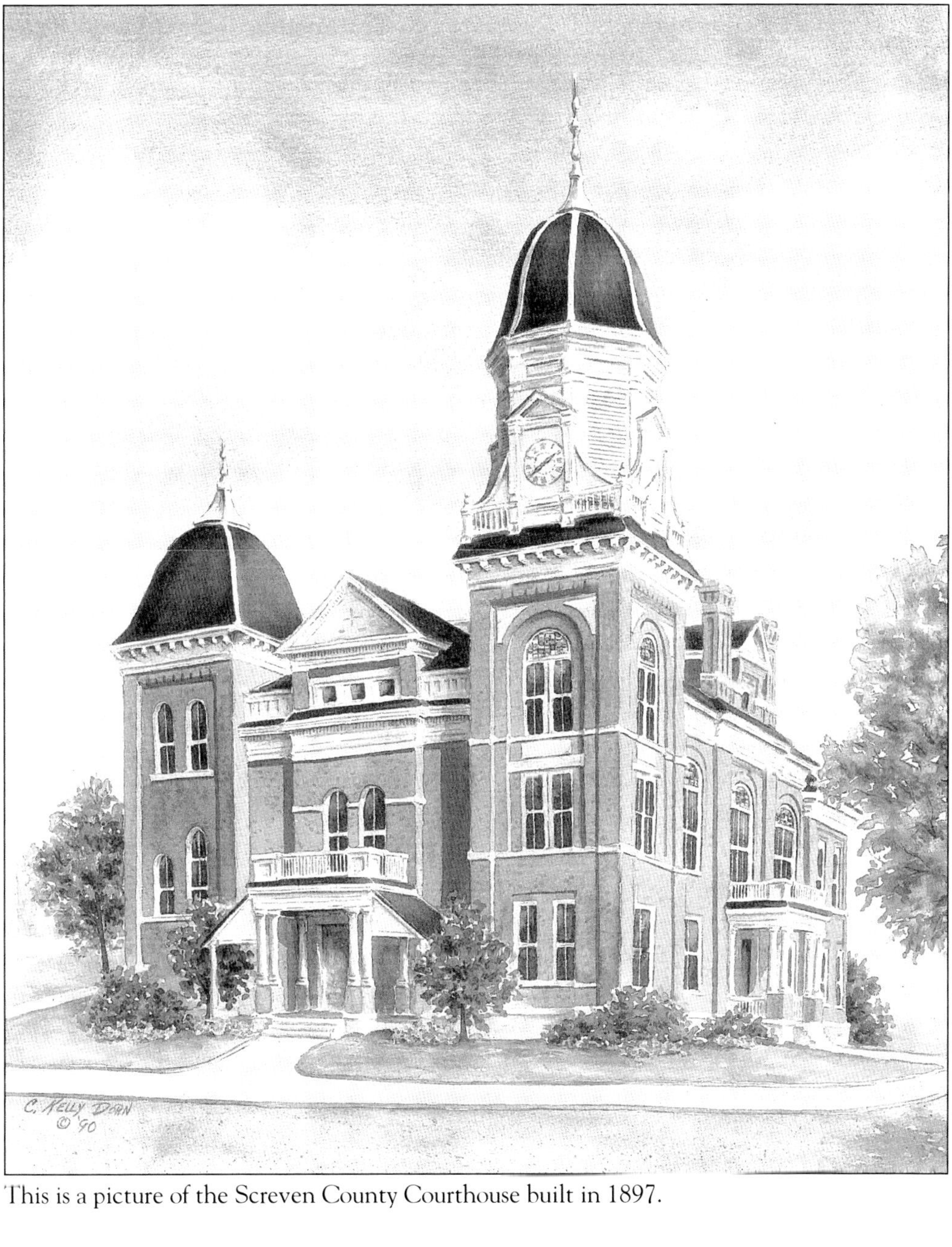

This is a picture of the Screven County Courthouse built in 1897.

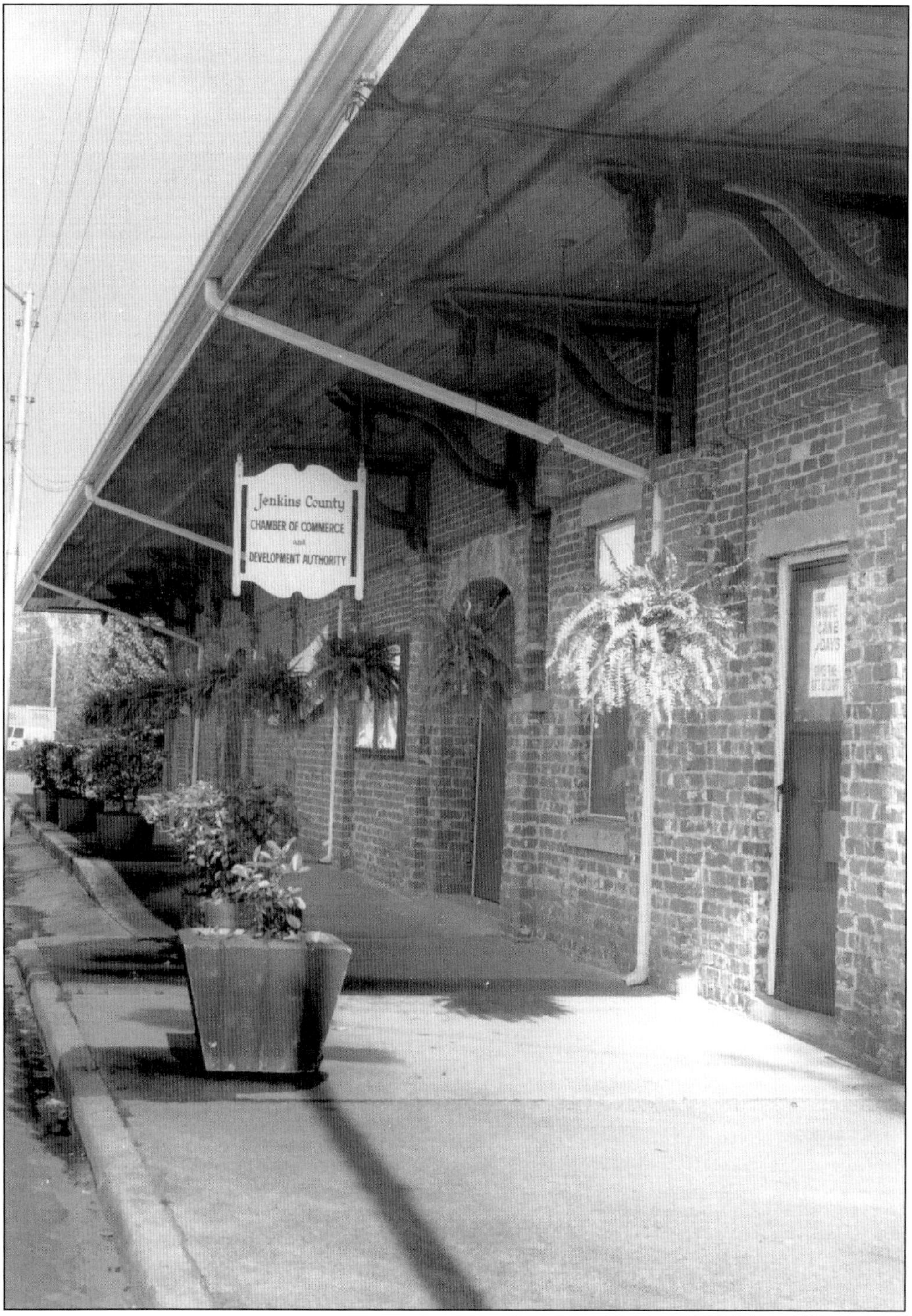
Jenkins County
CHAMBER OF COMMERCE
and
DEVELOPMENT AUTHORITY

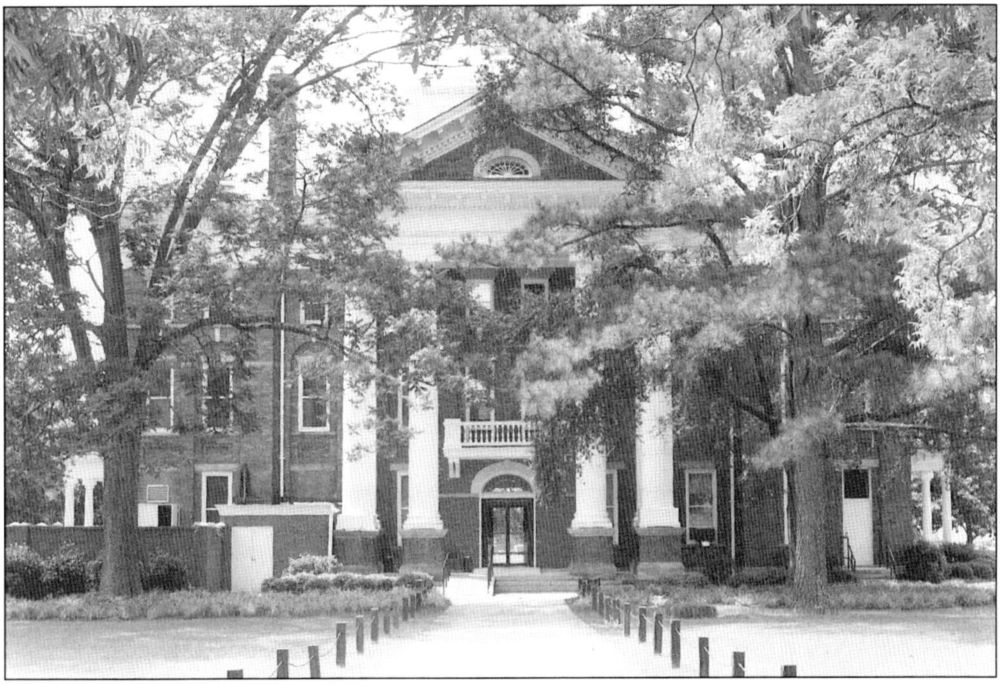

Millen was another of Screven County's early towns. Originally known as Millen Junction, the community dates back to the 1840s, when the Central of Georgia Railroad came through the area. The original village, a depot site located at the 80-mile marker on the Central of Georgia's main line and a junction point with a shorter railroad, was an important shipping point for the entire area. The town was named for John Millen, who was born in 1804 in Savannah. Millen was a lawyer who also served in the Georgia legislature. He died in 1843, ten days after he was elected to the U.S. House of Representatives, 28th Congress. The booming village was destroyed in December of 1864, when Union General William T. Sherman and his 62,000-man force visited the town, then located in Screven County.

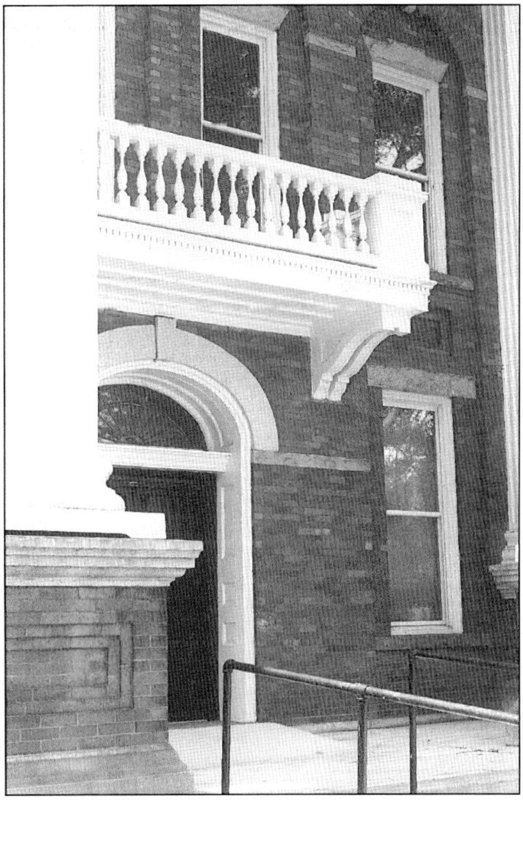

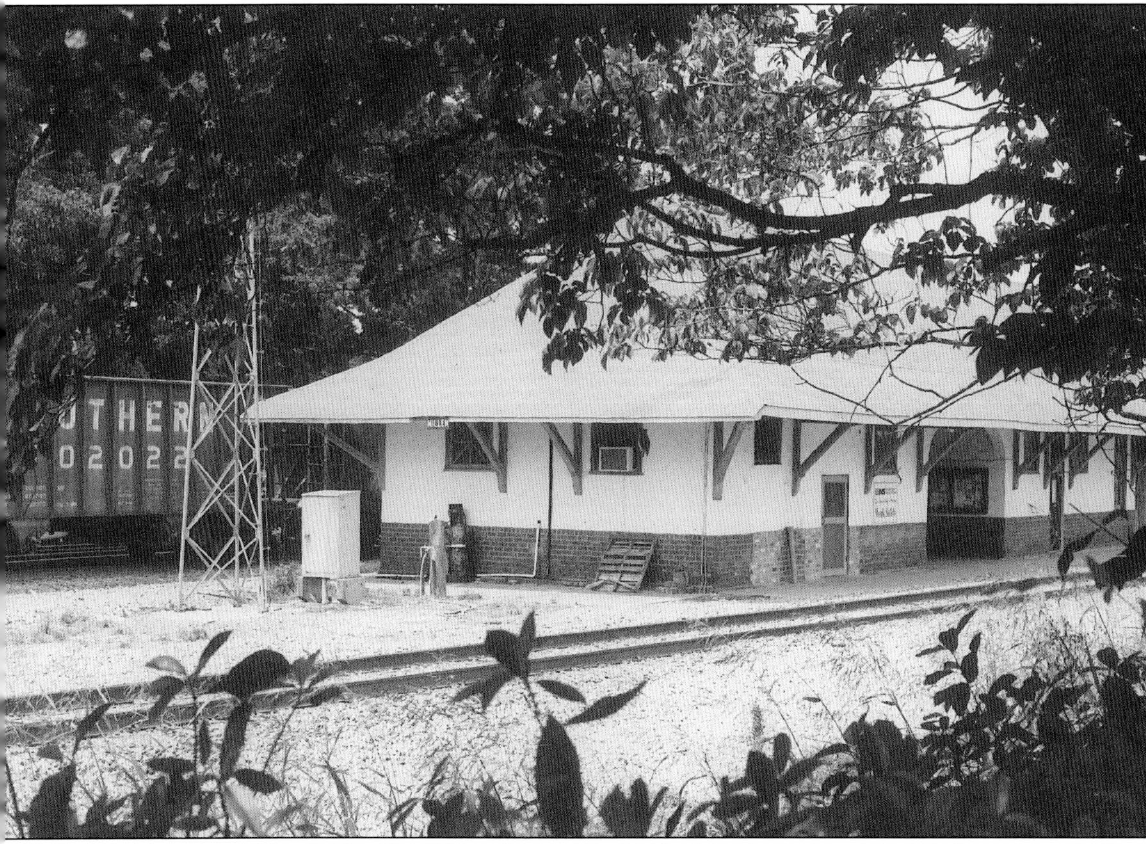

In the years following the Civil War, the town was rebuilt and once again became an important transportation hub for the region. Businesses sprang up, and new people moved into the area. The railroad remained the most vital part of the economy.

By 1900, the town was home to 411 people, and its militia district included 2,491. It featured a money order post office with free rural delivery, express and telegraph service, a bank, a cottonseed oil mill, a cotton yarn mill with 5,000 spindles, a large fertilizer warehouse, several successful stores, a school, and churches. Millen's merchants handled nearly 10,000 bales of cotton annually. In 1905, Millen became the governmental seat of the newly formed Jenkins County.

As the years passed, a decline in rail traffic through Millen changed the town from a bustling transportation hub to a calmer reminder of days past. The depot was closed, and daily passenger service was discontinued. Millen became a ghostly version of its former self.

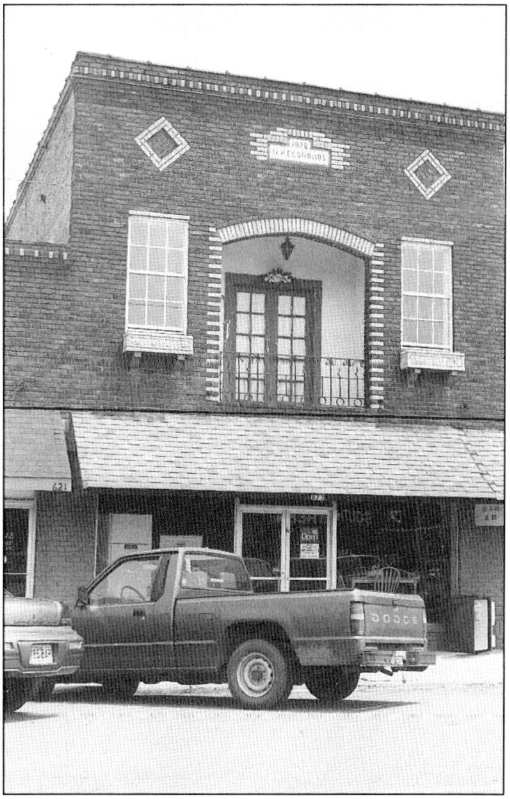

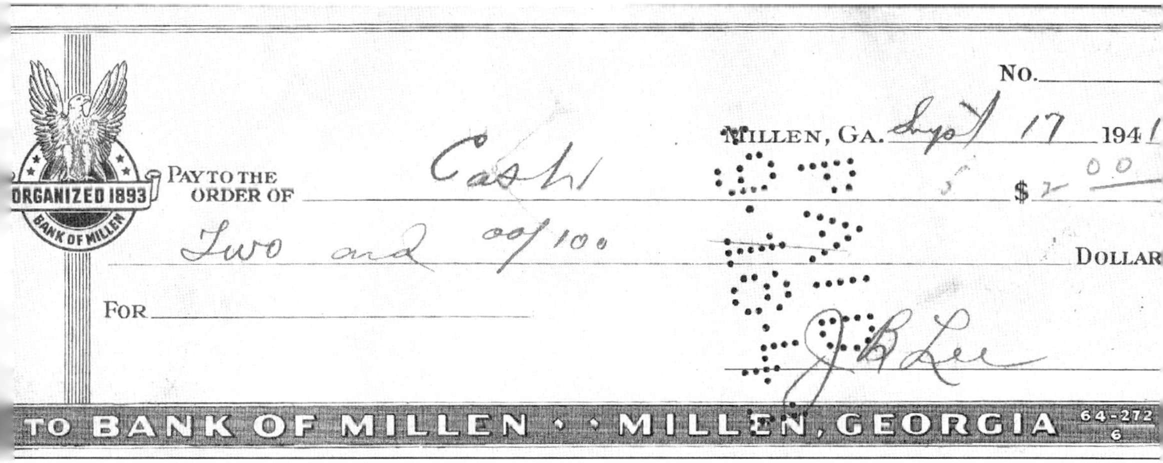

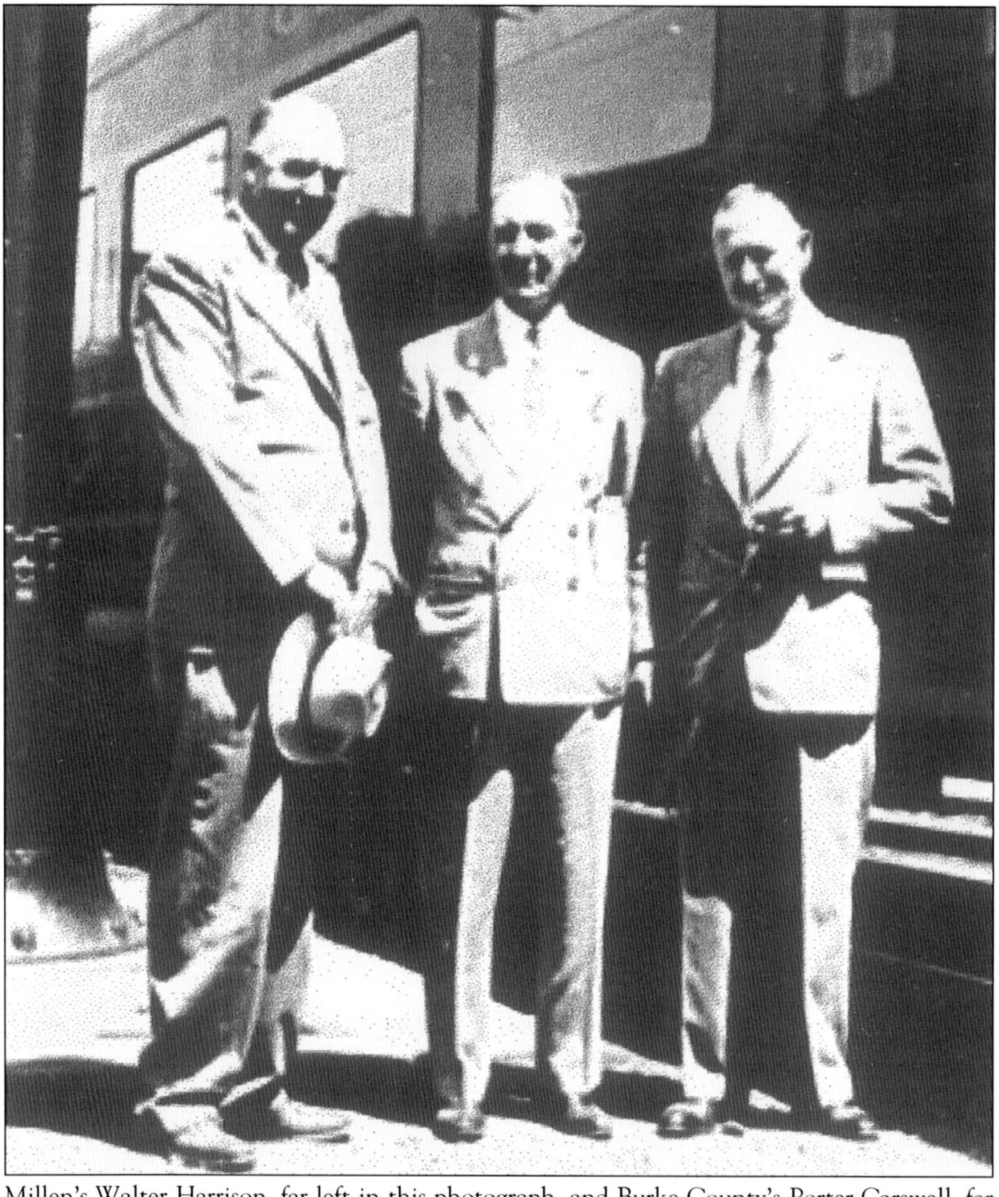

Millen's Walter Harrison, far left in this photograph, and Burke County's Porter Carswell, far right in the photograph, were instrumental in establishing a rural electric cooperative to provide electricity for residents of Jenkins, Screven, and neighboring counties. The cooperative began at Carswell's Bellvue Plantation on October 5, 1936, when the New Deal Power Association was formed. Carswell was elected president. The cooperative was subsequently renamed Planters Power Company, and in 1937, it became Planters Electric Membership Corporation. Harrison became a board member in 1937. Service began on August 25, 1937, with 91 connected customers. Shortly after that, the cooperative was serving three counties—Burke, Jenkins, and Screven—and a centrally located headquarters was established in Millen.

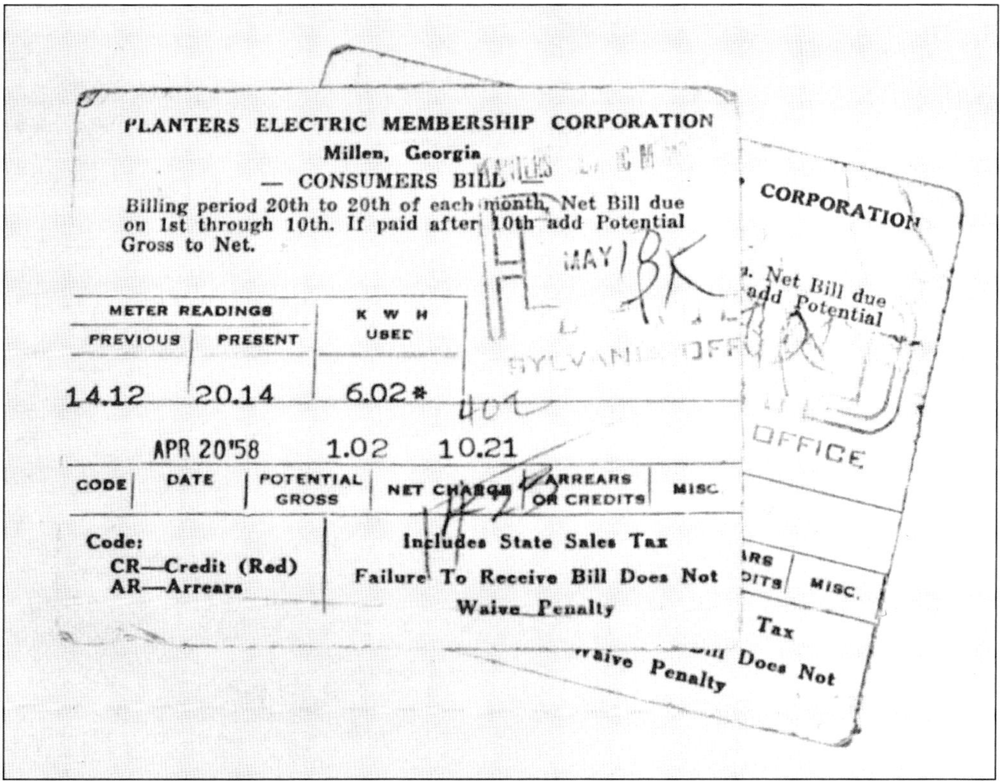

PLANTERS ELECTRIC MEMBERSHIP CORPORATION
Millen, Georgia
— CONSUMERS BILL
Billing period 20th to 20th of each month, Net Bill due on 1st through 10th. If paid after 10th add Potential Gross to Net.

METER READINGS		KWH USED
PREVIOUS	PRESENT	
14.12	20.14	6.02*

CODE	DATE	POTENTIAL GROSS	NET CHARGE	ARREARS OR CREDITS	MISC
	APR 20'58	1.02	10.21		

Code:
CR—Credit (Red)
AR—Arrears

Includes State Sales Tax
Failure To Receive Bill Does Not Waive Penalty

OFFICE

By the 1950s, Planter Electric was a vital part of the Screven and Jenkins Counties community. A modern headquarters building was built to meet the growing cooperative's needs.

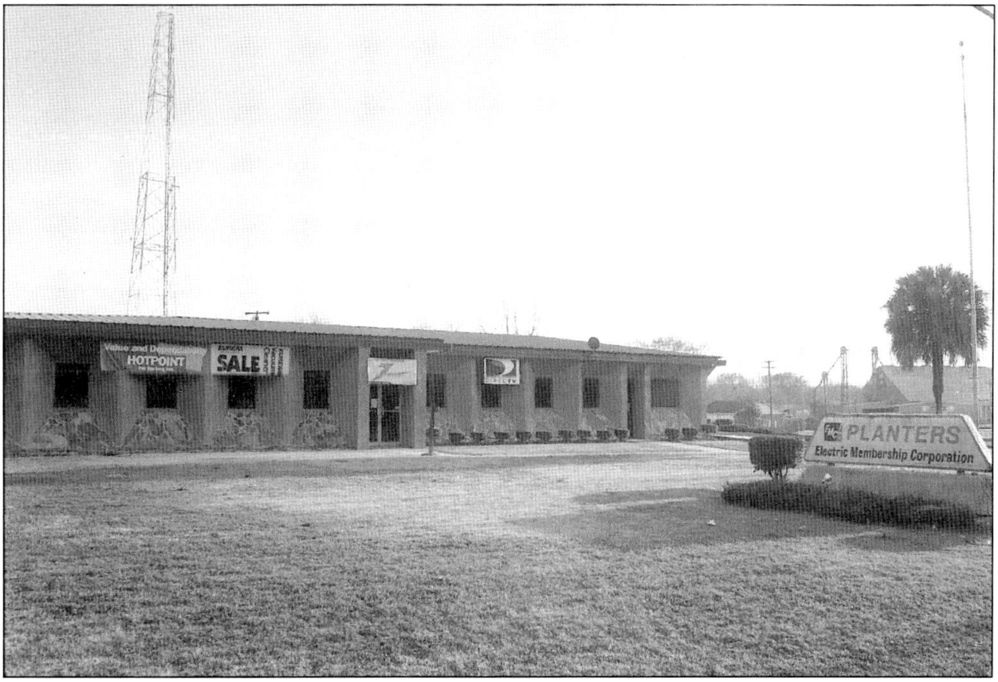

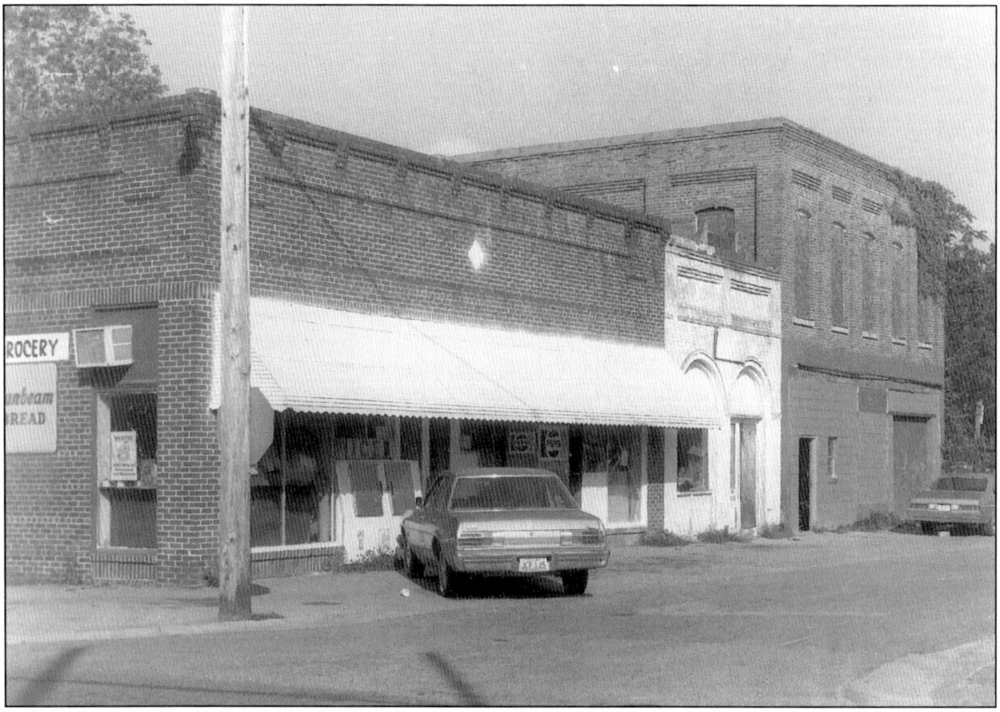

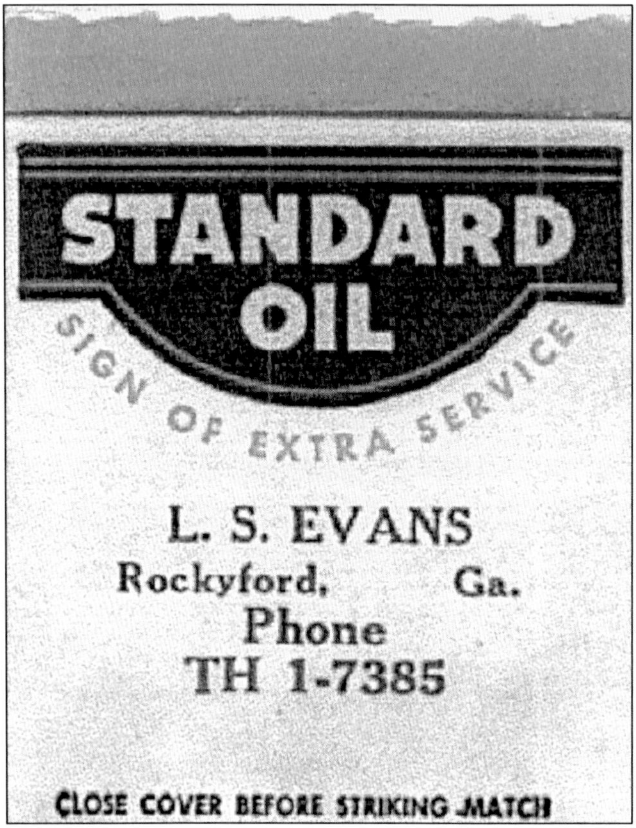

Rocky Ford may officially be one of Screven County's younger towns, but the area's reputation dates back to the mid-1700s. Situated on the Ogeechee River, the Central of Georgia Railroad, and the historic stagecoach route known as the Louisville Road, Rocky Ford served as Screven County's first governmental seat more than a century before the official town was created. Originally the area was known as The Rock, or The Ford, then later as No. 7, because it was located 65 miles above Savannah on the Central of Georgia Railroad. That changed around 1886, when the town's first post office was established.

An important farming community from its earliest days, Rocky Ford was the site of Benjamin Lanier's home, which legislation in 1793 had designated the central point for county operations, until a central location for the county seat and a permanent courthouse could be found. The area drew its name from the natural ford that settlers used regularly as a bridge across the Ogeechee River. George Heard, named postmaster in 1868, and his assistant, James M. Newton Jr., are the men who reputedly gave the town its name. When the U.S. Post Office directed Heard to submit a name for his establishment, he and Newton decided Rocky Ford would be a natural one.

Once established, the town grew rapidly, serving as a shipping point for the vast supply of lumber then harvested in the surrounding area. Little is known about community life between 1869 and the early 1880s. An item taken from the 1879–80 Gazateer Business Directory does shed some light on that period:

"Rocky Ford—Located near the Ogeechee River, 14 miles southwest of the Sylvania court house, 65 miles from Savannah, is a place of perhaps 35 inhabitants and ships principally cotton. Mail daily each way. William A. Edenfield Jr., postmaster; John M. Edenfield, artist; William A. Edenfield, grist mill; William A. Edenfield, Jr. General Store; Oliver Finch, grist mill; Elisha Shaw Mallory, machinist; George M. Wallace, justice."

The Central of Georgia Railroad reached Rocky Ford around 1840, and Central of Georgia officials soon recognized that the town was destined to become an important business center. Consequently, railroad facilities in the town were improved to accommodate increased business. A depot, well appointed for a small community, was erected, and a more modern one was built at a later date.

Rocky Ford became an important railway junction, thanks to the business generated by the Sylvania Central Railroad and the E.E. Foy Manufacturing Company, located across the Ogeechee just inside Bulloch County. Around 1890, the Central extended the run of its popular train, "The Shoofly," to the town in order to facilitate increased travel. This train made a round-trip journey between Rocky Ford and Savannah on a daily basis, leaving early and returning at night, until E.E. Foy Manufacturing Company moved its plant to Egypt, and "The Shoofly" did likewise.

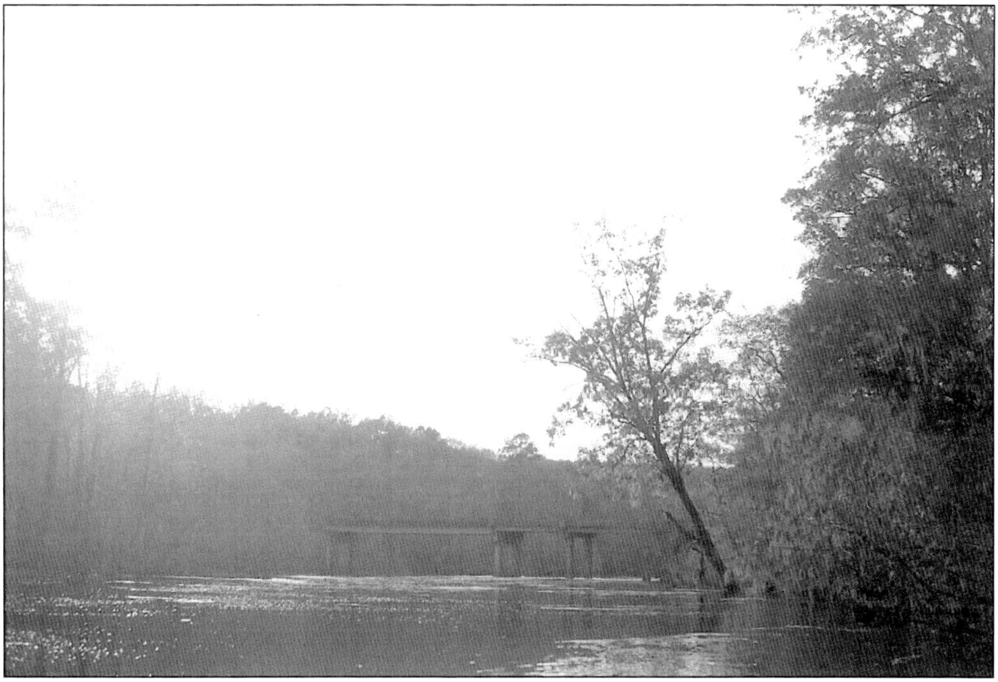

A concrete bridge made fording the Ogeechee a more pleasant experience.

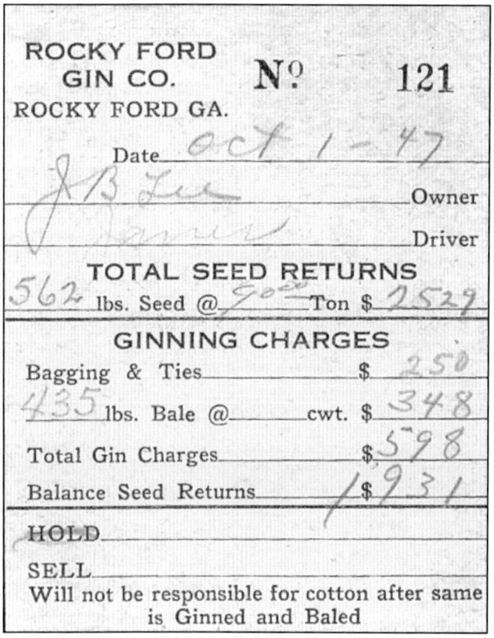

ROCKY FORD GIN CO. №. 121

ROCKY FORD GA.

Date Oct 1-47

J B Lee Owner

[illegible] Driver

TOTAL SEED RETURNS

562 lbs. Seed @ 90.00 Ton $ 25.29

GINNING CHARGES

Bagging & Ties $ 2.50

435 lbs. Bale @ cwt. $ 3.48

Total Gin Charges $ 5.98

Balance Seed Returns $ 19.31

HOLD

SELL

Will not be responsible for cotton after same is Ginned and Baled

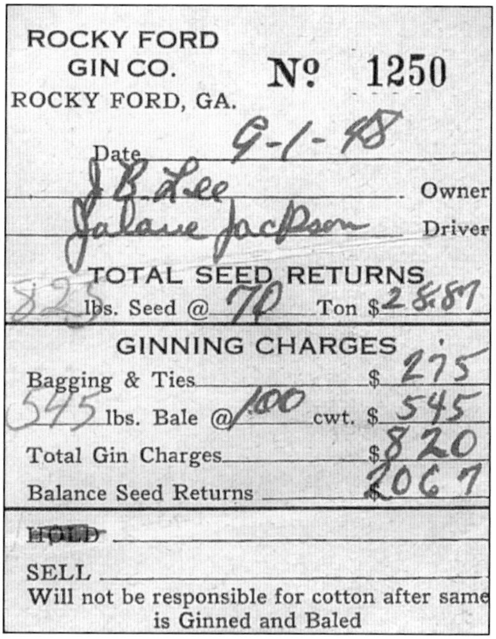

ROCKY FORD GIN CO. №. 1250

ROCKY FORD, GA.

Date 9-1-48

J B Lee Owner

Jalaue Jackson Driver

TOTAL SEED RETURNS

823 lbs. Seed @ 70 Ton $ 28.81

GINNING CHARGES

Bagging & Ties $ 2.75

545 lbs. Bale @ 1.00 cwt. $ 5.45

Total Gin Charges $ 8.20

Balance Seed Returns $ 20.67

HOLD

SELL

Will not be responsible for cotton after same is Ginned and Baled

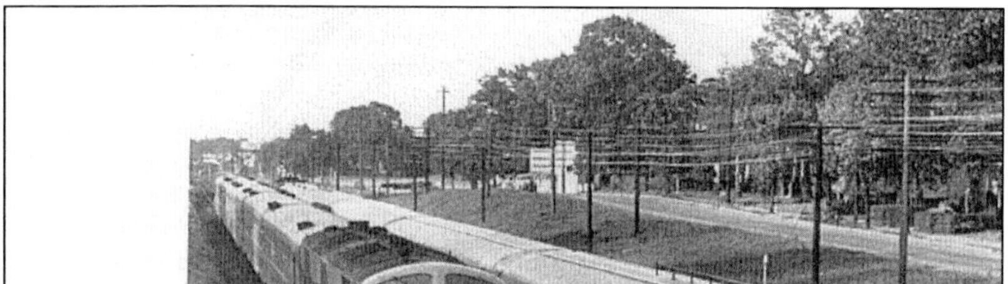

The railroad and cotton kept Rocky Ford on the map.

Three

War Comes Home

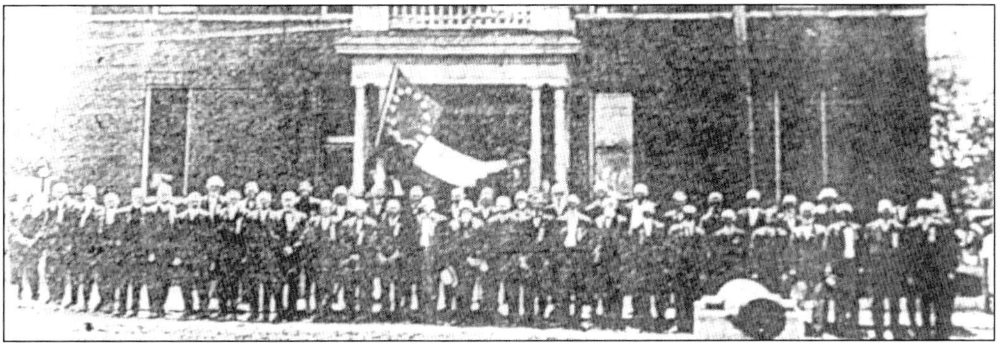

Screven Countians were preparing for war in 1861. The county's representatives, Curtis Humphries Sr. and J. Lawton Singellton, voted for secession when the Georgia Secession Convention met in January. Soon, men like the veterans above, who posed for a photograph in the early 1900s, were training for war all over the county.

The Screven Guards eventually became part of the 47th Regiment of Confederate Infantry. The Ogeechee Rifles, the Black Creek Volunteers, and Brown's Light Infantry were all accepted into the 25th Regiment.

Both regiments began the war fighting on the Georgia/Carolina coast, then were later transferred to Mississippi, where the Screven Countians served in the Jackson area during the summer of 1863. In September of that year, at Chickamauga, they were among the thousands in the Confederate Army of Tennessee who engaged the enemy heavily and suffered many casualties.

Most of 1864 saw the local soldiers help General Joe Johnston oppose Gen. W.T. Sherman in numerous battles around Atlanta. The 25th then followed General John Bell Hood to Tennessee, and the 47th returned to the South Carolina coast for the war's final months. The two regiments were reunited in the Army of Tennessee, when Johnston surrendered to Sherman at Greensboro, North Carolina, on April 26, 1865.

Some 800 Screven County men served the Confederacy. Most of those who saw extended duty and heavy combat were in the 25th and 47th regiments, but some were in other units, such as a company called the Screven Troop, which became Company F, 5th Cavalry Regiment; a company that became Company B, 7th Cavalry regiment; and a company that became Company D, 54th Infantry regiment.

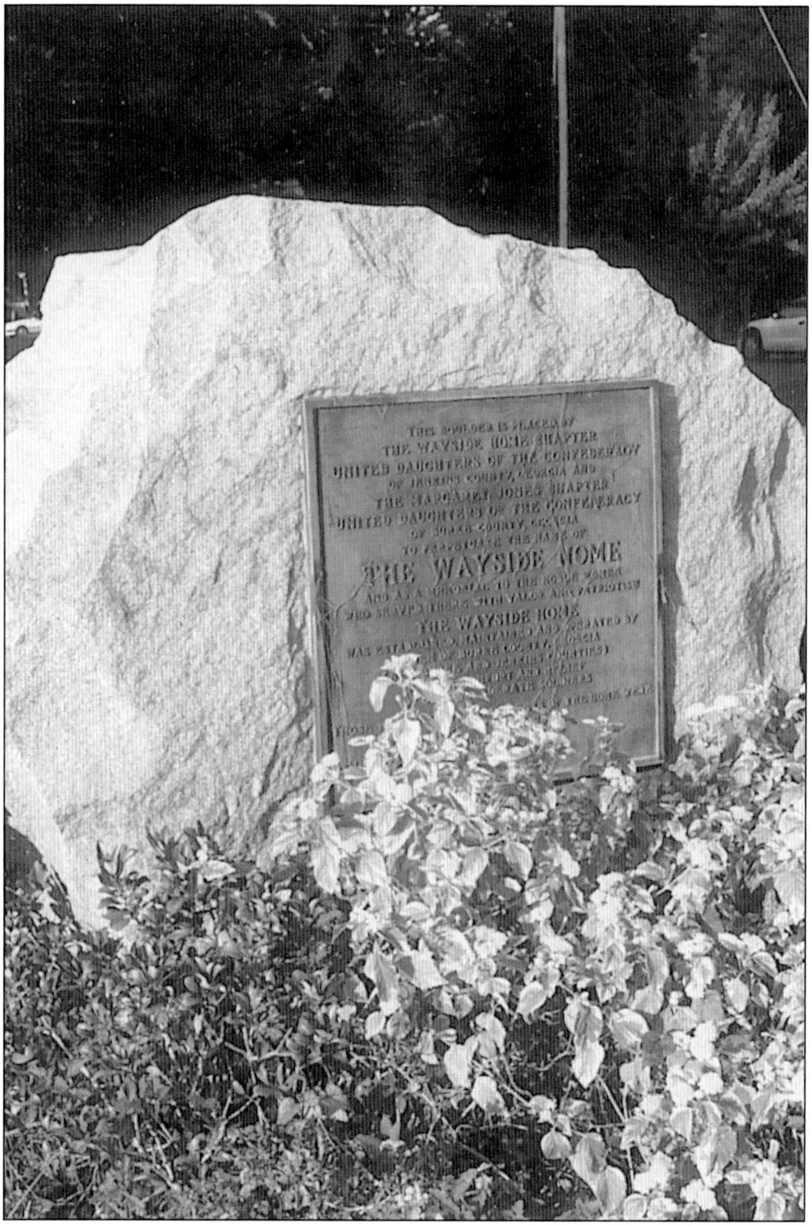

On the home front, the area's civilian population rallied to the cause. Men unable to serve in the Confederate Army served in other capacities that supported the war effort, and women did their part sewing uniforms, flags, and other things the troops desperately needed.

Among those women were the ladies who established the Wayside Home in Millen. On an around-the-clock basis, seven days a week, the Wayside Committee fed hungry soldiers, nurtured the sick and wounded, and provided a short respite from the rigors of war. Established in 1861, the Wayside Home made Millen a welcome spot for thousands of Confederate soldiers transported via the Central of Georgia Railroad and its supporting lines.

Situated next to the Central tracks in the heart of Millen, the Wayside Home operated throughout the war. Mary C. MacKenzie founded the home, and area ladies collected food, clothing, and medicine.

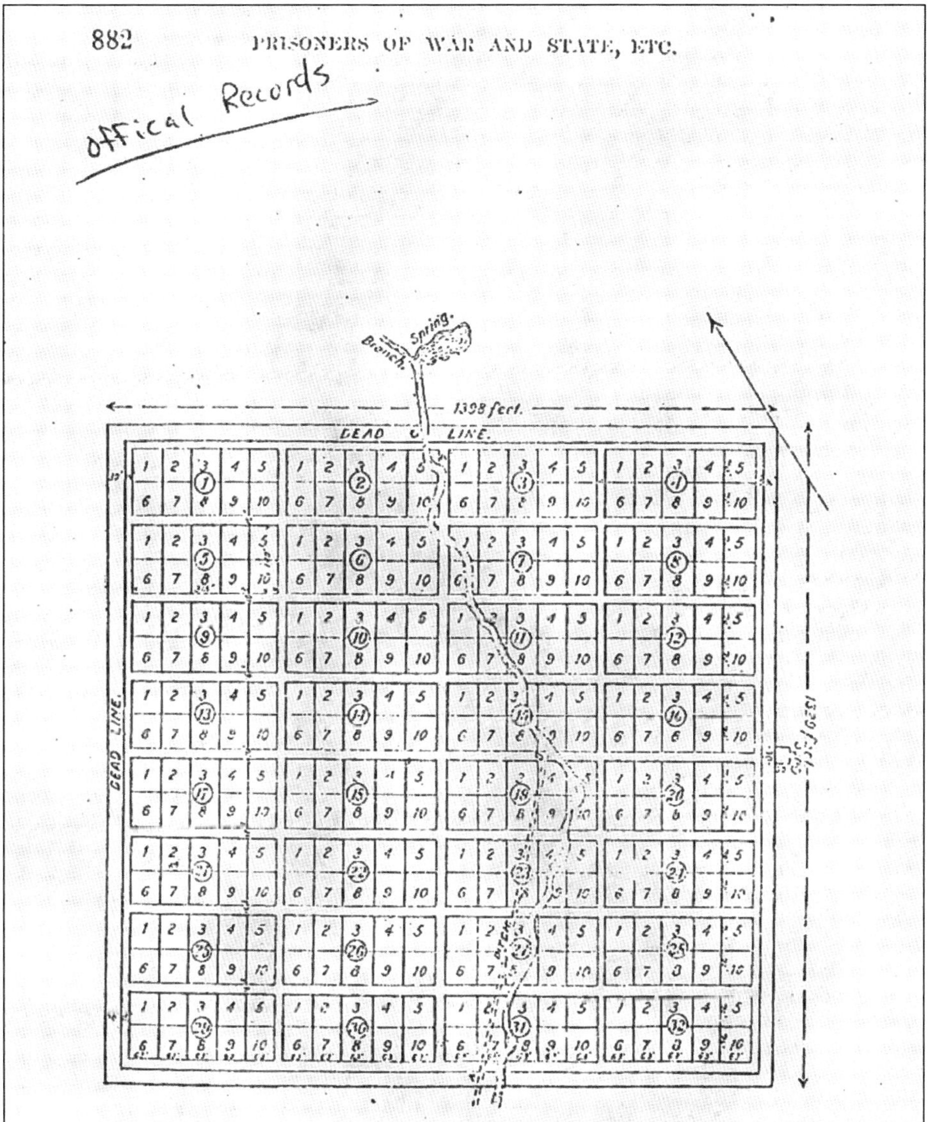

Millen was also the site of another war-time necessity. Camp Lawton prison camp was constructed and opened in 1864. Located 5 miles north of Millen, near the Augusta Railroad at Magnolia Springs, Camp Lawton was designed to accommodate excess Union prisoners that were previously held at Andersonville. It was one of 26 prominent stockades the Confederacy built, nine of which were in Georgia.

The facility was first scheduled to open in the summer of 1864, but the lack of funds and impressed labor delayed prison occupation until early October. Prisoners were shuttled by rail from Andersonville to Millen, where they arrived October 10th. The move included all Andersonville prisoners able to move, along with their guards. That number included 700 sick prisoners.

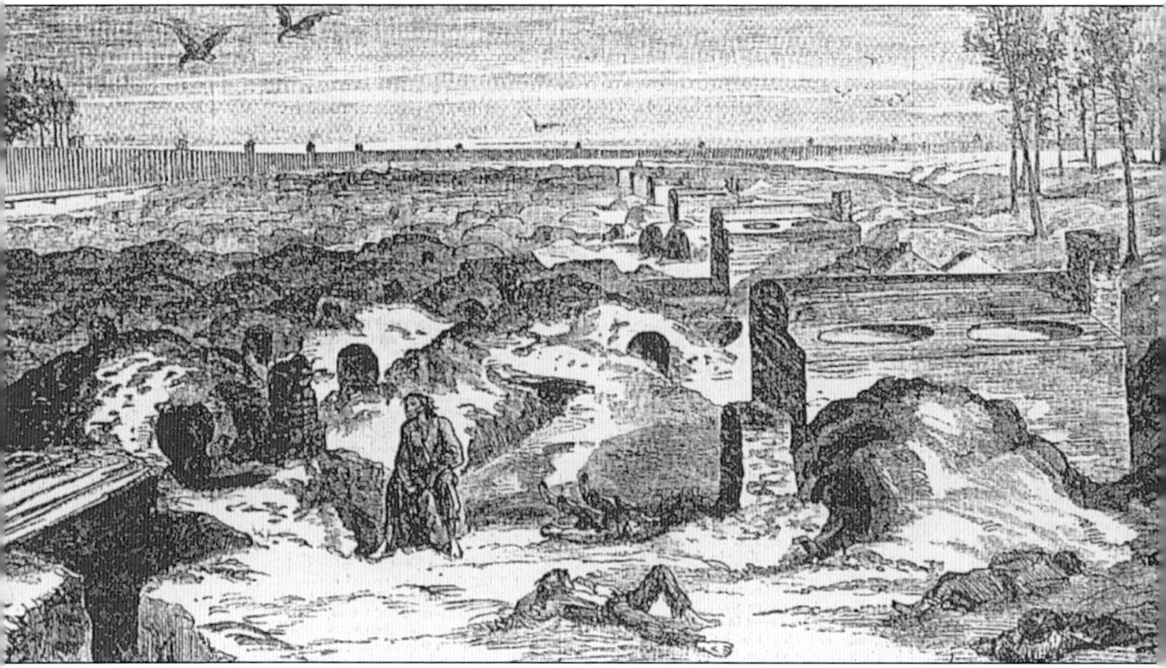

The Lawton stockade was one of the largest prisons in the world, built in the open style favored in that period. The facility was, in essence, a series of trees, standing one beside the other, in a huge square. A 30-foot-square gate, 15 to 20 feet high, with a catwalk along the top, dominated the east wall. Picket huts located every 50 feet served as sentry posts. A deadline stretched about 30 feet inside the stockade walls.

Camp Lawton measured 1,398 feet by 1,329 feet, enclosed 42 acres, and covered an area of nearly a quarter mile. It was designed to hold 32,000 prisoners and could hold some 40,000 if necessary. Andersonville covered about 26 acres and was built to hold 10,000.

The prison was divided into 32 sections, each of which held 1,000 prisoners. Each section was then divided into ten smaller areas designed to accommodate 100 prisoners. Consequently, each prisoner's living space amounted to about 44 square feet.

A stream (now known as Magnolia Springs) flowed through the middle of the prison, entering through the north wall and exiting through the south wall. Prisoners bathed and collected drinking water in the upper half. The lower half was reserved for sewage.

Three earthworks were built to guard the prison and its approaches. These were armed with 11 cannons manned by guards enrolled in the Georgia Reserves. The first prisoners used leftover lumber to build crude shelters. Later arrivals often draped blankets over holes they dug in the ground and filled the holes with brush for insulation.

Cooking facilities were incomplete. Hospital and health supplies were only slightly better than those at Andersonville. On November 8, 1864, Captain D.W. Vowles, commander of the prison, reported 486 deaths, 16 per day from early October to November 8th, among the 10,299 prisoners. The common ailments were diarrhea, dysentery, scurvy, and pneumonia. Vowles said 285 prisoners were detailed to work at the post, and 349 prisoners had enlisted in the Confederate service.

But the Millen prison camp's days were numbered. Union General William T. Sherman's army left Atlanta November 16th and moved rapidly across the state. By the end of November, Union troops were closing in on Camp Lawton, determined to free the prisoners. Consequently, on November 22nd, General Winder reported that all the prisoners had been sent to Savannah. Eventually, the majority was moved to Florence, South Carolina, although some were sent by rail to Blackshear and Thomasville in South Georgia.

The prisoner's life was one of suffering and despair. Housing facilities were deplorable under the best of situations, and food was scarce and lacked any variety whatsoever. George A. Hitchcock, a Massachusetts soldier who was among the prisoners moved from Andersonville to Camp Lawton, shared his experiences in his journal:

November 4, 1864
Packed like sardines and no change of position is possible. Eighty-three human breathers soon make the air of the shut up car very foul, but all through the night and the day in the one same sitting posture with the rain pelting against the car and nothing to eat, surely misery cannot much further go. We passed through Macon at daylight and turn on to the Charleston Railroad. Not the least idea can we gain of the country through which we pass. It is far into the night when we stop at Millen Station and are allowed to get out and stretch our aching limbs. As each car load is counted off, it is found that several have escaped during the journey while one of my own Mess was found dead in my car. He had been sick and the crowded condition of the car had killed him; one more victim to rebel cruelty. We are more than two hundred miles from Andersonville and none too far away either. March half a mile and come to the gates of another stockade [Camp Lawton], but we are kept outside until daylight.

November 4
The weather cleared during the night and the day opened very cold and windy. Suffered severely for lack of shelter and clothing. Have taken a cold. After arranging the shivering crowd into detachments as before, the rebs turned us into the pen where rations were issued to us: rice, meal, beef, beans and salt. Found the place a great contrast to Andersonville. Although about ten thousand of the old prisoners are here, the camp is laid out with some pretense of regularity and a considerable clear space covered with grass. There is a creek of good water running through camp and I camp down by its side, thinking if I could only keep warm I should be all right.

November 5
Drew two days rations; better in quality and quantity than at Andersonville. The men who arrived here first have made very comfortable winter quarters of logs. Several hundred, who thought they were going to be exchanged, in their disappointment and despair, have taken the oath of allegiance and gone into the rebel army. Poor soldiers they will make for a falling cause.

November 10
Rain in the morning but cold and windy at night. A rebel officer has been in camp looking up and taking the names of those most destitute of clothing, presumably to prepare our men for the coming winter.

November 11
Clear and cold. A recruiting officer has been in camp, enticing prisoners to enlist into the rebel army. Several went from our division. Pretty hard up must be the cause that accepts such service as that. The clothing inspector examined our division in the afternoon. For sale in abundance: roast chicken, boiled sweet potatoes, eggs, biscuits, butter, pumpkin and potato pies, rice and bean soups, soda cakes and molasses, but our experience is the same as the Ancient Mariner - "Food a everywhere, but not a morsel for us."

November 21
Storm all day. As soon as the 2nd Division had vacated its comfortable quarters, I with others arose at one o'clock in the night and occupied one of the fine shanties. We enjoyed it until dark of this day - when lo! we are ordered to pack up and leave. We start off in the rain in great wonderment as to the meaningof this haste. Rumors are rife that Sherman has something to do with it and our suspicions are confirmed when we reach the depot and see train after train hurrying down past us toward Savannah, laden with every description of household goods: furniture, countrymen and their families and negroes of all ages. Numberless trains of all sorts arrive and deposit their freight along the side of the railroad. We, meanwhile, have to stand waiting in a terrible freezing, biting wind for hours.

November 22
But at last near four o'clock in the morning, more dead than alive and chilled to the heart, we are packed on a train—sixty to a car and glide away on one of the smoothest railroads I ever passed over. Our three weeks imprisonment in Millen was in several ways beneficial to us: the change of sights and opportunity to breath pure air, pleasant surroundings and the knowledge that more humane counsels prevailed with those in authority. All these causes served to raise our well-nigh despairing spirits so that when we drew out of Millen in such a pitiable condition, our hearts had taken new courage. The belief that Sherman was not far off gave new courage for us to hold out a little longer. The country through which we passed was a monotonous level—almost entirely covered with great stretches of pine forests.

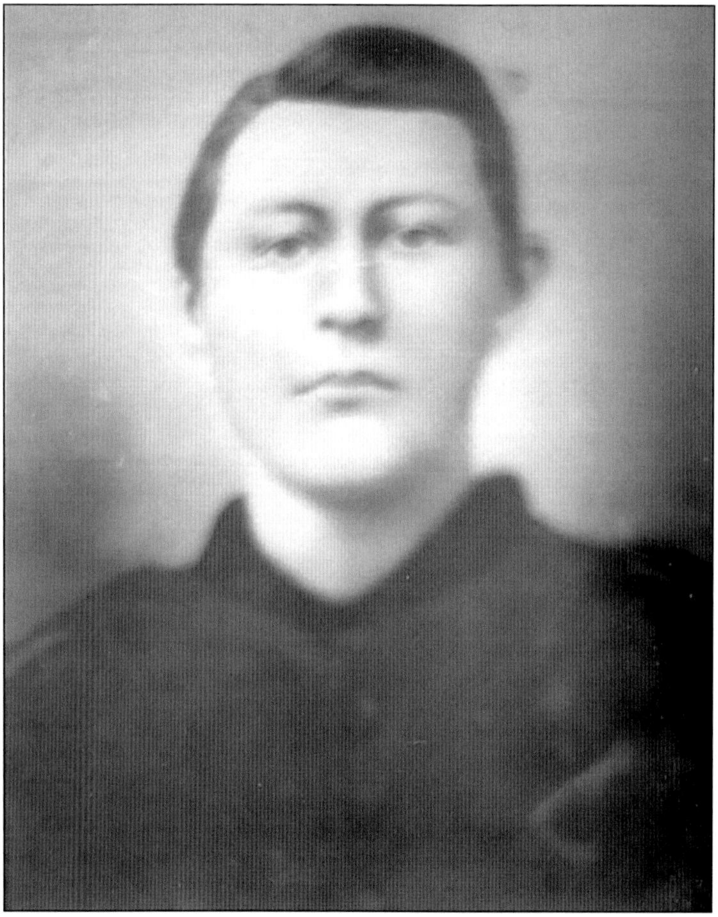

Area soldiers, like this one named Perkins, fought diligently far from home.

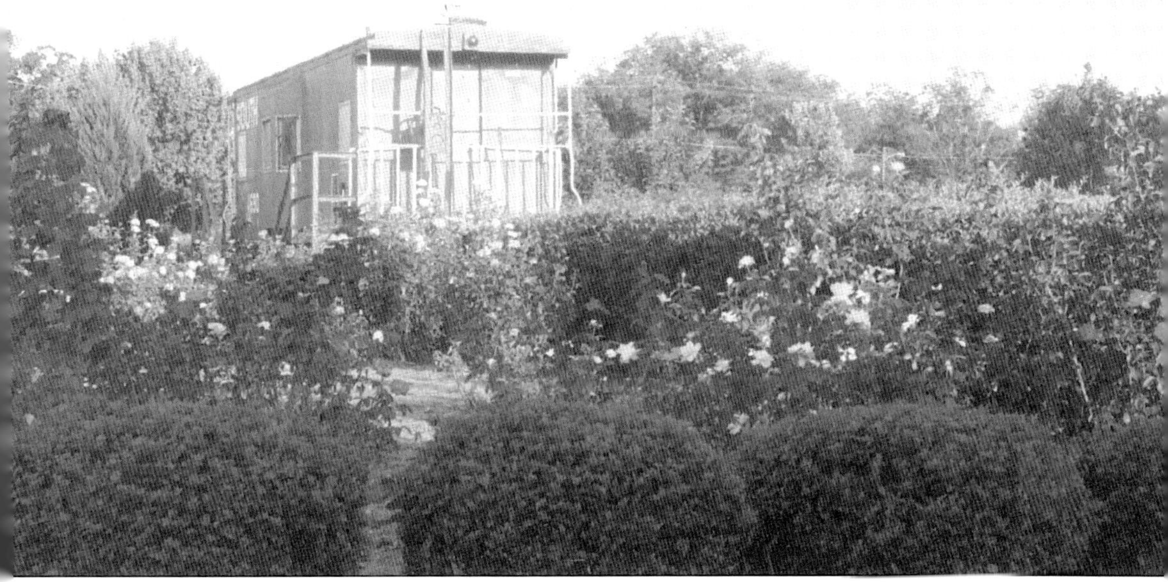

This is a current shot of the Millen depot area. This spot, where the 1864 conflagration occurred, is now a beautiful spot where people gather to remember the past and plan for the future.

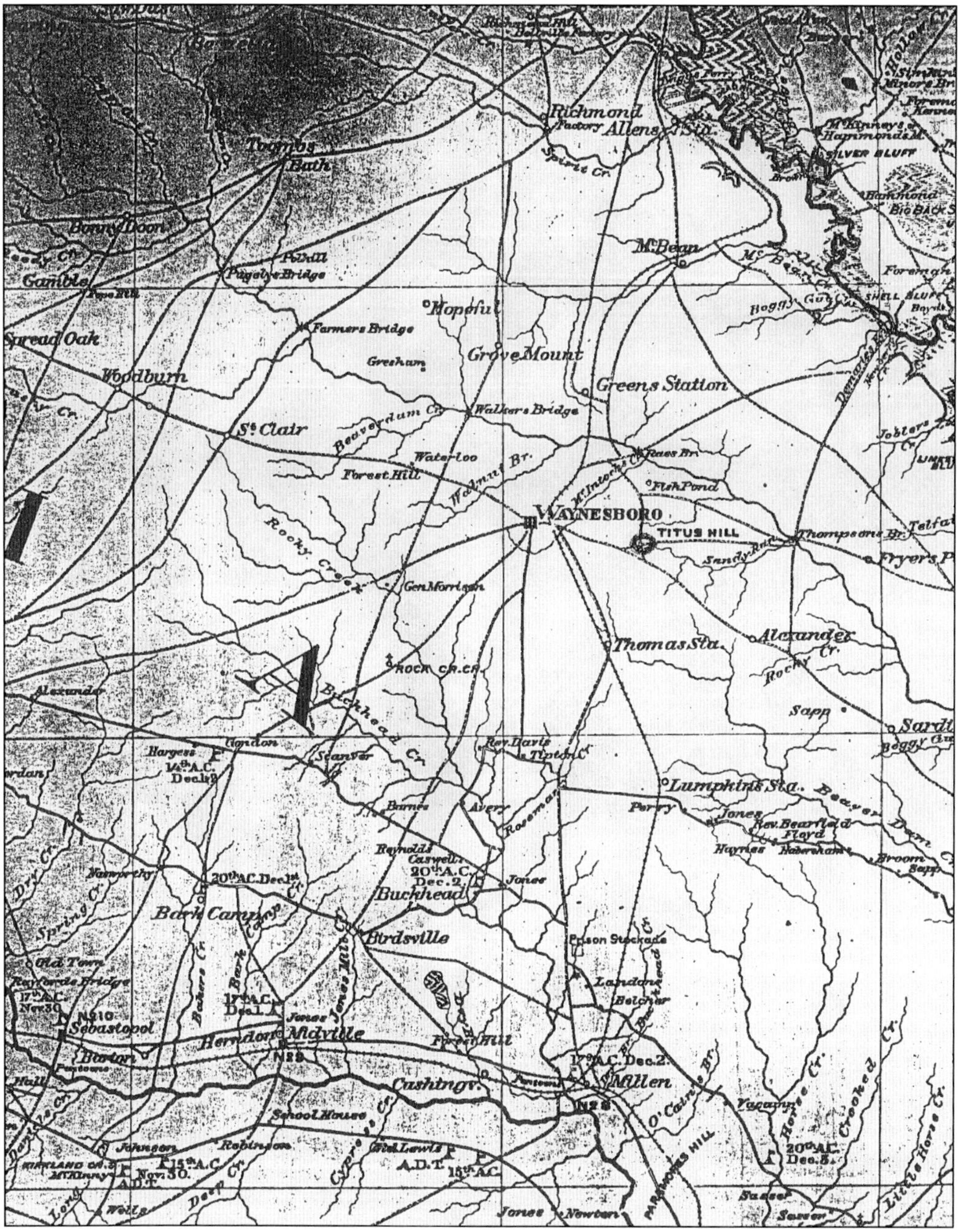

Within days, Union General William T. Sherman and his troops were prowling the countryside in and around Millen. This map shows where the Federal troops were during the week-long struggle between Federal and Confederate cavalry operating in the area. Known as the Battle of Waynesborough, the series of skirmishes occurred in late November and early December of 1864. It was probably the last all-out battle between Union and Confederate troops before Sherman's army took Savannah.

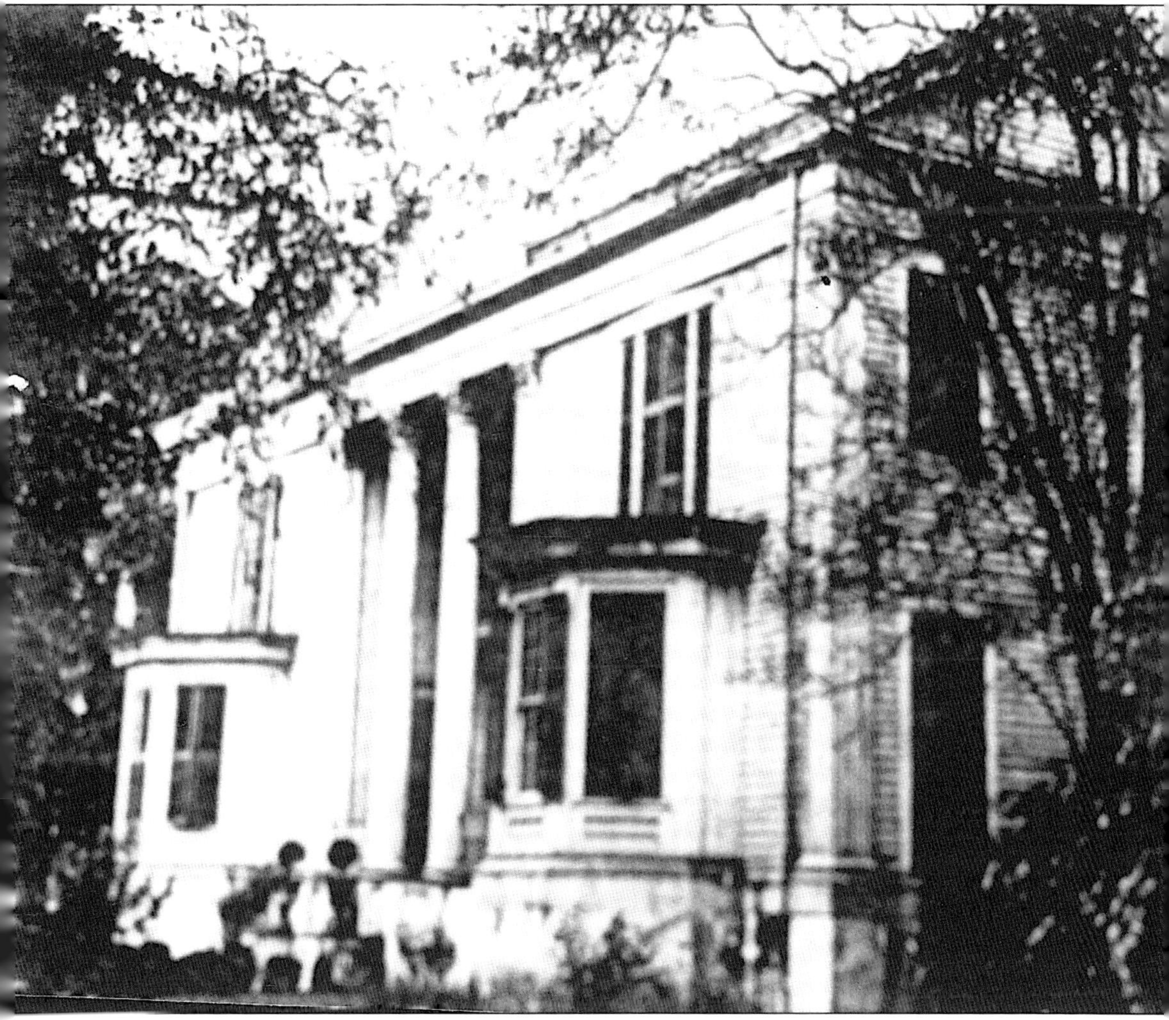

At Birdsville Plantation, about 10 miles northwest of Millen, Union soldiers ransacked the house and outbuildings, then threatened to burn the place to the ground. But the mistress of the house, bedridden following the birth of twins (who had quickly died), saved the mansion when she refused to leave her chamber.

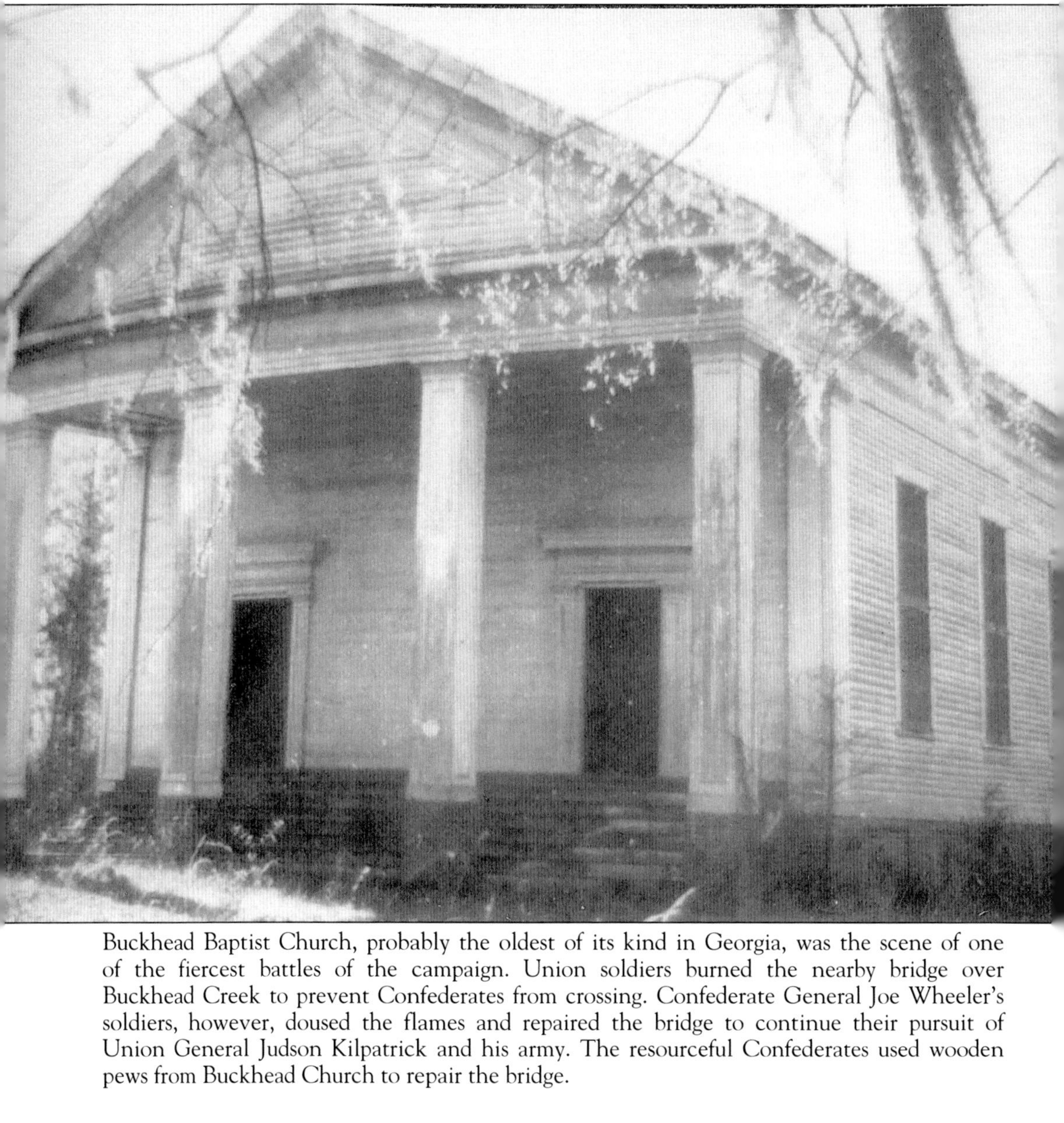

Buckhead Baptist Church, probably the oldest of its kind in Georgia, was the scene of one of the fiercest battles of the campaign. Union soldiers burned the nearby bridge over Buckhead Creek to prevent Confederates from crossing. Confederate General Joe Wheeler's soldiers, however, doused the flames and repaired the bridge to continue their pursuit of Union General Judson Kilpatrick and his army. The resourceful Confederates used wooden pews from Buckhead Church to repair the bridge.

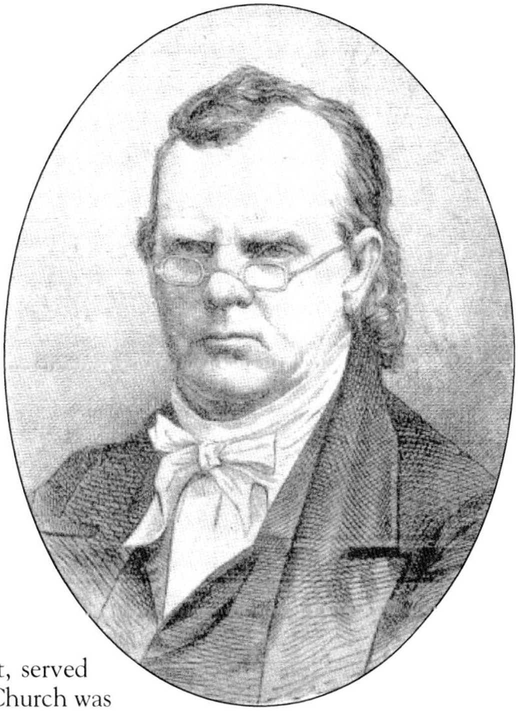

The Reverend J.H.T. Kilpatrick, at top right, served Buckhead for many years. Nearby Fairhaven Church was also ransacked.

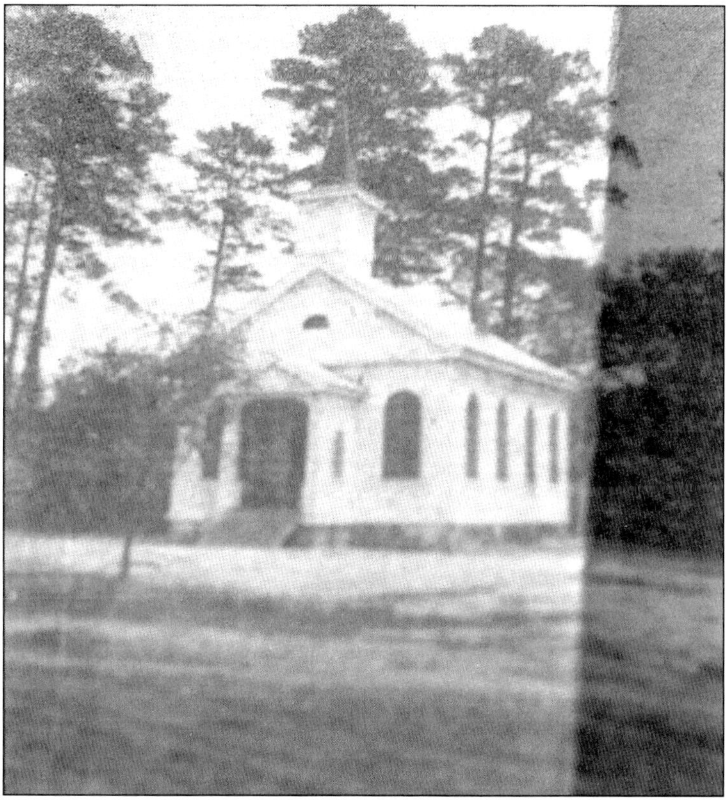

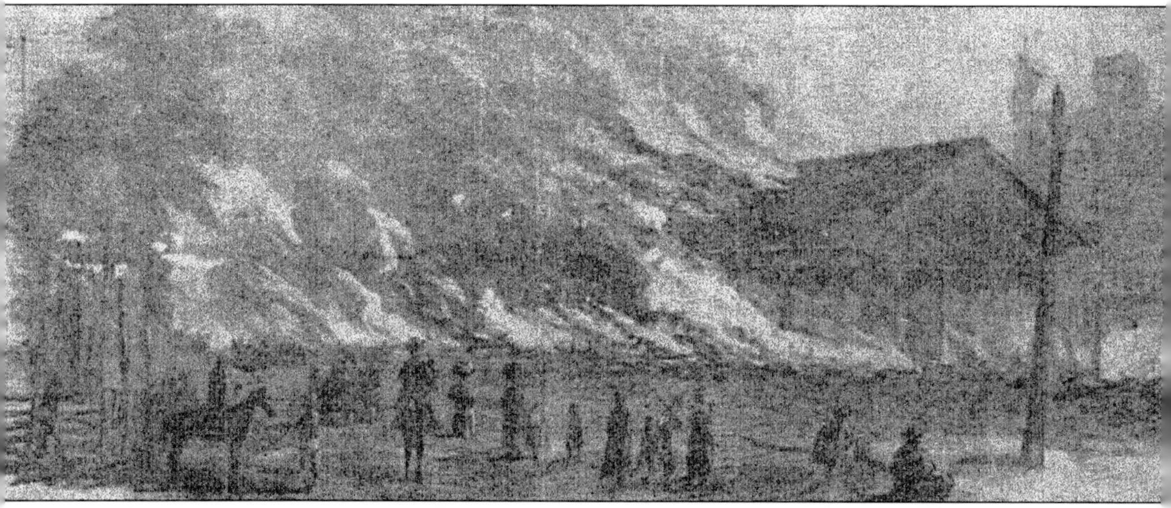

The Union army arrived in Millen on December 3, 1864, and promptly burned the town down. Major Henry Hitchcock, a member of Sherman's staff, recorded the event in his diary:

But there are hardly any—that is, were hardly any but railroad buildings here. Over the R.R. track stood when we came a really fine frame R.R. depot,—of which Davis is making a capital sketch for Harpers' Weekly—some 200 feet long, I should judge, open at the sides the roof resting on wooden arches springing longitudinally from wooden columns. On the E. Side of this was a handsome little station house, apparently used for ticket and other offices and perhaps cold refreshments. I didn't get into it. On the West side, facing the Stationhouse, say 100 feet off, was a large two story frame hotel, with many rooms, large dining hall, and quite a number of outbuildings, also a gasometer and gas apparatus in the yard and the house lit with gas. In front of this was a yard or garden filled with handsome trees, bushes, etc. Further down the railroad on t'other (E) side stood three large frame storehouses, 100 feet deep X 40 to 50 feet wide each, side by side, and facing and very near the R.R. tracks, and good high board fences around three sides. They were evidently built and had been used for Confederate storehouses.

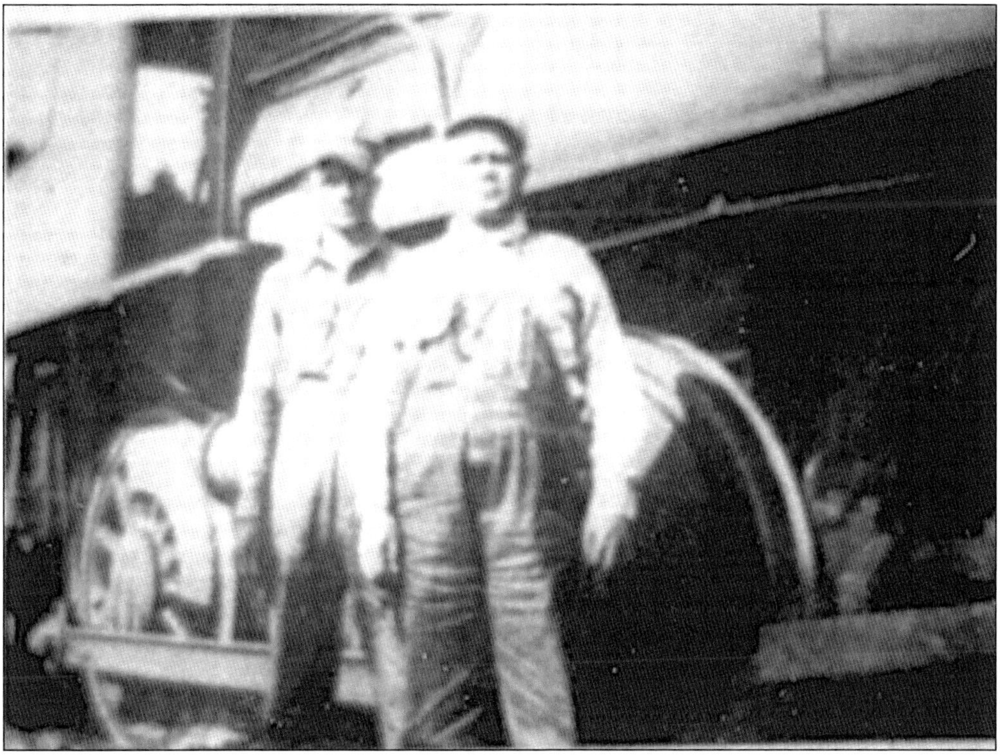
Along the way, Sherman's men destroyed the railroad.

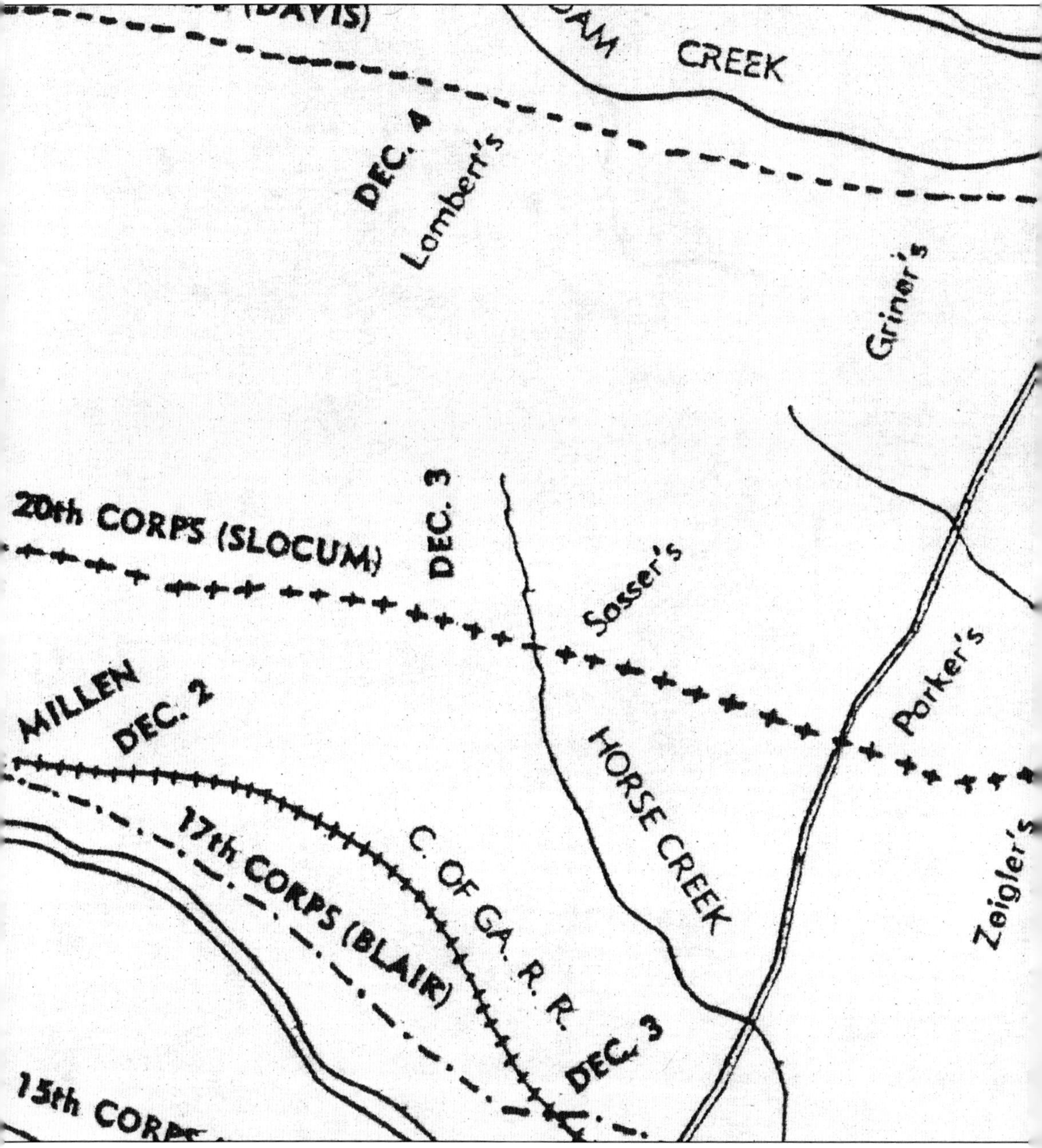

With Millen in ashes, Sherman and his troops turned south toward Savannah. Howard's Corps marched below the Ogeechee River on the Bulloch side. Blair's column, which included Sherman himself, continued down the Old Louisville Road, now Highway 17. Soldiers destroyed Central of Georgia tracks as they went along, passing through Scarborough, Rocky Ford, Dover, and Oliver. Davis Corps came into Screven on the Habersham Road, passing below Beaver Dam Creek and Brier Creek, then marching southward along a path roughly corresponding to Highway 24. Sherman's 62,000 men met no organized opposition during the three-day period required for the army to pass through the county.

During that time, the Federals visited Parker's Station near today's Rocky Ford, the home

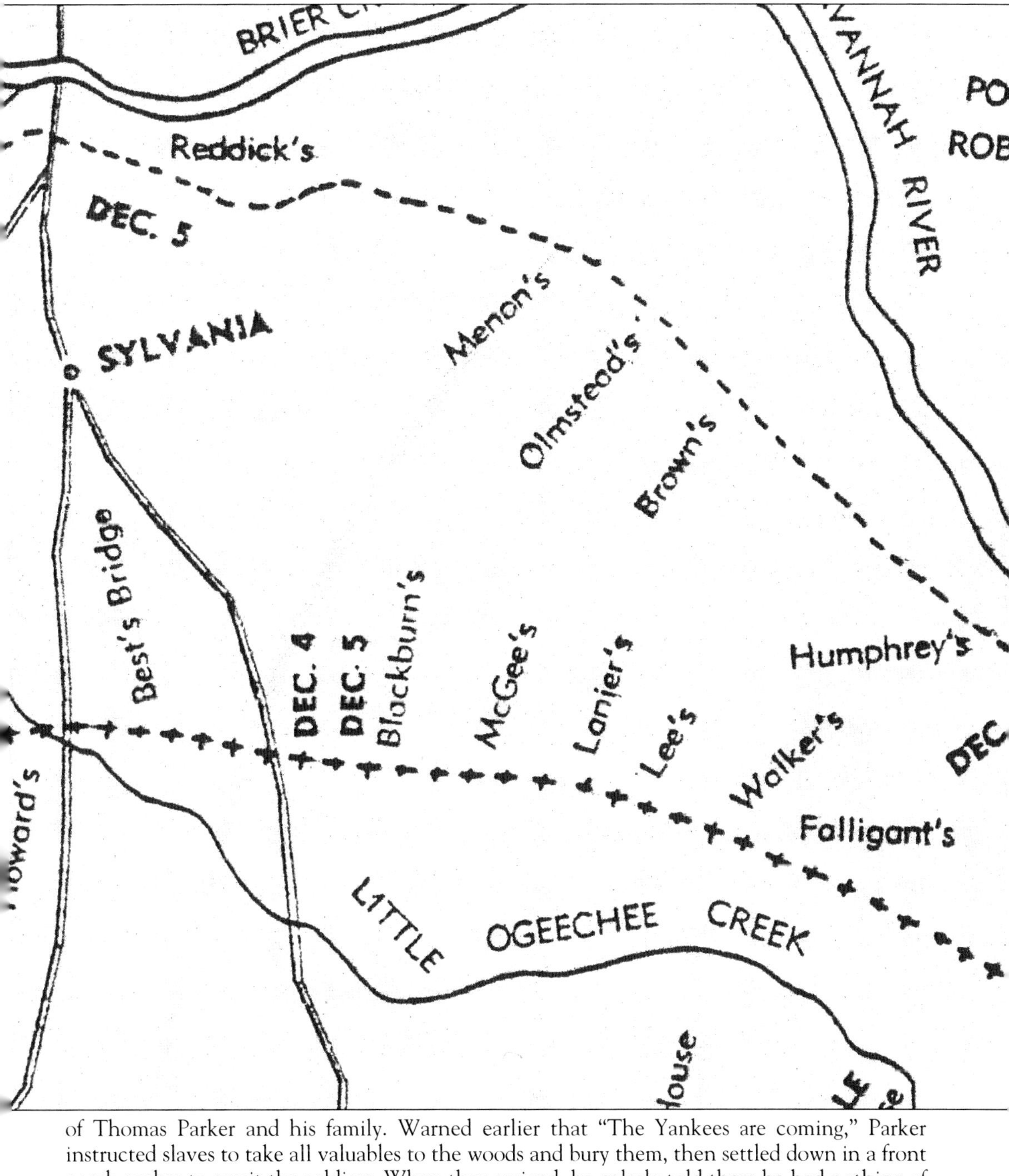

of Thomas Parker and his family. Warned earlier that "The Yankees are coming," Parker instructed slaves to take all valuables to the woods and bury them, then settled down in a front porch rocker to await the soldiers. When they arrived, he calmly told them he had nothing of any value, a statement proven valid during a search that followed. And so the Yankees moved on, leaving Parker right where they had found him.

The soldiers then moved on to the Screven County community known as Halcyondale, where the army established headquarters for the night. Sherman spent his final night in the county at the Lufburrow house in nearby Oliver.

Battle of Waynesboro Dec. 4, 1864

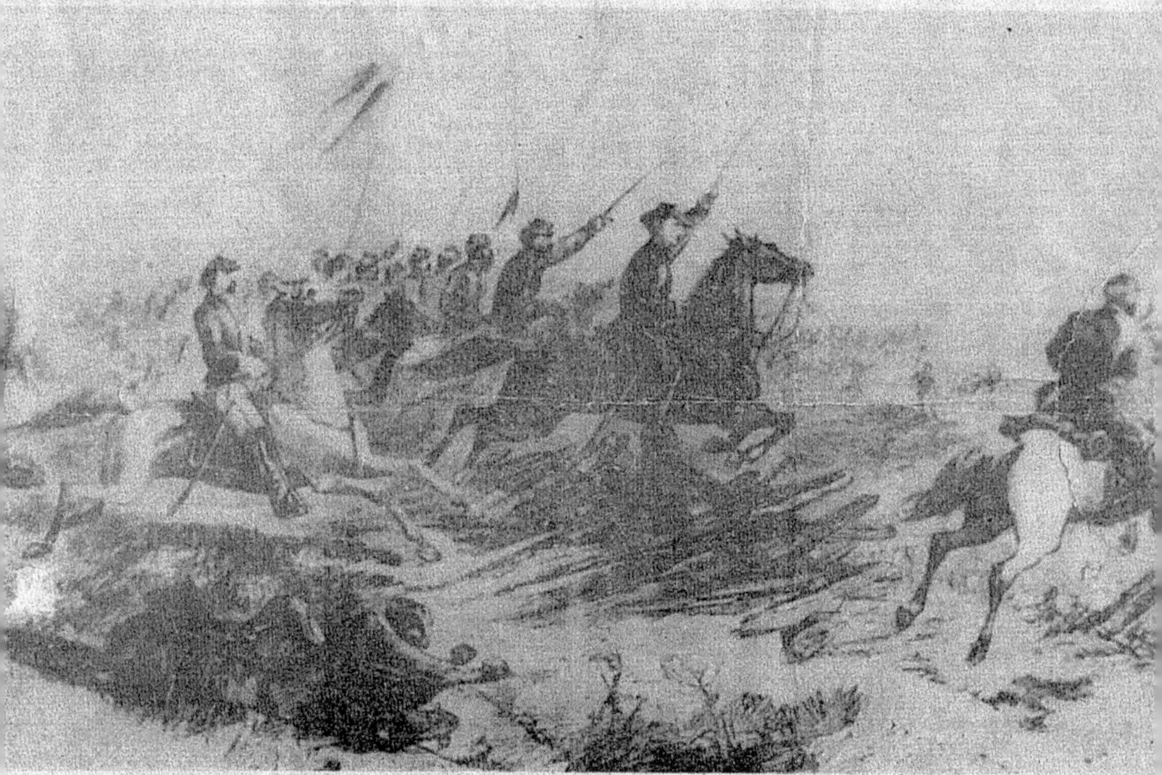

KILPATRICK'S LAST CHARGE AT WAYNESBORO ROUTED WHEELER'S CAVALRY
This was one of the few fierce battles of Sherman's March to the Sea.

Decades after the war, Screven County's Captain William Henderson shared his experiences as a soldier participating in the Battle of Waynesboro: "I was color bearer in my company. Well, the fight began near the little creek below here—McIntosh, and we fought all over the field to the right. It was in that field that I dismounted an adjutant of a Michigan regiment with my flag-staff and would have killed him if it had not bent double. Afterwards I was glad I did not kill him for he was a handsome fellow. In a few minutes, I began to retreat and had reached the town and were right in front of Dr. Whithead's home. I was standing shoulder to shoulder to Captain Bess when he fell mortally wounded. Being color bearer I always felt that he received the shot intended for me. We could not stop to remove him, but we heard that some of the enemy picked him up and carried him into the house. That night, we camped near Briar Creek—I think it was nearly Christmas time."

Four

THE THREE "RS" AND PRAYER

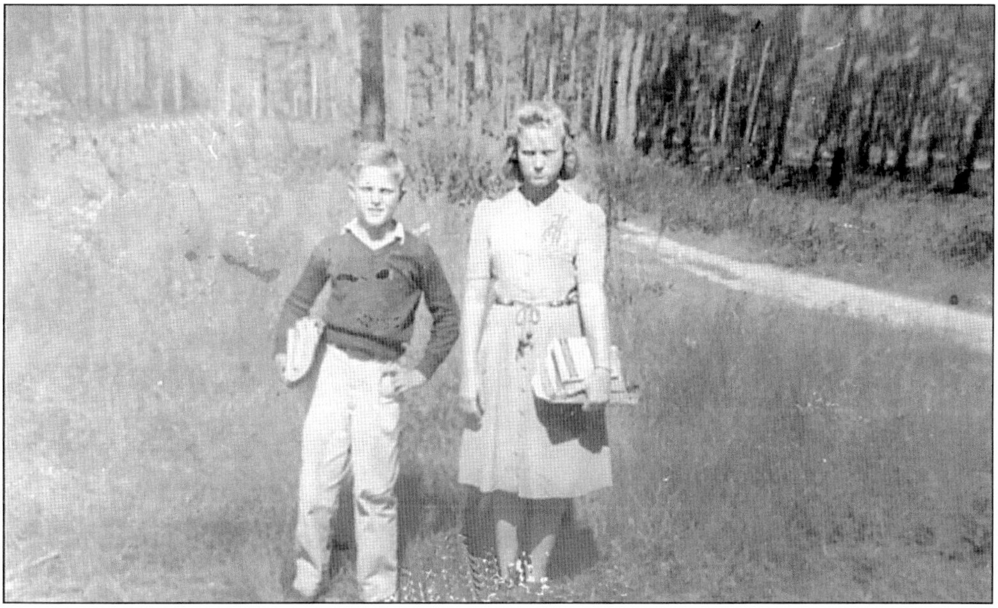

Education for Screven County's children was a subject that interested area officials from the earliest days. But more than a century passed before an effective, tax-supported school system was developed. By the 1940s, however, the county provided timely instruction in modern facilities for students like Brantley and Emily Bazemore.

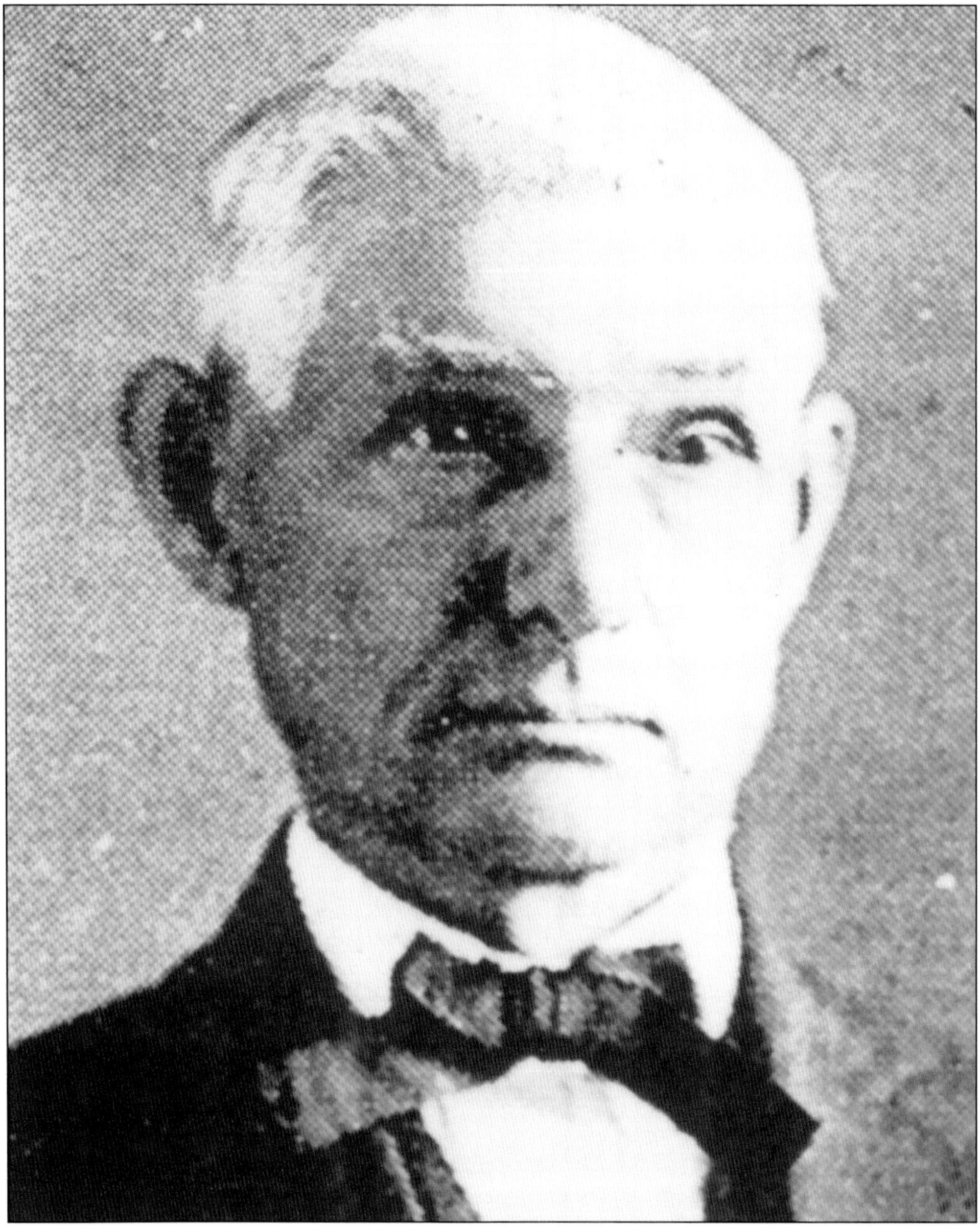

The esteemed and respected Reverend Hamilton John Arnett was the county school superintendent during the early 1900s, a significantly progressive time in the history of Screven County education. He was also the pastor of several Baptist churches in the county and, for 24 years, Screven County's tax collector. This beloved school superintendent worked tirelessly for nearly 30 years to mold the county's school system into a viable educational system that prepared students for their adult lives. He finally stepped down from the post in 1928.

Arnett's efforts brought about the 1924 completion of a school building large enough to house students throughout the school years. School children began their schooling in the north end of the building and gradually worked to the other end. The 11th grade was the highest, and most students were just 16, or barely 17, when they graduated.

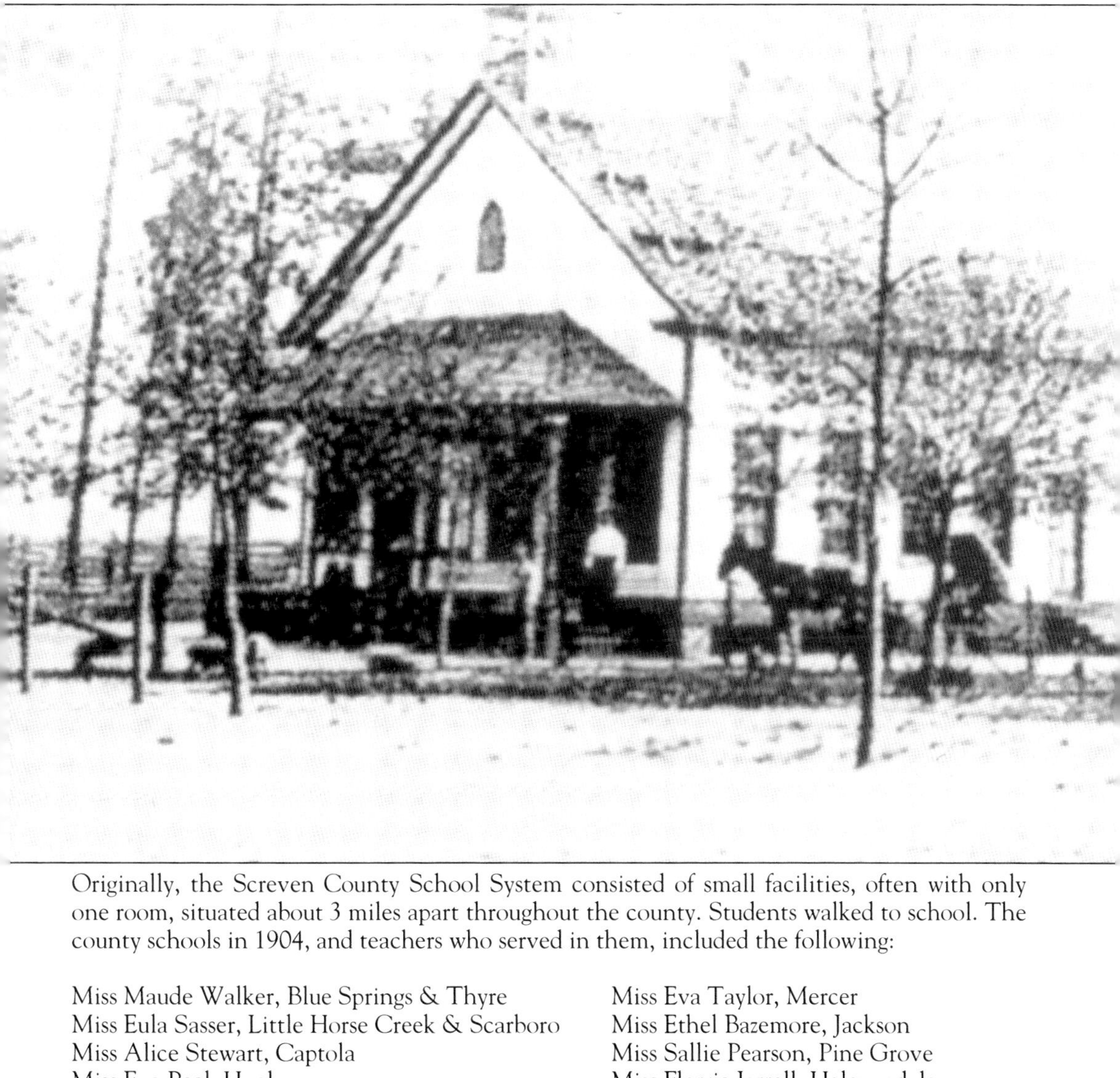

Originally, the Screven County School System consisted of small facilities, often with only one room, situated about 3 miles apart throughout the county. Students walked to school. The county schools in 1904, and teachers who served in them, included the following:

Miss Maude Walker, Blue Springs & Thyre
Miss Eula Sasser, Little Horse Creek & Scarboro
Miss Alice Stewart, Captola
Miss Eva Peel, Hook
Miss Susie Overstreet, Wesley & Midway
Miss Hessie Newton, Oliver
Miss Isabel Hollingsworth, Sylvania
D.J. Wallace, Pine Vale & Oak Hill
A.B. Jenkins, Bascom
J.P. Dell, Cave Springs
U.O. Thompson, Middleground
W.M. Scott, Maple Branch
J.M. Bazemore, Elmwood & Lee-Evans
J.L. Lee, Hamilton & Williamson
H.L. Howard, Bradwell & Gilgal
Miss Eva Taylor, Mercer
Miss Ethel Bazemore, Jackson
Miss Sallie Pearson, Pine Grove
Miss Florrie Jarrell, Halcyondale
Mrs. C.M. Cooper, Cooperville
Miss Lessie Crawford, Sylvania
W.C. Howard, Harwell & Gilgal
S.P. Rhodes, Spring Branch
Berry Jenkins Jr., Lee & Hurst
J.C. Irvine, Newington
J.H. Waters, Goloid
S.R. Sowell, Newton
R.J. Mincey, Friendship
D.S. Lafitte, Rocky Ford
J.H. Jarrell, Marlow

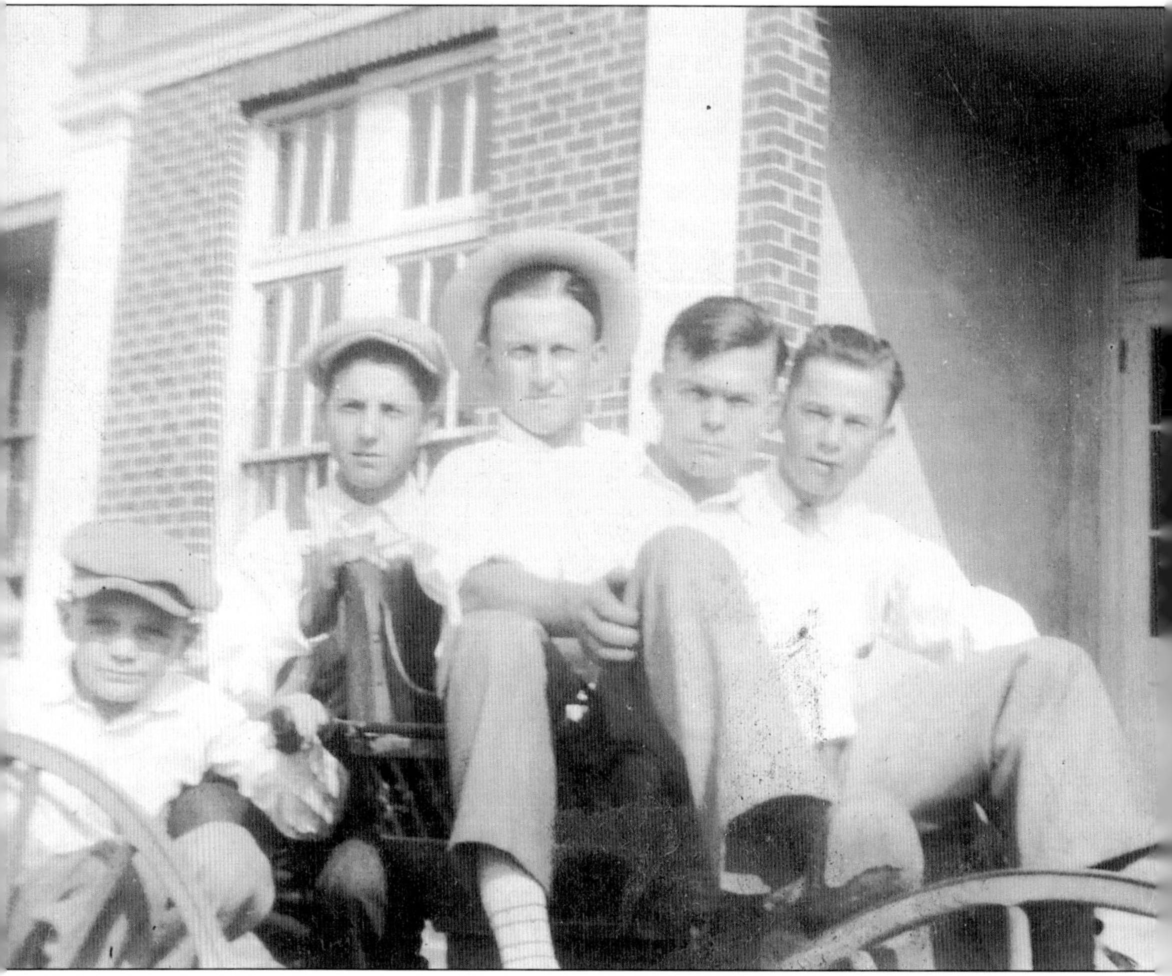

Rocky Ford's first schoolhouse, a one-room facility torn down years ago, played a vital part in Screven County's early development. It served as schoolhouse, church, meeting place, etc., for some 20 years. During many of those years, J.E. Irving, a teacher of many attainments, often taught 60 students, from beginners to bookkeeping pupils. The curriculum included drawing, Latin, algebra, and English composition. Other teachers who taught in the one-room schoolhouse included G.W. Bailey, Daisy Wallace, David Lafitte, Colonel A.S. Anderson of Millen, and Miss Lilla Burke.

Around 1908, Rocky Ford's Masonic lodge and Screven County officials banded together to build a new schoolhouse. It was a two-story building located across the street, adjacent to the Baptist church. The Masons used the building's upper level, and the lower portion, two or three rooms, served as the school. Teachers who taught in that building included Annie Lane, Marvin Vincent, Virginia Fitts, L.M. Earnest, Dolly Hunter, Mary Grubles, and Mada Wyant.

In 1925, the Rocky Ford district was bonded to build a $35,000 brick schoolhouse, pictured above. C.L. Daughtry bought the bonds. Clayton Hollingsworth of Dover was the first school superintendent to serve in the new building. Among teachers who served there were Cassie Bolton, Gussie Miller, Annie Lane Sharpe (the school's second superintendent), Waldo Pafford (the third superintendent), Annie Moore Morris, Vivian Polk, and Wylly Johnston, superintendent.

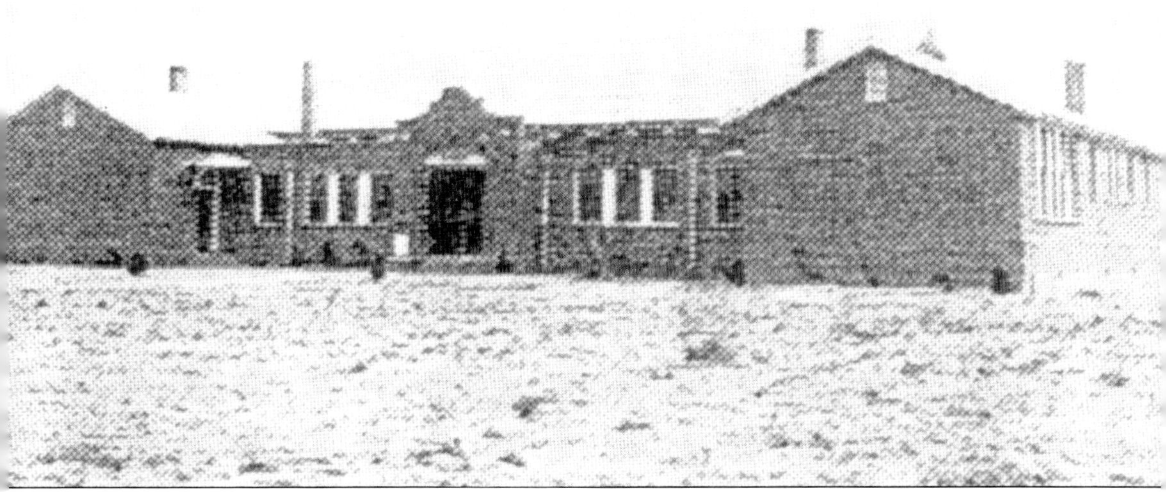

School facilities for African-American students received scant notice in the 19th century. Apparently there were no such schools before emancipation. The situation began to change in the late 1800s. But in those days, when the school system for rural-area whites was decidedly primitive, the system for children of color was even more so.

The 1916 report on the county school system listed 23 Negro schools but gave no details about them. Accompanying pictures indicated that almost all of them were one-room buildings, which were not much more than shacks. In 1915, a respected African-American teacher named C.J. Smith helped prepare a petition requesting a new school building to replace Sylvania's existing facility for African Americans.

A year later, as a principal, he announced that "the colored people of Sylvania and vicinity have united in one common effort to erect an adequate school house for the training of their children." He said a fundraising drive was underway and "hardly a white man approached has failed to subscribe to this worthy cause. If I haven't reached your office, I am now on the way." The effort required time and hard work, but a new school for Screven Countians of African-American descent eventually did materialize. By 1930, the Screven County Training School, pictured above, was ready for occupancy.

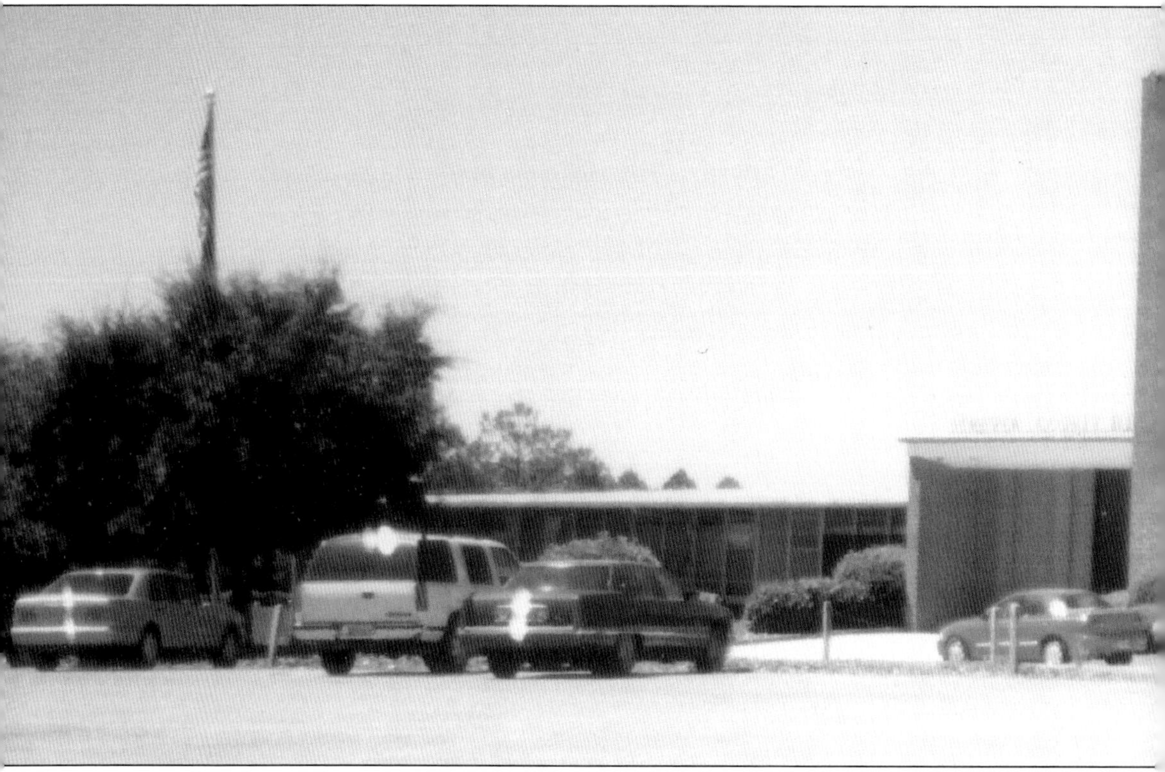

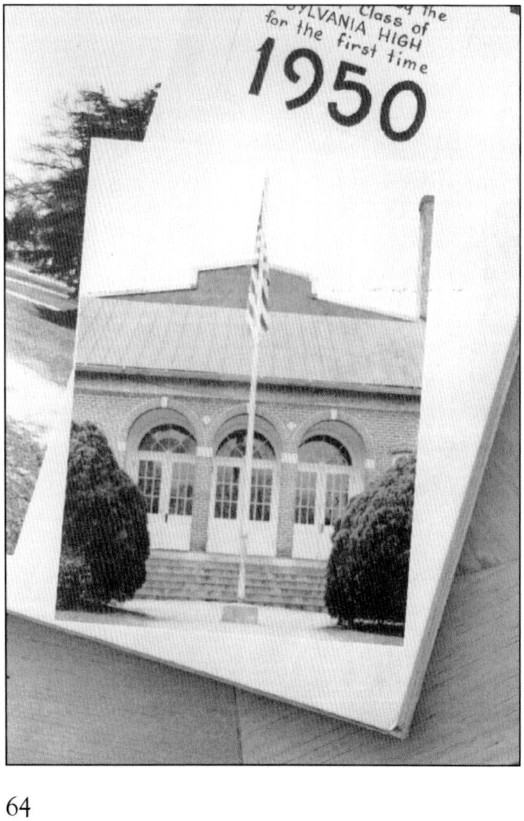

By 1916, Screven County's school tax, approved by voters in 1907 and levied at 3.5 mills, yielded more than $7,876 to support the county's schools. That figure supplemented a state school fund appropriation of $20,239. Each school had its own trustees, and in 1916, eight schools were listed as "standard." Only two were so categorized the previous year.

In all, some 62 schools were in operation, despite the fact that consolidation was already the policy of the board of education. Sylvania High School (bottom right), of course, was the largest, with 8 teachers, 10 grades, and 350 pupils. The school year lasted eight months, and the school library included 350 volumes.

Some schools in outlying areas featured substantial buildings, including Bay Branch, Cooperville, Gilgal, Millhaven, Oliver, and Rocky Ford. Others were apparently one-room shacks.

In Sylvania, the 1924 building (at left) continued to be known as Sylvania High School until 1951, when a new Screven

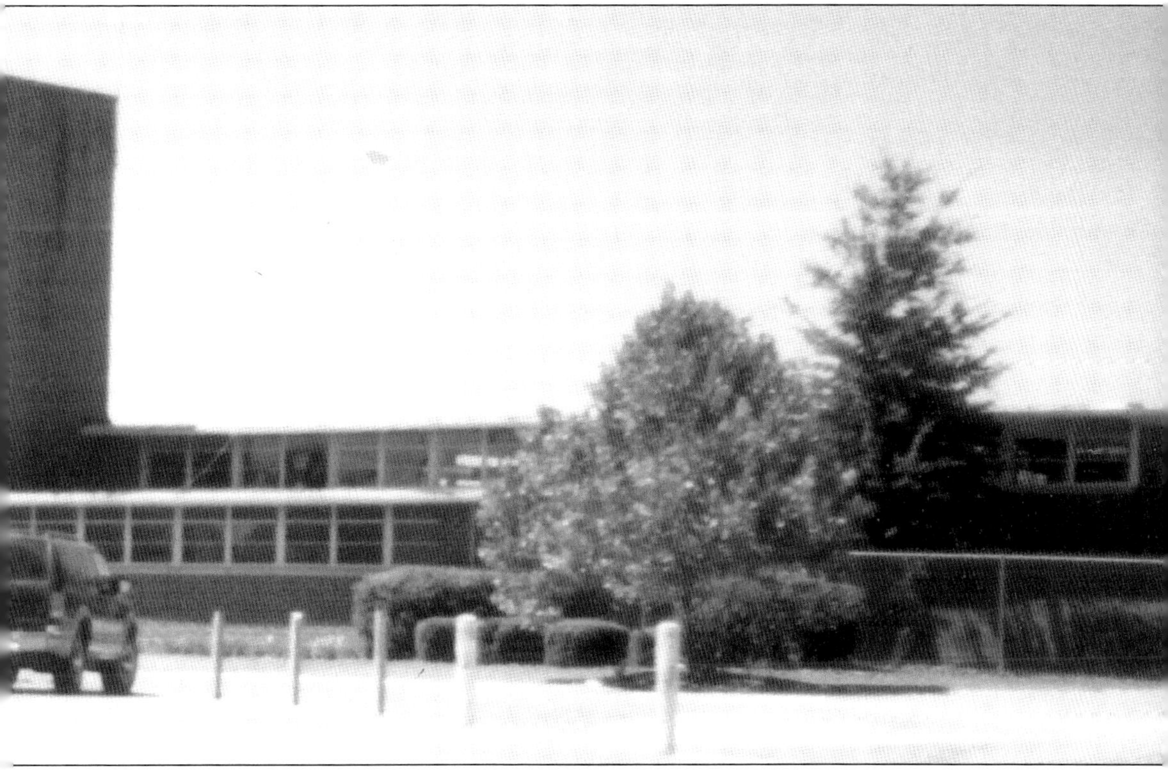

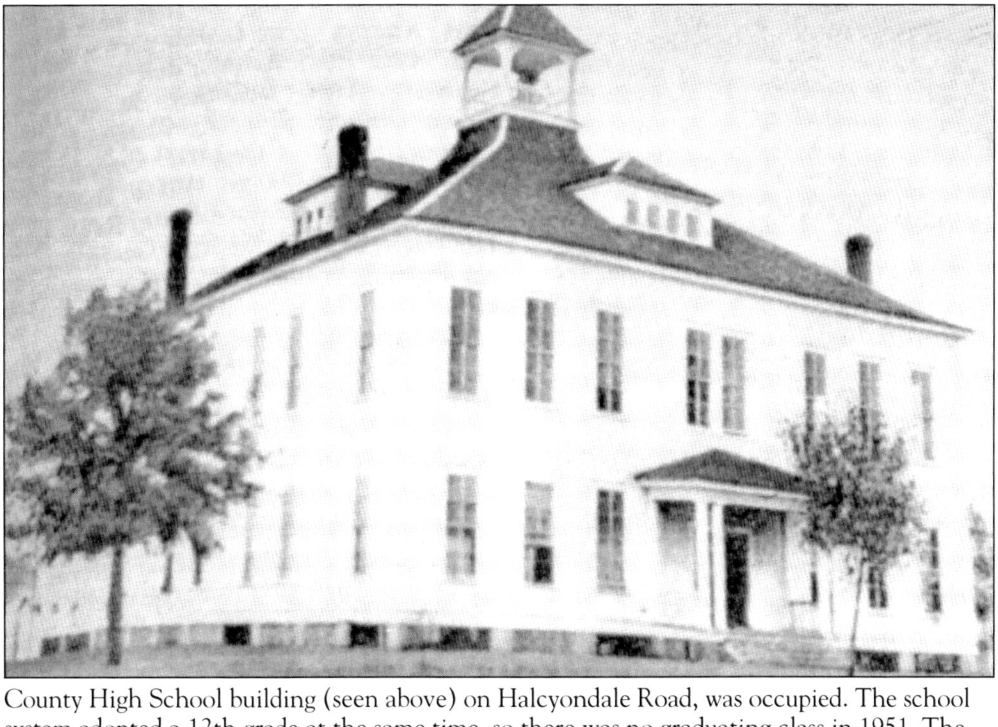

County High School building (seen above) on Halcyondale Road, was occupied. The school system adopted a 12th grade at the same time, so there was no graduating class in 1951. The last 11th-grade graduating class received diplomas on May 29, 1950.

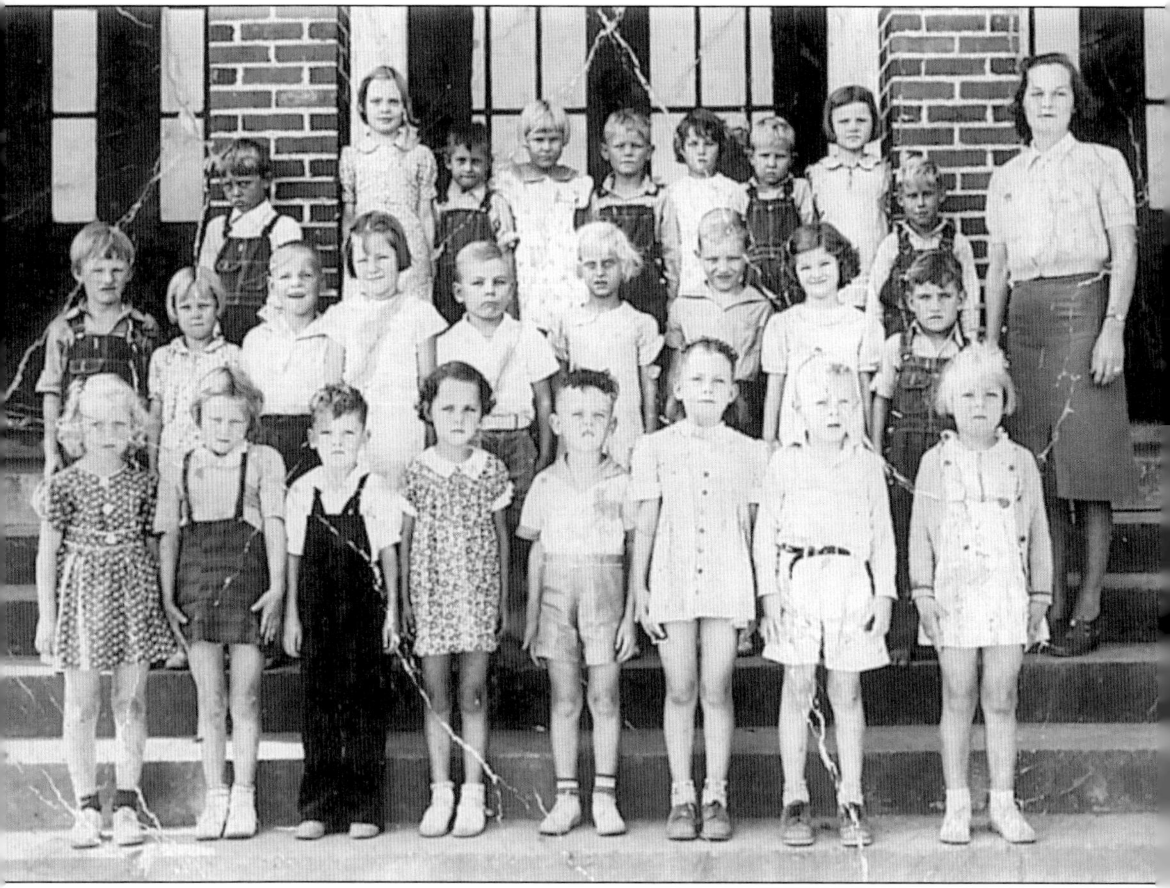

Sylvania High School's Class of 1950 began its school days in 1939, in the school building constructed in 1924. Eleven years later, the class, pictured at right, ended its local school days at the other end of the same hall. Class members graduating in 1950, the last Sylvania High School class, included J.C. Anderson, Chris Bazemore, Emily Bazemore, Rosemary Bazemore, Donnie Bennett, Bettie Bragg, Gene Brant, Roy Brinson, Rose Brinson, Exodyne Brower, Emory Burke, Charles Cleary, Margaret Daughtry, G.W. Davis, Nell Davis, Billy DeRolf, Thomas Dickey, Ann Evans, Helen Evans, Estelle Freeman, Lillian Hagan, Jacqueline Hall, Elizabeth Hartley, Vernon Hodges, Christie Lariscy, Jewel McBride, Valeria Mills, Johnie Mincey, Dorothy Mock, Cathryn Parker, Edwin Parker, Seigmund Parker,

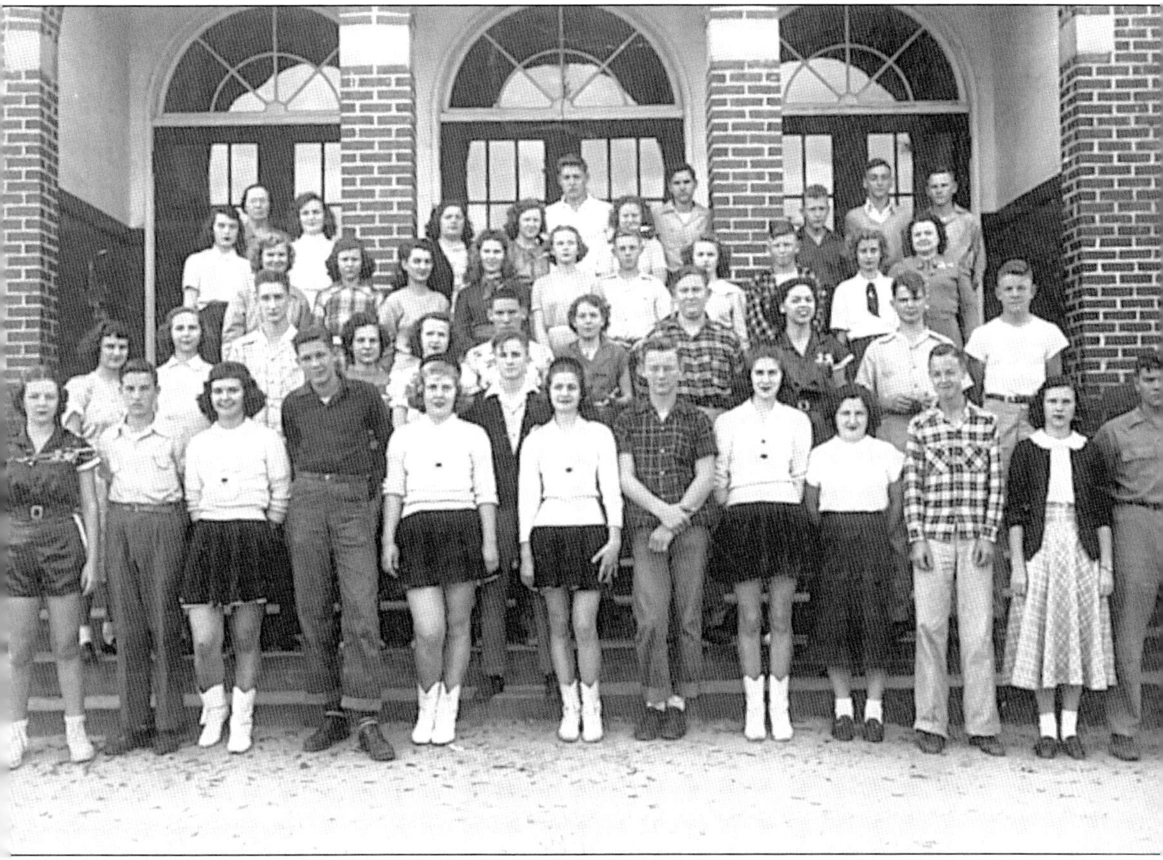

George Patrick, Bayne Pierce, Harold Lee Prescott, LaVaughn Reddick, Robert Reddick, Shirley Ann Sasser, Harold Lee Scott, Helen Sharpe, Jewel Smith, Runnel Stregles, Wallace Taylor, Bernard Thompson, Mack Thompson, Barbara Waters, Lavonia Waters, Lucy Ann Wells, and Jerry Zeigler.

Diplomas were also awarded to four veterans: William R. Lovett, Carlton E. Weaver, Charles Hilton Ferguson, and John Wilbur Cail.

Jim Jordan was the last principal of SHS and the first principal of SCHS. The old SHS building continued to serve the county as Sylvania Elementary School for the next 40 years, until it was finally abandoned in 1990.

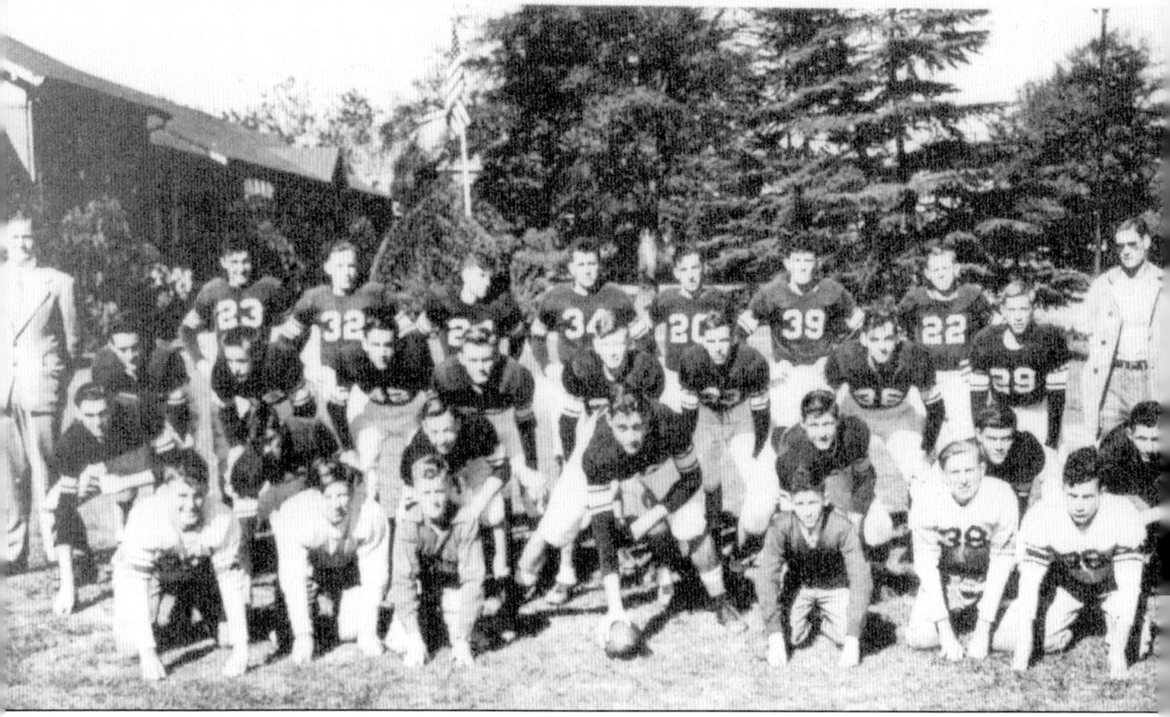

The 1949 Sylvania High School Gamecocks enjoyed a successful season with six wins, three losses, and no ties. Harold Waters took over as coach that year, and three of the 22 boys made the Region 2, Class B, second team—Wallace Taylor, center; Edwin Parker, guard; and Bernard Thompson, back. Team members, shown above, include the following, from left to right: (front row) Douglas Frieze, Billy Ansley, Rabun Waters, and Ben Turner (all managers); (second row) Clyde Lane, Donalt Williams, Lavaughn Reddick, Wallace Taylor, Edwin Parker, Charles Cleary, and Leonard Mock; (third row) J.C. Anderson (manager), Billy DeRolf, Roy Brinson, Bayne Pierce, Jerry Zeigler, Seigmund Parker, Gordon Walker, Mack Wooten, Waldo Boyd, and Coach Harold Waters; (fourth row) Herschel Evans, Wensley Sheley, Earl Miller, "Noony" Lariscy, Harold Prescott, Bernard Thompson, and Mack Thompson.

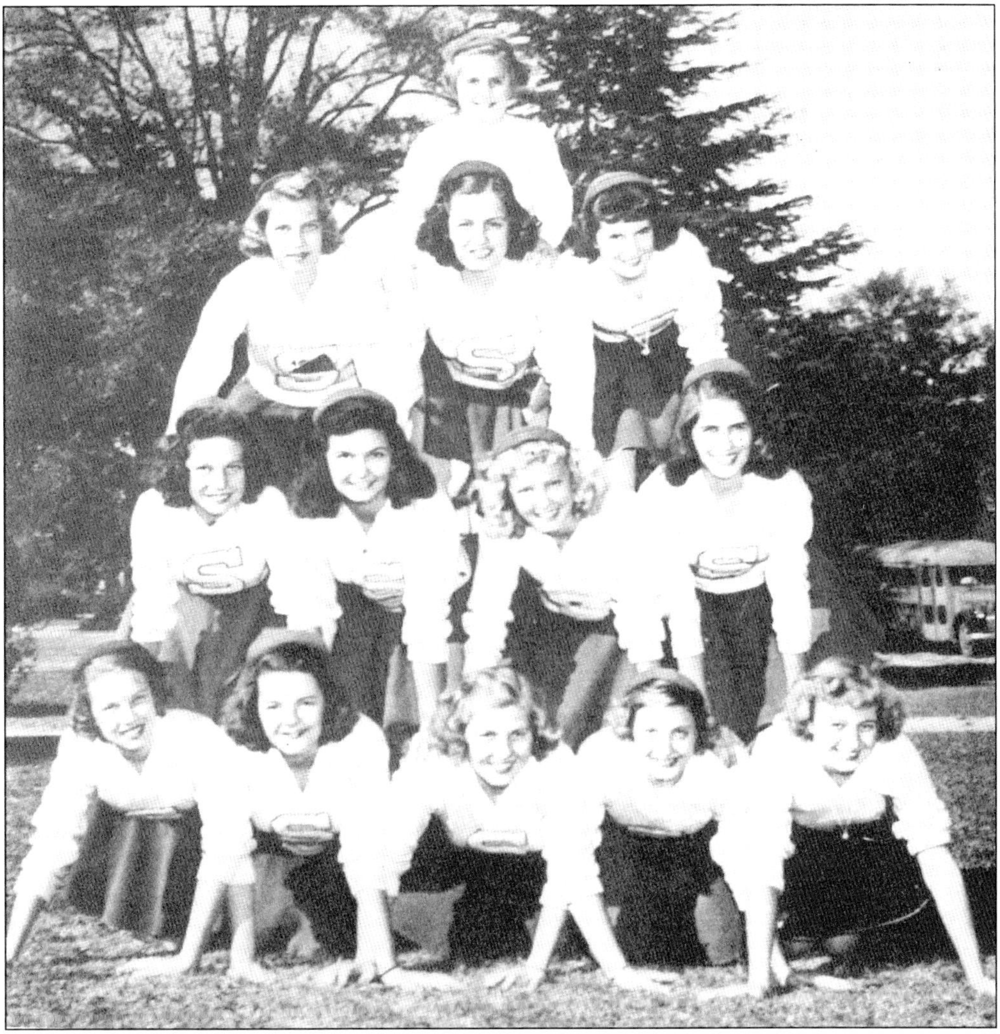

Pictured above, the 1949 cheerleading squad was there to provide the needed encouragement. Shown here, from left to right, are as follows: (front row) Shirley Rouse, Helen Sharpe (captain), Jacqueline Hall, Edna Durden, and Jane Cochrane; (second row) Margaret Daughtry, Ann Evans, Miriam Glisson, and Liz Hartley; (third row) Mary Hobby Mills, Mary Dean Miller, and Anne Ria Boyd; and at the top is Kathryn Louise "Henry" Mobley.

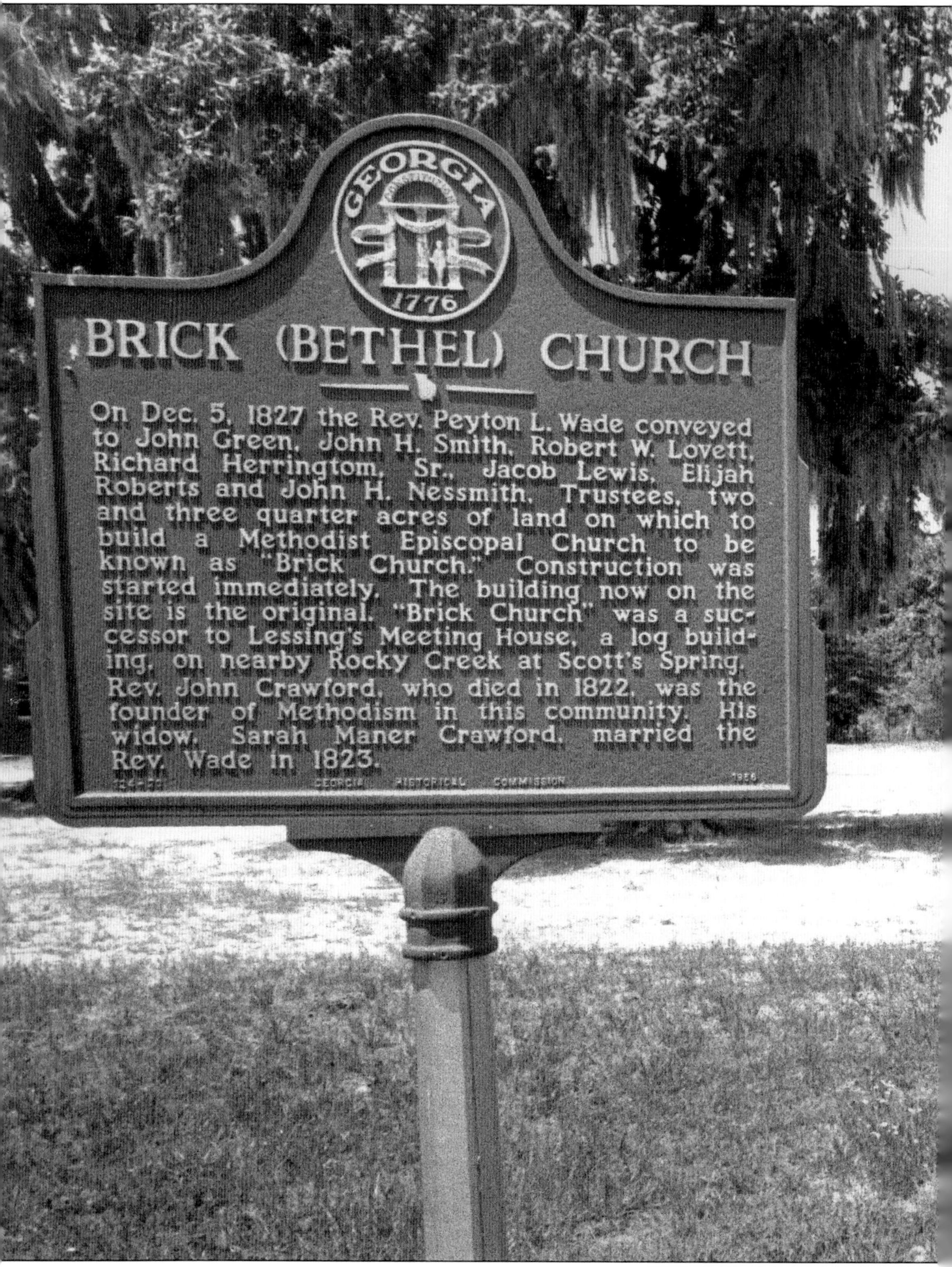
GEORGIA
1776
BRICK (BETHEL) CHURCH
On Dec. 5, 1827 the Rev. Peyton L. Wade conveyed to John Green, John H. Smith, Robert W. Lovett, Richard Herringtom, Sr., Jacob Lewis, Elijah Roberts and John H. Nessmith, Trustees, two and three quarter acres of land on which to build a Methodist Episcopal Church to be known as "Brick Church." Construction was started immediately. The building now on the site is the original. "Brick Church" was a successor to Lessing's Meeting House, a log building, on nearby Rocky Creek at Scott's Spring. Rev. John Crawford, who died in 1822, was the founder of Methodism in this community. His widow, Sarah Maner Crawford, married the Rev. Wade in 1823.
GEORGIA HISTORICAL COMMISSION

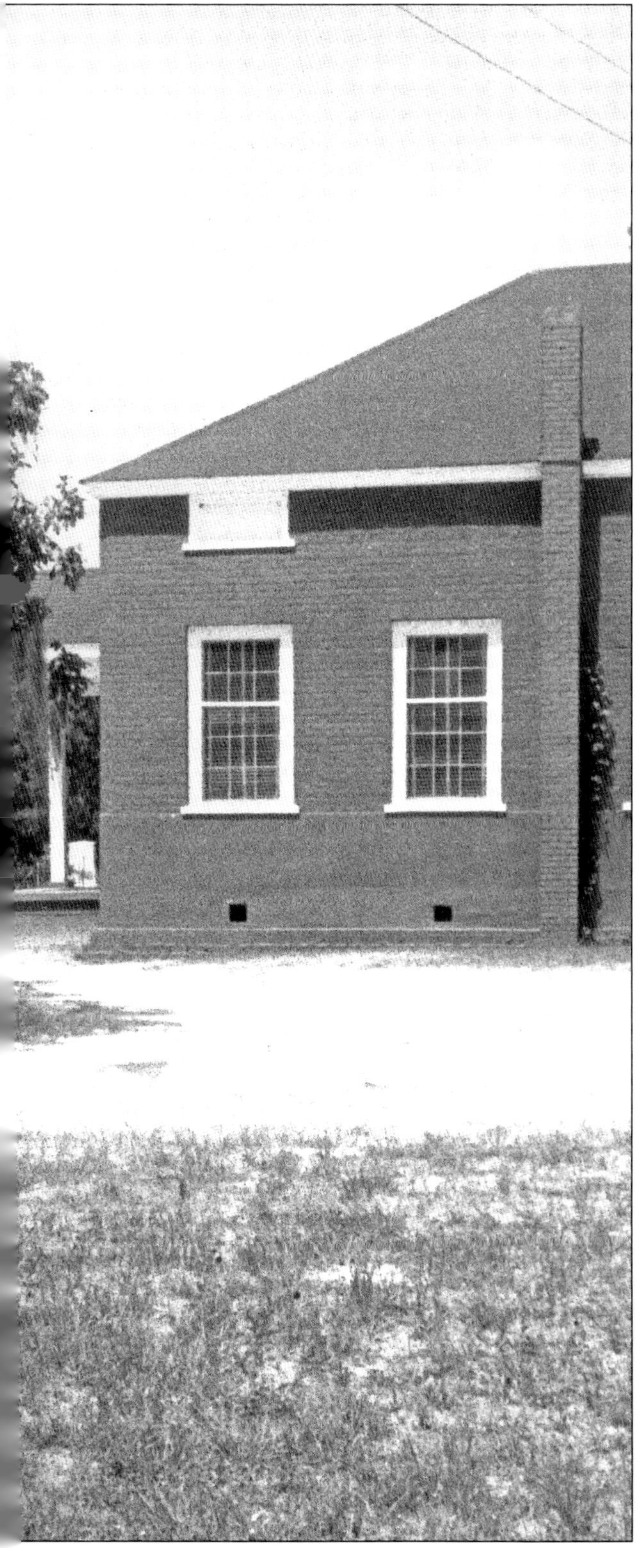

The church was an integral part of Screven County life from its earliest days. The county's first organized house of worship was Oliver's Little Ogeechee Baptist Church. It was established in 1790, with the Reverend William Cone as pastor. Still a vital part of life in the Oliver community, the church survives today as an historic building constructed in 1912.

The oldest church building in Screven County is the 1827 Bethel "Brick" Church, located near the Wade Plantation, pictured at left. The church was established when the Reverend Payton L. Wade gave 2.75 acres of land to church trustees John Green, John H. Smith, Robert W. Lovett, Richard Herrington Sr., Jacob Lewis, Elijah Roberts, and John H. Nessmith, stipulating that a Methodist Episcopal church, to be known as "Brick Church," be built there. The building now standing on the site is that structure.

The establishment of the "Brick Church" was a direct result of activities at Lessing's Meeting House, a log building located at Scott's Spring on the nearby Rocky Creek. The Reverend John Crawford, who died in 1822, was the leading force in the establishment of Methodism in the community. His widow, Sarah Maner Crawford, married the Reverend Wade in 1823.

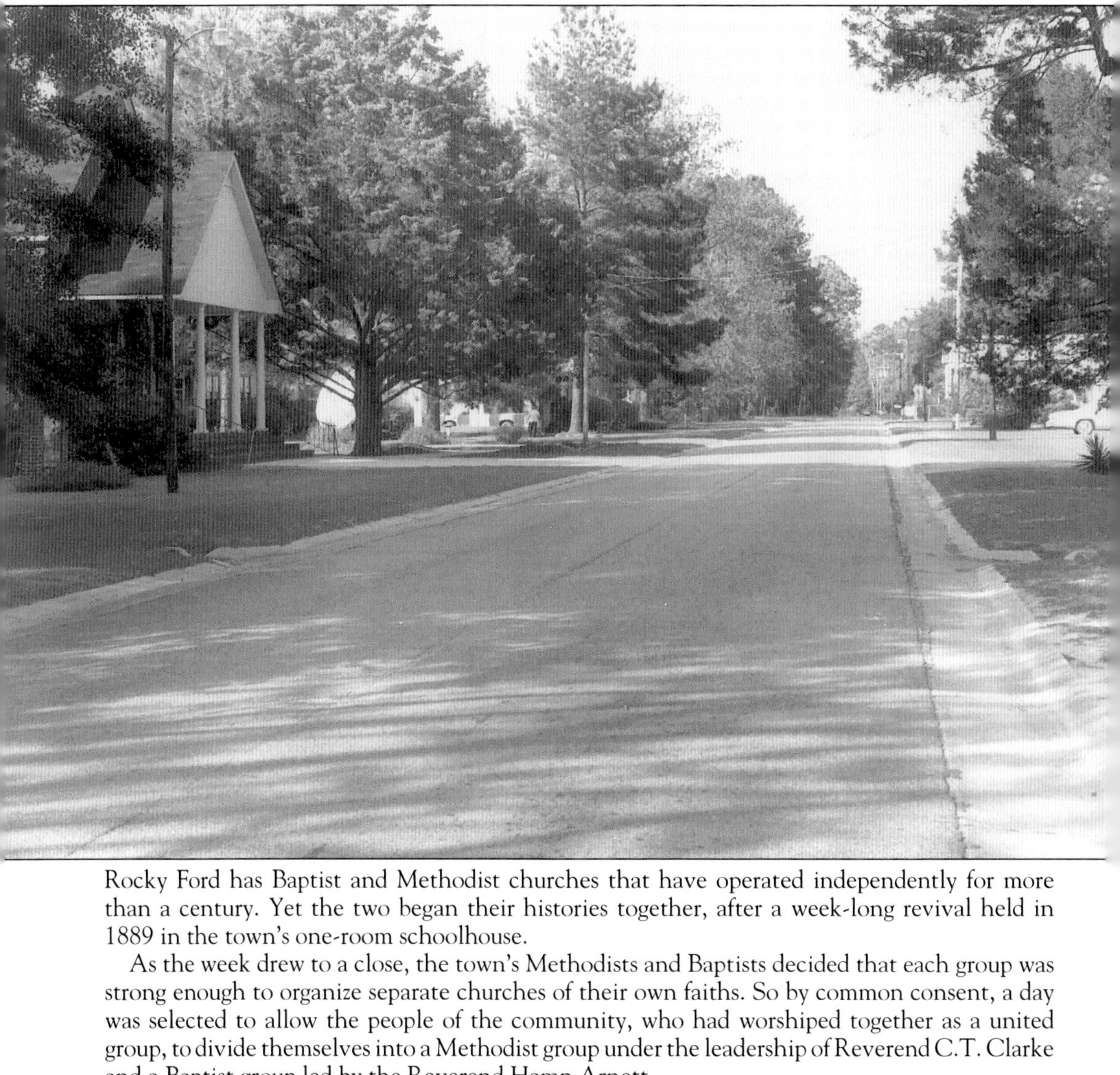

Rocky Ford has Baptist and Methodist churches that have operated independently for more than a century. Yet the two began their histories together, after a week-long revival held in 1889 in the town's one-room schoolhouse.

As the week drew to a close, the town's Methodists and Baptists decided that each group was strong enough to organize separate churches of their own faiths. So by common consent, a day was selected to allow the people of the community, who had worshiped together as a united group, to divide themselves into a Methodist group under the leadership of Reverend C.T. Clarke and a Baptist group led by the Reverend Hamp Arnett.

Few, if any, other churches can claim that the first steps in their organization were taken together in a one-room schoolhouse, in a selection process that went something like the old-fashioned spelling bee. Clarke stood on one side of the building, and Arnett stood on the other. Those present expressed their church preference by joining the line they preferred.

Those who selected the Methodist church that day included Mr. and Mrs. A.J. Brinson, Mr. and Mrs. James M. Newton Sr., Mrs. George Heard, Miss Florence Heard, Mrs. Esther Wallace, R. Allen Williams, Mr. and Mrs. W.H. Hawkins, John Ingram, George Hagan, and Jas Calhoun.

Those who chose the Baptist church were Mr. and Mrs. H.C. Kittles, J.R. Rosier, Sam Cail, Ed Sikes, John Duggan, and Joseph T. Phillips.

The Rocky Ford Missionary Baptist Church began when a presbytery, including the Reverend Arnett, H.G. Edenfield, and A.L. Brantley, met on September 9, 1889, to constitute the church. Edenfield was elected chairman and Brantley the secretary. Arnett preached the first sermon. The church elected J.T. Phillips, Samuel Cail, and W.A. Edenfield as deacons.

On September 16, 1889, George Heard deeded a lot to the church trustees that measured 100 feet by 125 feet, and he stipulated that a church building of no less than 20 feet by 30 feet be erected there. He said the building should be placed on brick pillars, good materials should be used, the church should be painted, and all this must be completed within 12 months. The church paid Heard "the sum of one dollar cash-in-hand."

And so the small-town church served its members well until the spring of 1934, when fire destroyed the structure. Despite lean times brought on by the Great Depression, church members built another church that was larger than the first one. The Reverend J.W. Harper preached the first sermon in the completed building on January 15, 1939.

The Rocky Ford Methodist Church's first conference was held in the schoolhouse on March 23, 1890. The new pastor, the Reverend W.J. Robertson, was in charge. J.M. Newton was elected secretary.

When the second conference was held in September, the following names were added to the church roll: Dr. H.W. Doster, Blanche Wallace, Daisy Wallace, Eula Wallace, Elizabeth Tilley, Lena Tilley, and Valentine Tilley.

The two churches were built at the same time. George Heard donated the lots on which the structures were erected. They were practically within sight of one another but on opposite sides of the street. Mr. Jones, who operated the sash and door factory, provided materials for both churches.

A third church, the Rocky Ford Christian Church, joined the town's religious community in 1907, when the membership moved its headquarters from Millerville. The Reverend Daughtry was that church's first pastor.

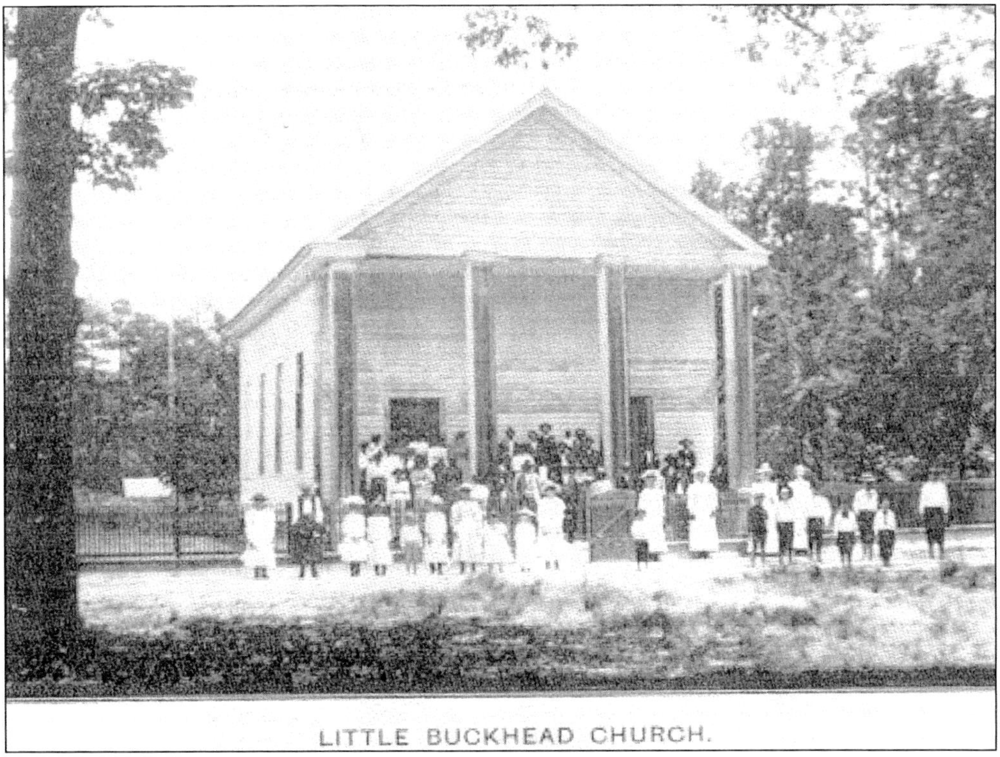

Little Buckhead Church in Jenkins County was established by former slaves, who separated from Buckhead Baptist Church after the War between the States.

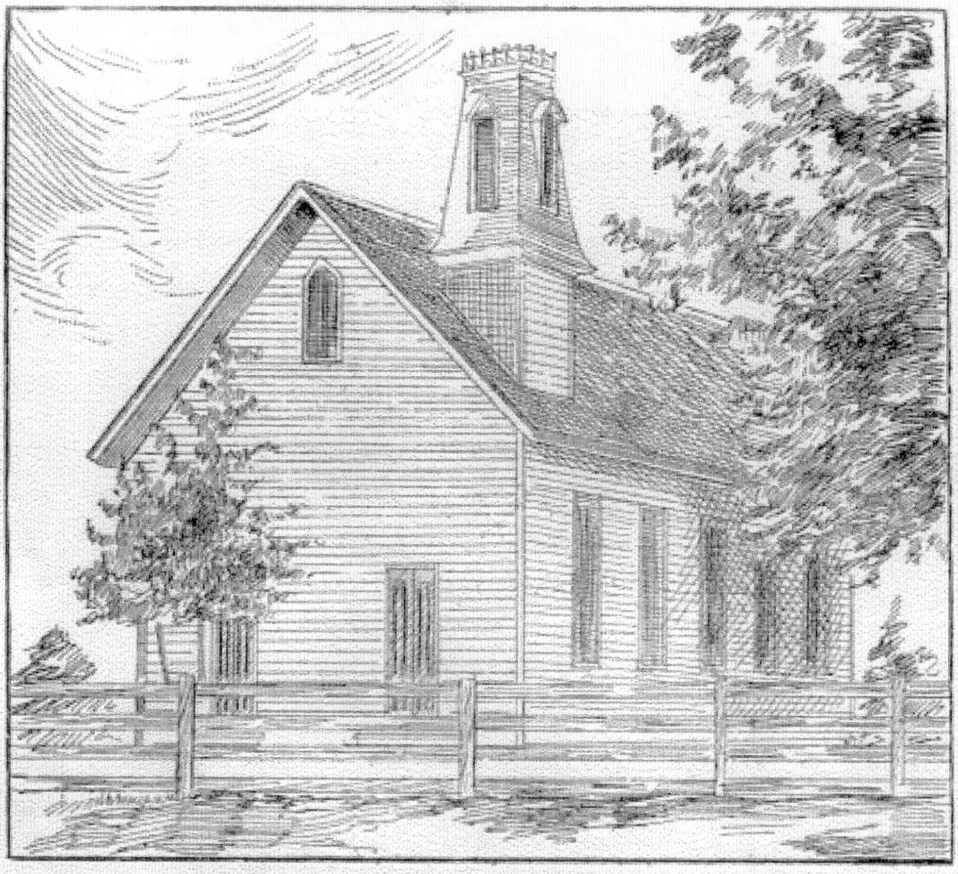

MAGNOLIA CHURCH.

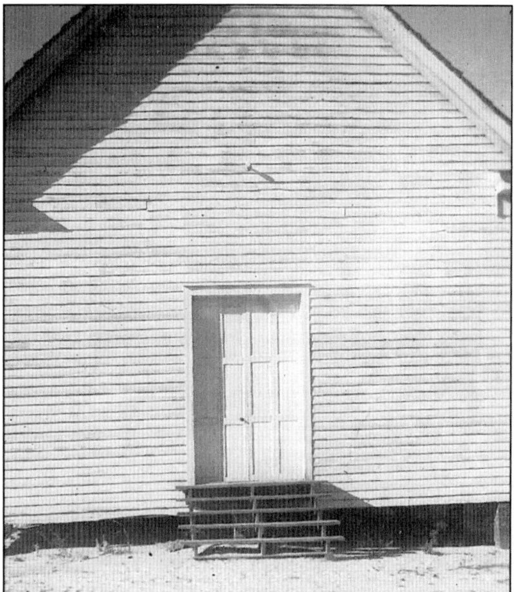

Jenkins County's Magnolia Baptist Church, at Perkins, is pictured above. It is one of the older houses of worship in the area. Established in the 1800s, the church has served as a spiritual home for numerous community leaders over the years. Dry Branch Baptist Church, seen at left, has also been a part of the Jenkins County community for generations.

Five

Chugging Through the Years

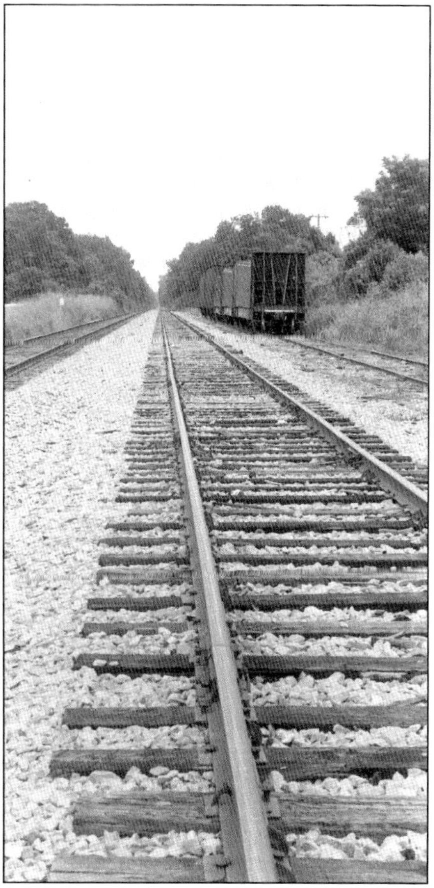

Sylvania Central's short railroad connected with the Central of Georgia at Rocky Ford. Sylvania, being the terminus, prospered markedly. The town's 1900 population was 545, and its militia district population was 3,135. An important shipping point for Screven County, the county seat handled large quantities of lumber, turpentine, cotton, sugar cane, fruits, and vegetables. Located in the town were express and telegraph offices, a money order post office with free rural delivery, a bank, several successful mercantile houses, a lumber yard, an oil mill, and a courthouse and jail valued at $20,000.

One of the town's most metropolitan mercantile firms was the L.H. Hilton Company, built in 1903 by L.H. Hilton. Located opposite the east front of the courthouse on Main Street, the Hilton firm dominated an entire block. Built of pressed brick, the two-story mercantile house featured Georgia-marble trimmings, modern equipment, and other accessories. Lighting was provided by acetylene gas, and the business was supplied with artesian water. Together the company's main building and warehouse included some 26,000 square feet.

The firm sold a little bit of everything—general merchandise, farm implements, machinery, buggies, furniture, hardware, etc. Hilton, a native Screven Countian, also served as president of the Screven County Bank and Screven County Oil Mills.

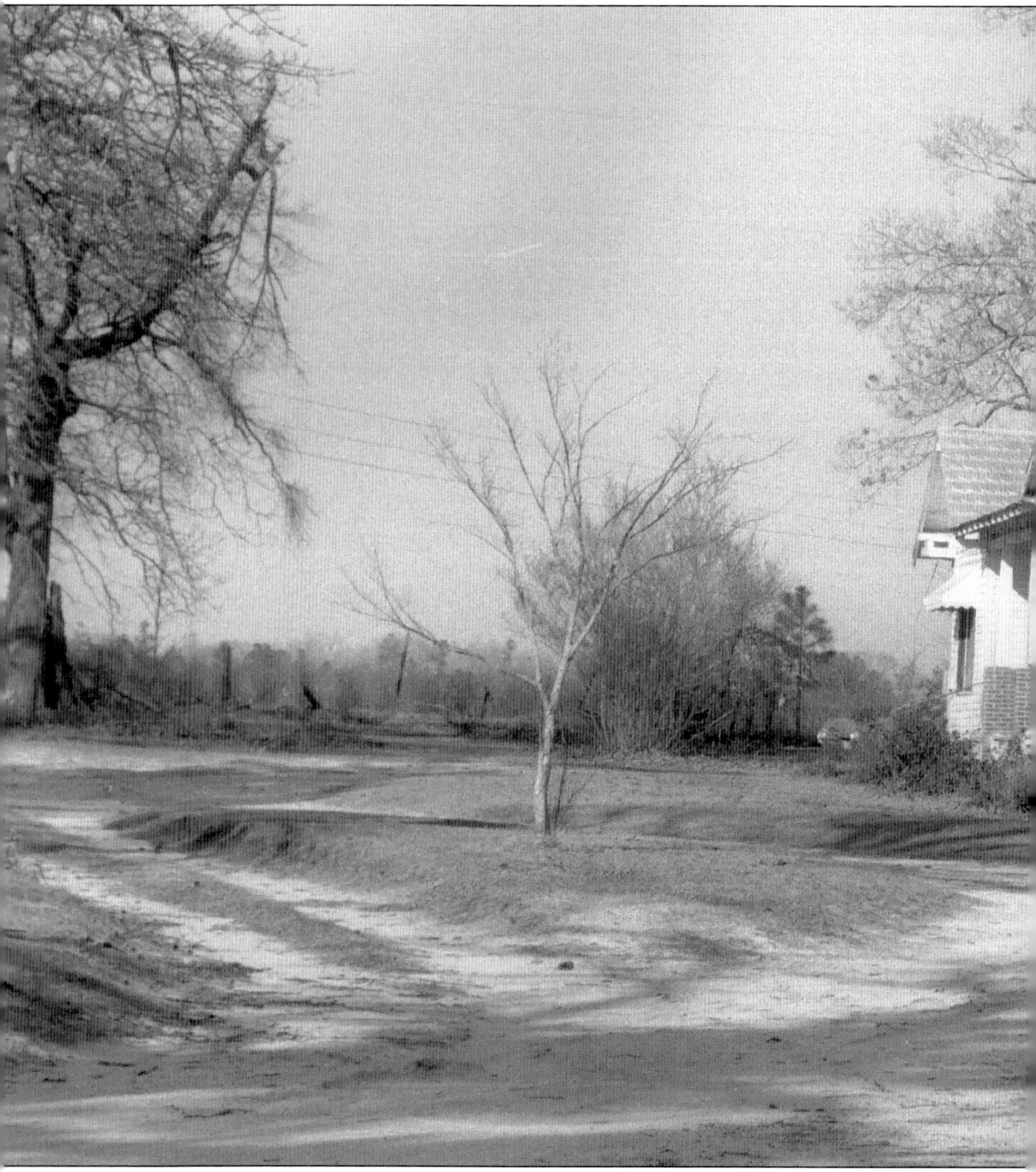

This Rocky Ford homestead, built in 1923, was probably the first rural home in Screven County to have electricity. When his house burned in October of 1922, Joshua A. Lee built this new home with all the conveniences of the day. He also powered it with electricity supplied by a Delco Light System, which included 24 motor-charged batteries. Lee kept the system until 1937, when electricity became available through the REA (Rural Electrification Administration).

A prominent farmer and community leader, Lee grew up near Cooperville. He was the third son of a Civil War widow. Although Lee received little education, he grew up to

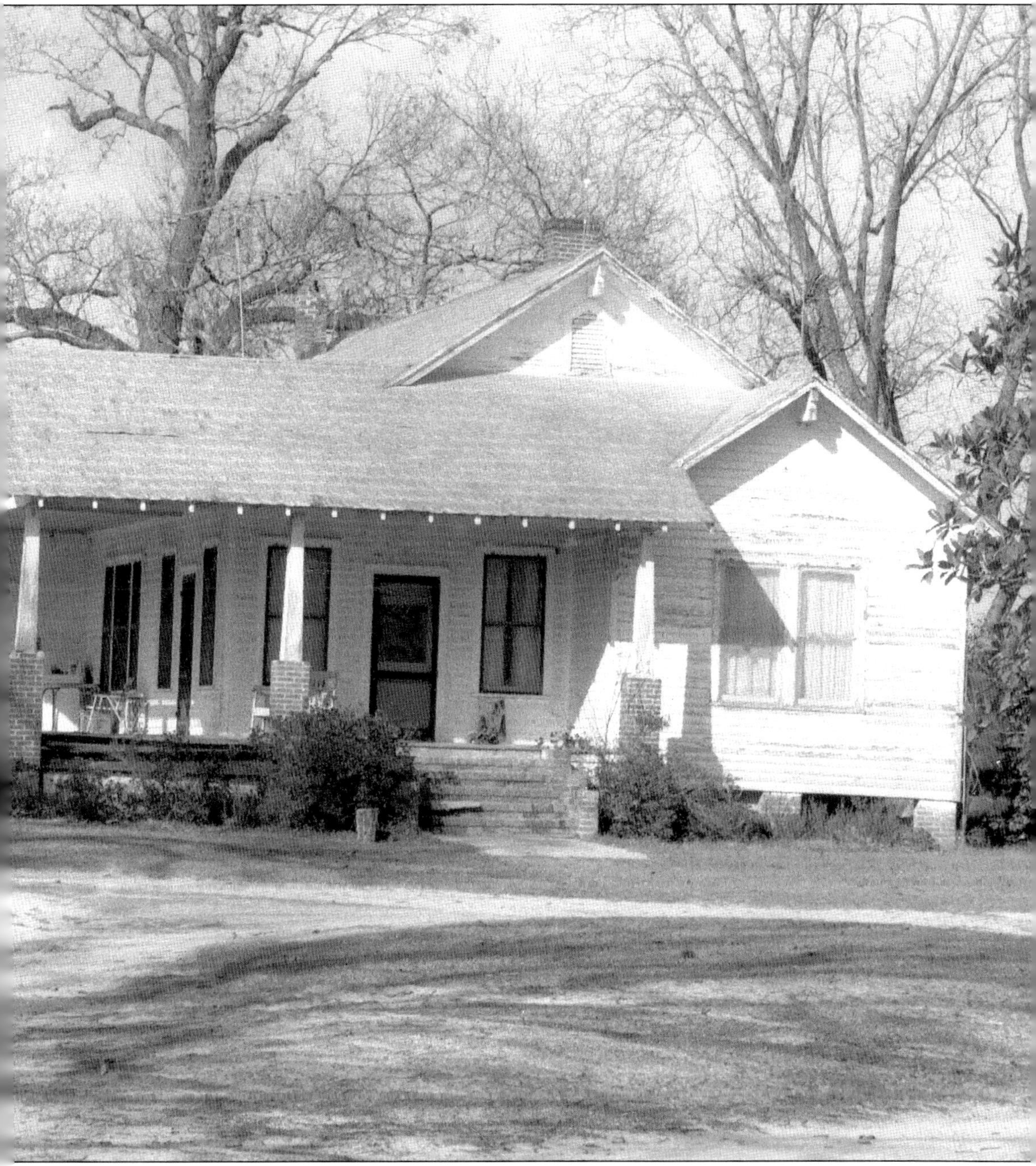

become a large landowner and a county commissioner. He was elected to serve two terms in the Georgia House of Representatives, in 1927 and 1929.

During his time in the legislature, Lee went to Atlanta on Monday mornings, taking the Number 1 from Rocky Ford, and returned on Friday night or Saturday morning on the Number 2 train. While in Atlanta, he purchased mules, which he later sold to neighbors in Screven County.

He died at home on January 20, 1928, of pneumonia, shortly before he was to begin his second term.

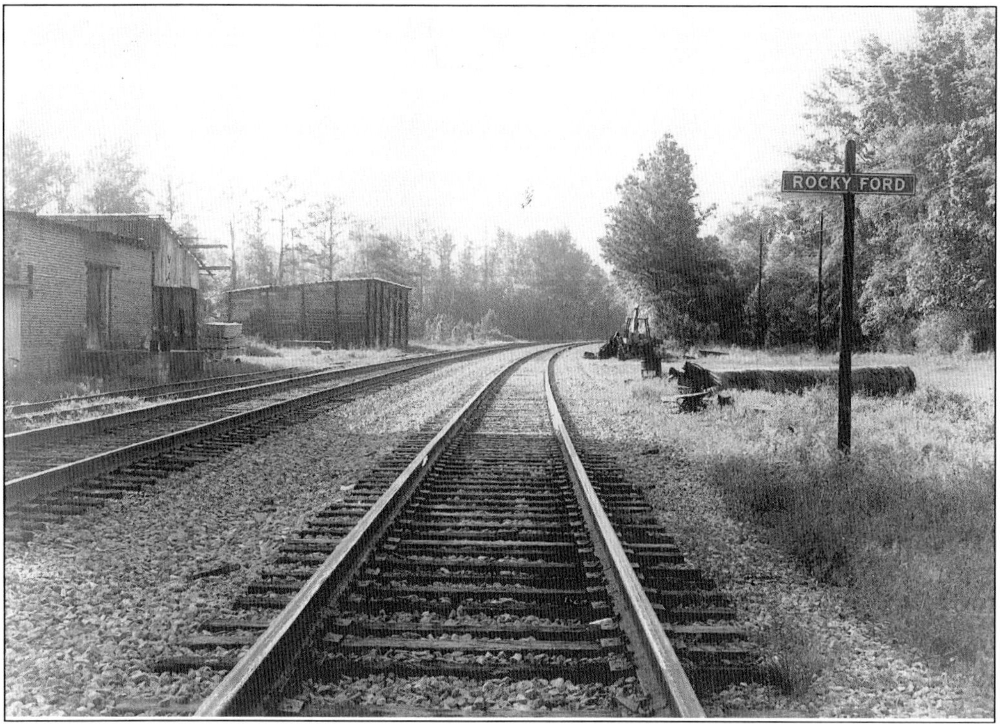

Life in and around Rocky Ford changed in 1886, when George R. Heard built the first bridge across the Ogeechee so that he could move lumber from his sawmill at Bellwood to the Central of Georgia station at Rocky Ford. A second, smaller bridge that crossed nearby Horse Creek and a road through the swamp completed the primitive thoroughfare. It was a toll bridge for a number of years.

Heard sold the mill to the E.E. Foy Manufacturing Company around 1887, and Foy built a large mill across the river in Bulloch County, where 100 workers sawed and planed lumber and manufactured laths and shingles. Later, the county built one long bridge across the creek and river. Foy then erected a railroad trestle across the river near The Rocks and purchased a small train engine to haul the mill's products to the Central Railroad to be shipped to market.

Rocky Ford grew steadily, and soon the town numbered among the busiest shipping points on the Central of Georgia Railroad. Then, in 1887, a sash and door factory/planing mill, one of the region's largest industries, was established. In addition to sawed and planed lumber, sashes, and doors, this factory produced ready-cut houses, which were shipped throughout the country for erection. The company even sent carpenters to put these houses together on-site. A part of Rocky Ford life for about 12 years, the mill stimulated physical and economic growth in the town. Some 30 houses and a hotel were built for company employees and associates.

Meanwhile, George Heard purchased the entire acreage upon which the town of Rocky Ford was later built, selling home sites and business lots to those moving to the area. He and his son, Rollo, owned and operated the Rocky Ford Brick Yard, which shipped top-quality brick throughout the United States. At one time, the brickyard produced and shipped 2.5 million bricks per year.

The brickyard remained a fixture in the community well into the 20th century. W.J. Chapman bought the brickyard from the original owners and operated it from about 1908 to 1918, then sold it to Arthur Burke, who operated the facility until 1927, when bank failure brought about the company's collapse.

The "Sam Hotel," operated by Sam Kea, was another long-time landmark in Rocky Ford. Then came the Barber Hotel, pictured at right, which was a town landmark for decades, reaching into the 1960s. This two-story brick structure, overlooking the Central of Georgia Railroad track, offered a large, attractive lobby and a dining room equal to many found in large cities. It also housed the town's barber shop. Operators over the years included a Mrs. Gunby, Bessie Chapman and Mrs. Angus Parker, Mrs. Wacker, and, in later years, Mr. and Mrs. B.B. Barber, owners and final operators.

The Rocky Ford Bank, which served its namesake town from July 3, 1907, until 1927, was a positive determining factor in the growth of the town. At one time rated one of the strongest of the smaller banks, it was operated by W.H. Parker, president, and W.E. Jenkins. Mr. Thorpe and Thomas (Prince) Parker were cashiers at a later date, and Mrs. DeWaul D. Newton was an assistant with Thomas Parker. Arthur Burke was the second and last president.

The bustling town's largest industry was probably the Ogeechee River Stave & Heading Company, a progressive company with international connections. This company was established in 1918 and was sponsored by Bartol Krulic, a native of Austria who, before his immigration to Rocky Ford, was associated with a stave exporting company.

Stockholders were Krulic, Arthur Burke, John A. Brinson, J.T. Parker, B.W. Miller (all of Rocky Ford), B. Fisher of Millen, and Mr. Wacker of Kentucky. When business at the factory peaked, the weekly payroll totaled $3,000 at the Rocky Ford plant alone, where approximately 100 men worked. Auxiliary plants were scattered all over South Georgia.

Ogeechee River Stave & Heading Company shipped staves, barrel headings, and completed barrels to the Standard Oil Company at Bayonne, New Jersey, and exported them to Barcelona, Spain, and to France. On the local level, the company purchased large timber tracts needed to manufacture its highly sought-after products. The substantial orders the company filled for French wine dealers required specially prepared staves for wine barrels.

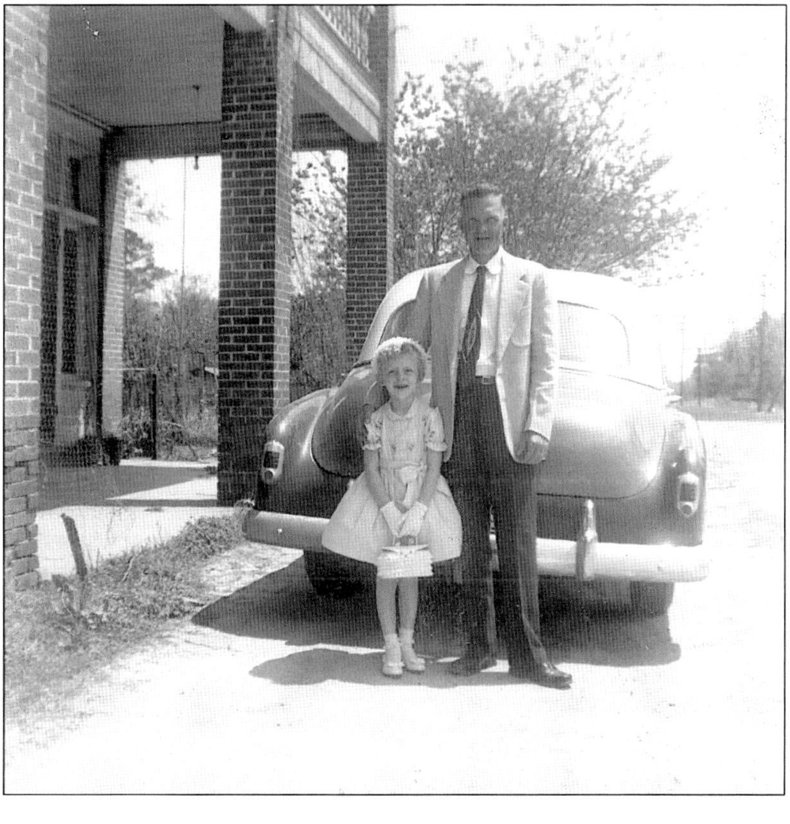

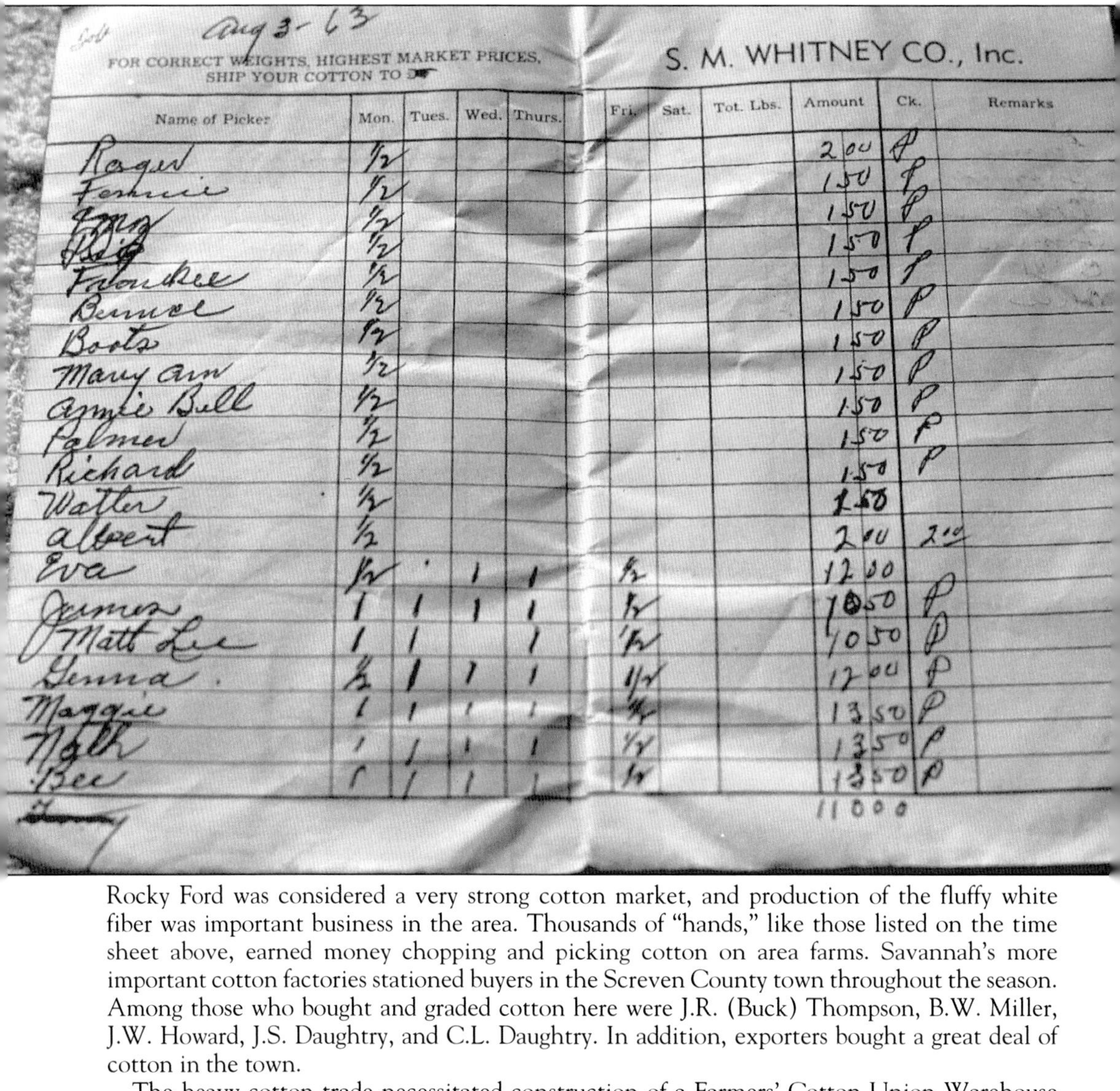

Aug 3-63

FOR CORRECT WEIGHTS, HIGHEST MARKET PRICES, SHIP YOUR COTTON TO

S. M. WHITNEY CO., Inc.

Name of Picker	Mon.	Tues.	Wed.	Thurs.	Fri.	Sat.	Tot. Lbs.	Amount	Ck.	Remarks
Roger	½							2 00	P	
Fernnie	½							1 50	P	
Emma	½							1 50	P	
Big	½							1 50	P	
Frankie	½							1 50	P	
Bennie	½							1 50	P	
Boots	½							1 50	P	
Mary Ann	½							1 50	P	
Annie Bell	½							1 50	P	
Palmer	½							1 50	P	
Richard	½							1 50	P	
Walter	½							1 50		
Albert	½							2 00		2.00
Eva	½		1	1	½			12 00		
James	1	1	1	1	½			10 50	P	
Matt Lee	1	1		1	½			10 50	P	
Gemma	½	1	1	1	1½			12 00	P	
Maggie	1	1	1	1	½			13 50	P	
Nath	1	1	1	1	½			13 50	P	
Bee	1	1	1	1	½			13 50	P	
								110 00		

Rocky Ford was considered a very strong cotton market, and production of the fluffy white fiber was important business in the area. Thousands of "hands," like those listed on the time sheet above, earned money chopping and picking cotton on area farms. Savannah's more important cotton factories stationed buyers in the Screven County town throughout the season. Among those who bought and graded cotton here were J.R. (Buck) Thompson, B.W. Miller, J.W. Howard, J.S. Daughtry, and C.L. Daughtry. In addition, exporters bought a great deal of cotton in the town.

The heavy cotton trade necessitated construction of a Farmers' Cotton Union Warehouse and other storage facilities. Around the turn of the 20th century, the brick warehouse held 2,000 bales, plus platform space. The Farmers' Cotton Union Warehouse was a stock company organized in 1906 by community farmers.

Other business assets of the area included its several large gins, one conveniently located on the railroad. A frequent, seasonal tableau featured countless wagons and trucks loaded with cotton and parked in every available space around the gin, each awaiting its turn.

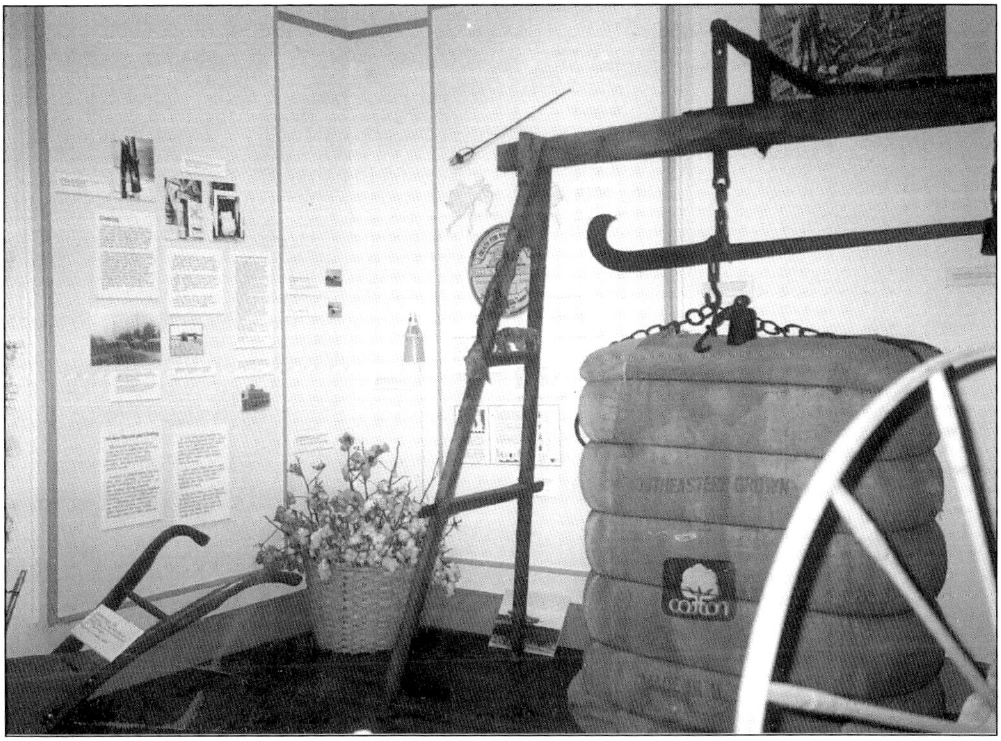

On the stalk or in the bale, King Cotton has reigned supreme in Jenkins and Screven Counties since the 1800s.

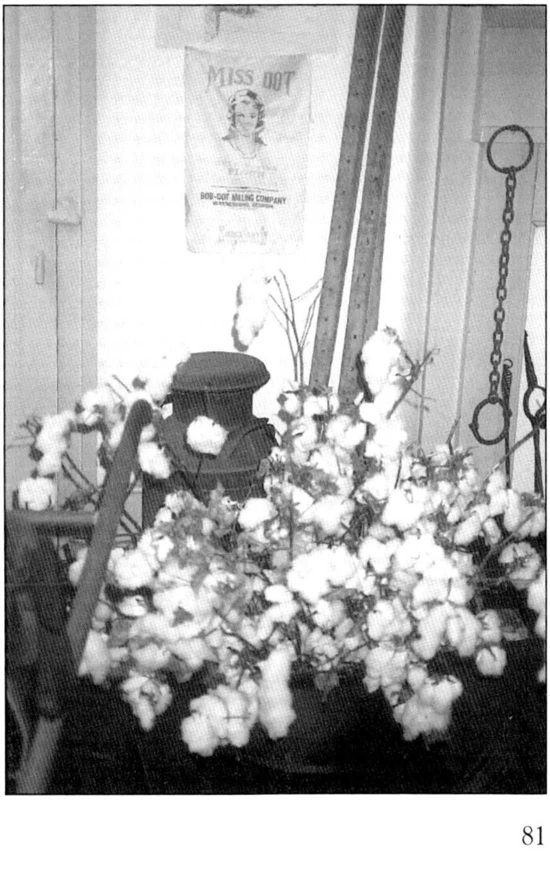

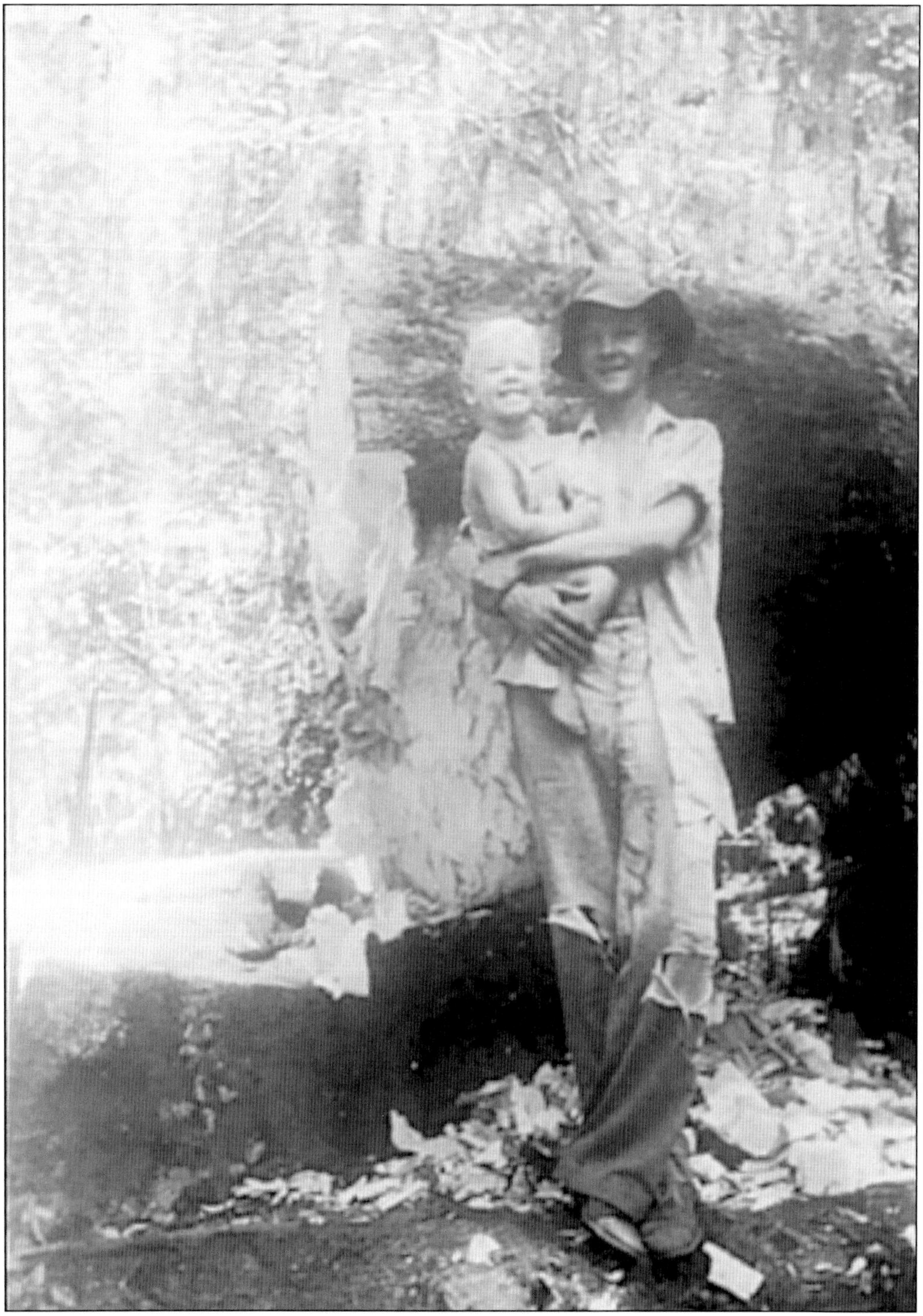

The pulpwood industry also generated economic growth in Screven County. Slack farm seasons often caught farm boys like Weyman Lee, pictured above with his younger brother Charles, deep in the woods working diligently.

One small store became the cornerstone for a larger concern started by the Silver Brothers, who moved from Rocky Ford to Sylvania, where they started the mother store of a chain. Other stores located in the town for a short time included H. Minkovitz, and Mirsky and M. Cohen.

Substantial buildings were erected during this period, including four brick stores, owned by Orren Burke, W.H. Parker, and J.T. Parker, and a concrete store that belonged to G. Morris.

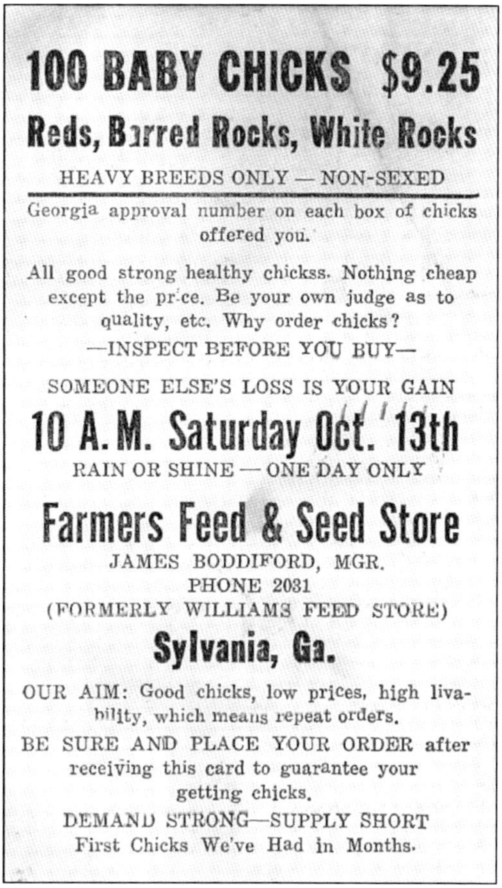

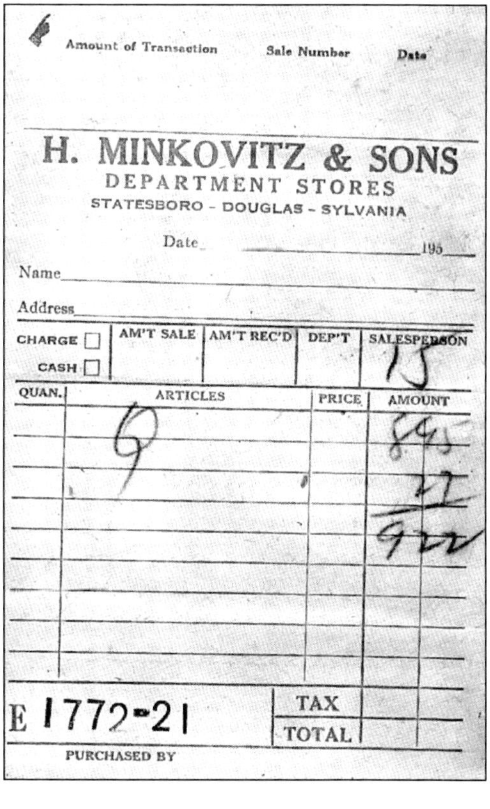
Amount of Transaction Sale Number Date

H. MINKOVITZ & SONS
DEPARTMENT STORES
STATESBORO - DOUGLAS - SYLVANIA

Date ______ 195__
Name ______
Address ______

CHARGE / CASH	AM'T SALE	AM'T REC'D	DEP'T	SALESPERSON

QUAN.	ARTICLES	PRICE	AMOUNT

E 1772-21 TAX TOTAL

PURCHASED BY

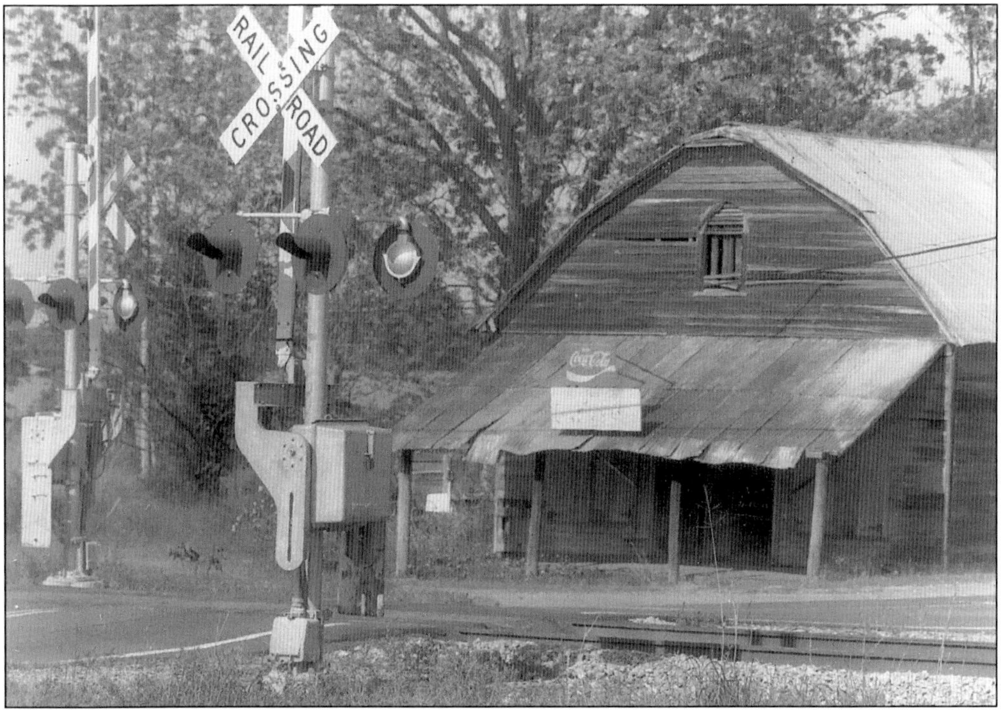

The Jenkins County village of Perkins, once the bustling headquarters of the Perkins brothers railroad, sawmill, and other businesses, saw a decline in the 20th century. Townspeople carried on though, despite the fact that few trains passed through and few businessmen walked its streets.

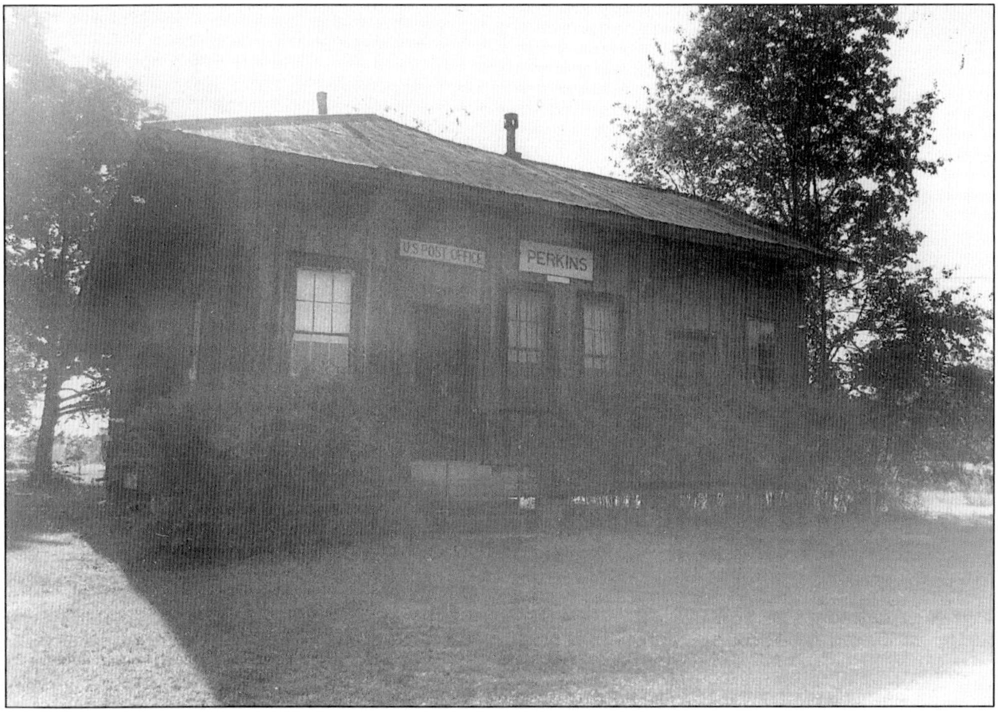

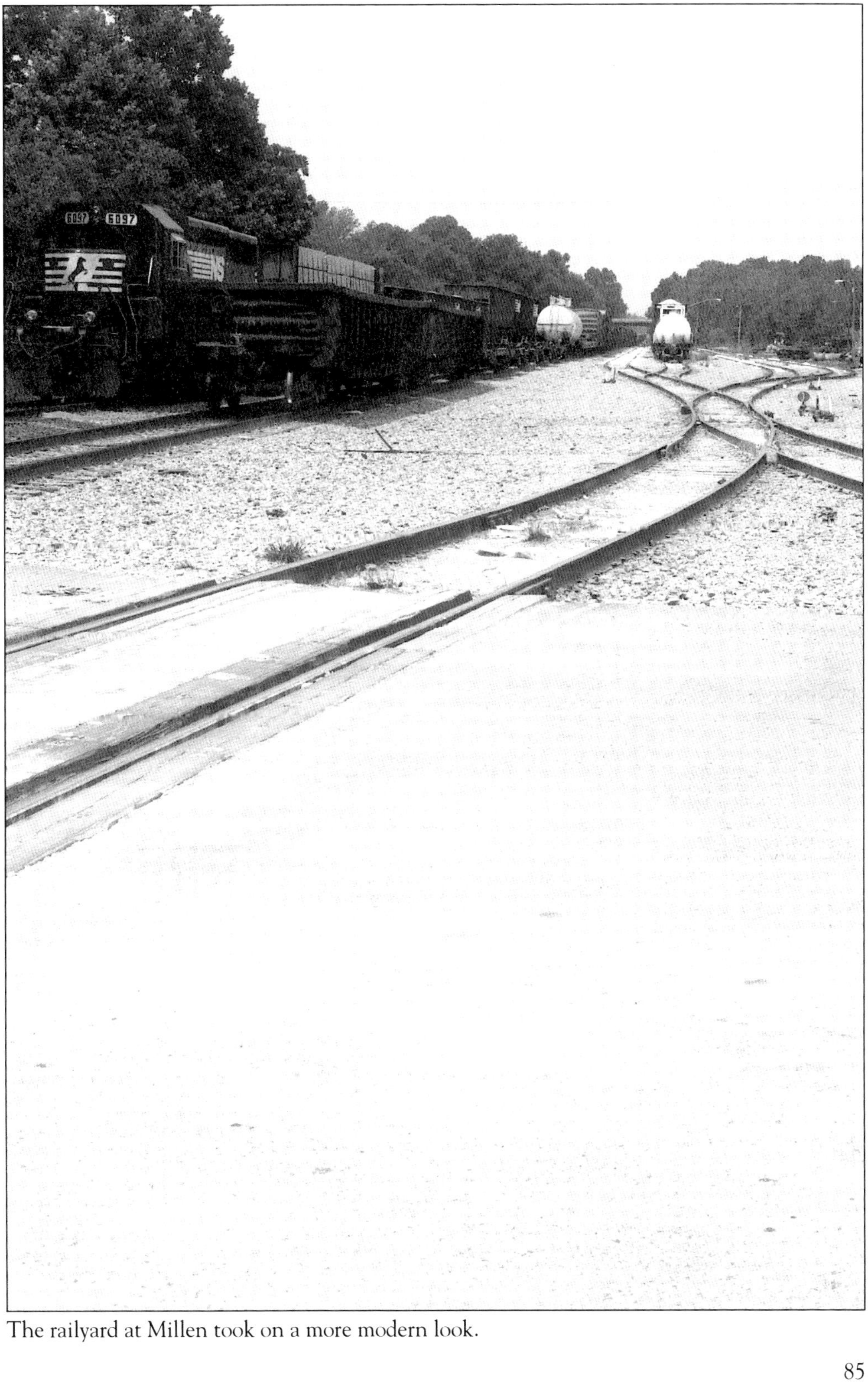

The railyard at Millen took on a more modern look.

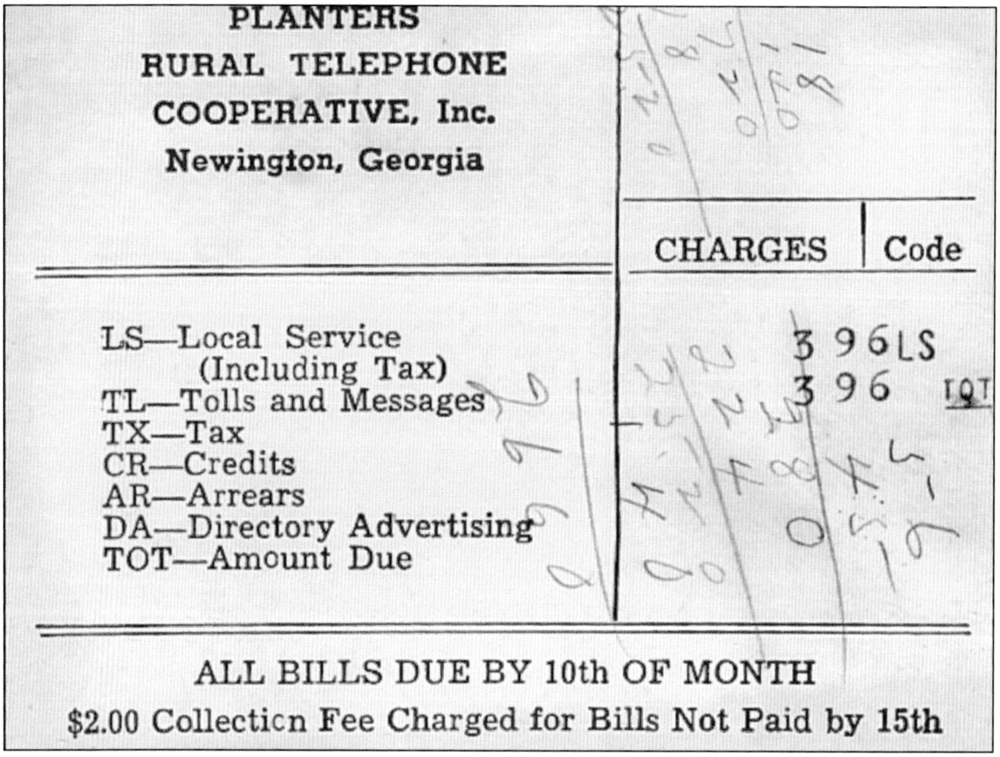

PLANTERS
RURAL TELEPHONE
COOPERATIVE, Inc.
Newington, Georgia

	CHARGES	Code
LS—Local Service (Including Tax)	3 96	LS
TL—Tolls and Messages	3 96	TOT
TX—Tax		
CR—Credits		
AR—Arrears		
DA—Directory Advertising		
TOT—Amount Due		

ALL BILLS DUE BY 10th OF MONTH
$2.00 Collection Fee Charged for Bills Not Paid by 15th

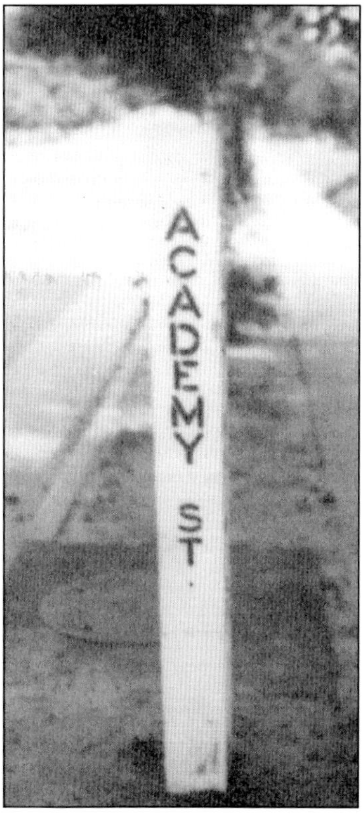

Communications in the area became easier when Planters Rural Telephone Cooperative, Inc., was established during the summer of 1950. Incorporators held their first meeting at the Jenkins County Courthouse on July 6, 1950. In March of 1951, the directors completed the purchase of Effingham Telephone Company, which included two exchanges at Guyton and Pineora. Meanwhile, negotiations continued with the REA's telephone program officials in efforts to secure a loan to build a new system to cover Screven County and to expand the project to Effingham. Word came at the annual membership meeting on August 14, 1952—REA funds would be available to construct 100 miles of telephone line and install switching equipment. The expansion was designed to serve 1,000 members.

The majority of those facilities were in place by the end of 1955. By July of 1956, 699 subscribers in Screven and Effingham Counties were being served, with another 200 patiently waiting. Steady growth continued into the 1960s, when underground cable and new switching equipment were installed. In 1962, Planters Telephone completed its new headquarters building in Newington. By the end of 1966, 2,000 subscribers were being served throughout the area.

In Sylvania, street markers, like the one pictured at left, went up at intersections as local woman's club members worked to improve the community.

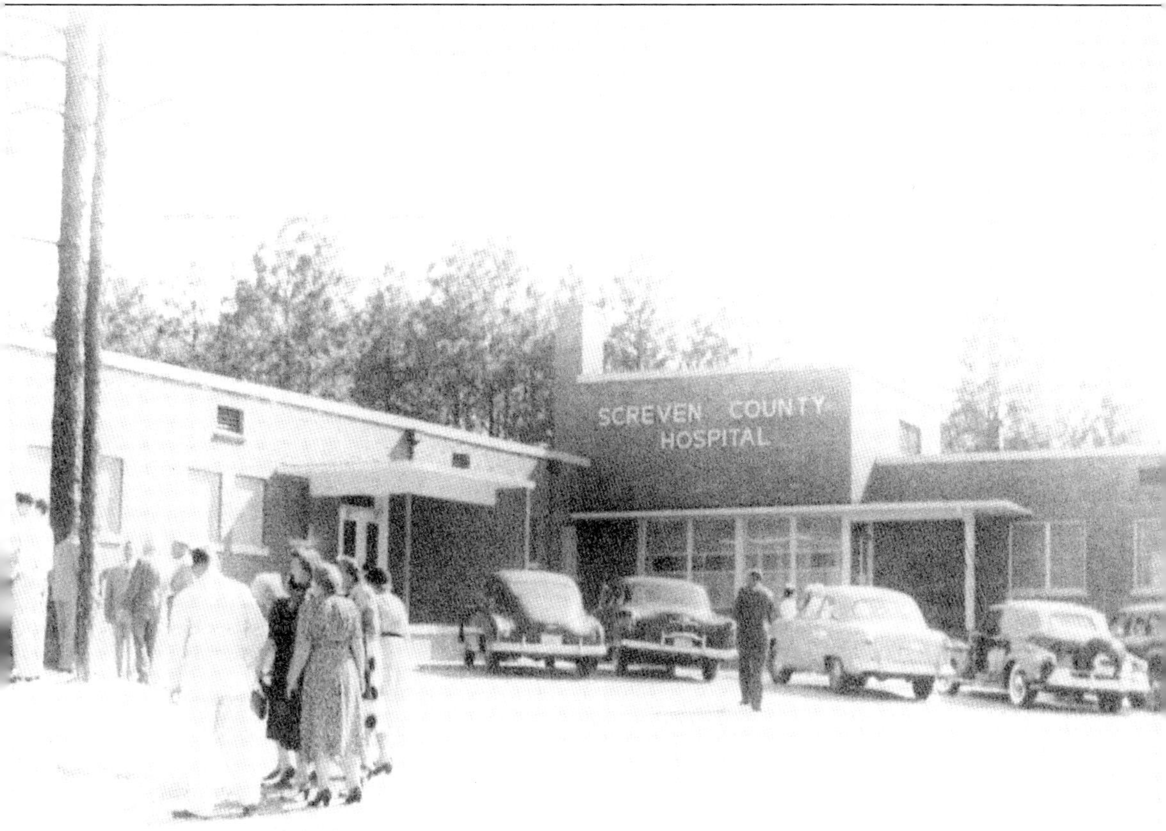

Screven County residents inspected their new hospital when the $332,000 facility opened in 1951. The Screven facility was the first Georgia hospital built under the Hill-Burton health care act. Officials said Screven County supplied its share of funds entirely from surplus money.

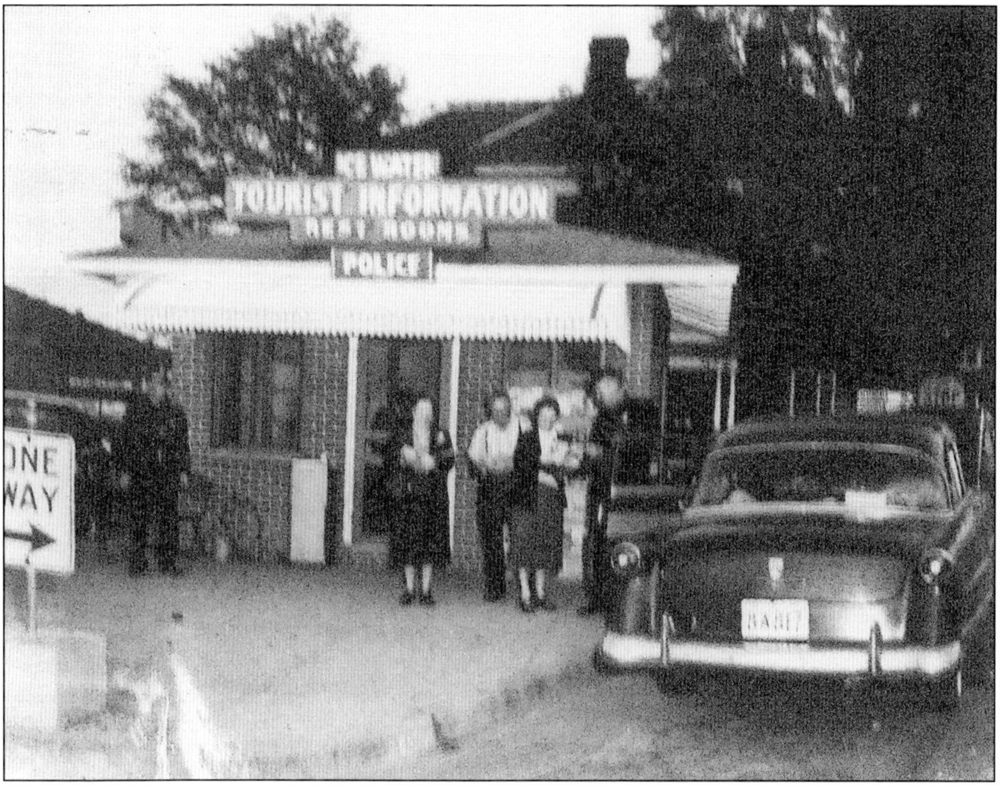

Sylvania's Tourist Information Center opened its doors in 1954, just in time for the heavy traffic season on U.S. Highway 301, which opened in 1947. The brick hut, armed with a big sign and lots of local information, was located right in the heart of Sylvania, where motorists could not help but see it. The highway, for decades a popular north-south route in the eastern United States, brought 5,000 cars a day through Sylvania and Screven County. In its heyday, Sylvania boasted 11 motels, several restaurants, numerous service stations, and other businesses geared towards the tourist trade. Traffic on the highway dropped drastically when I-95 was constructed.

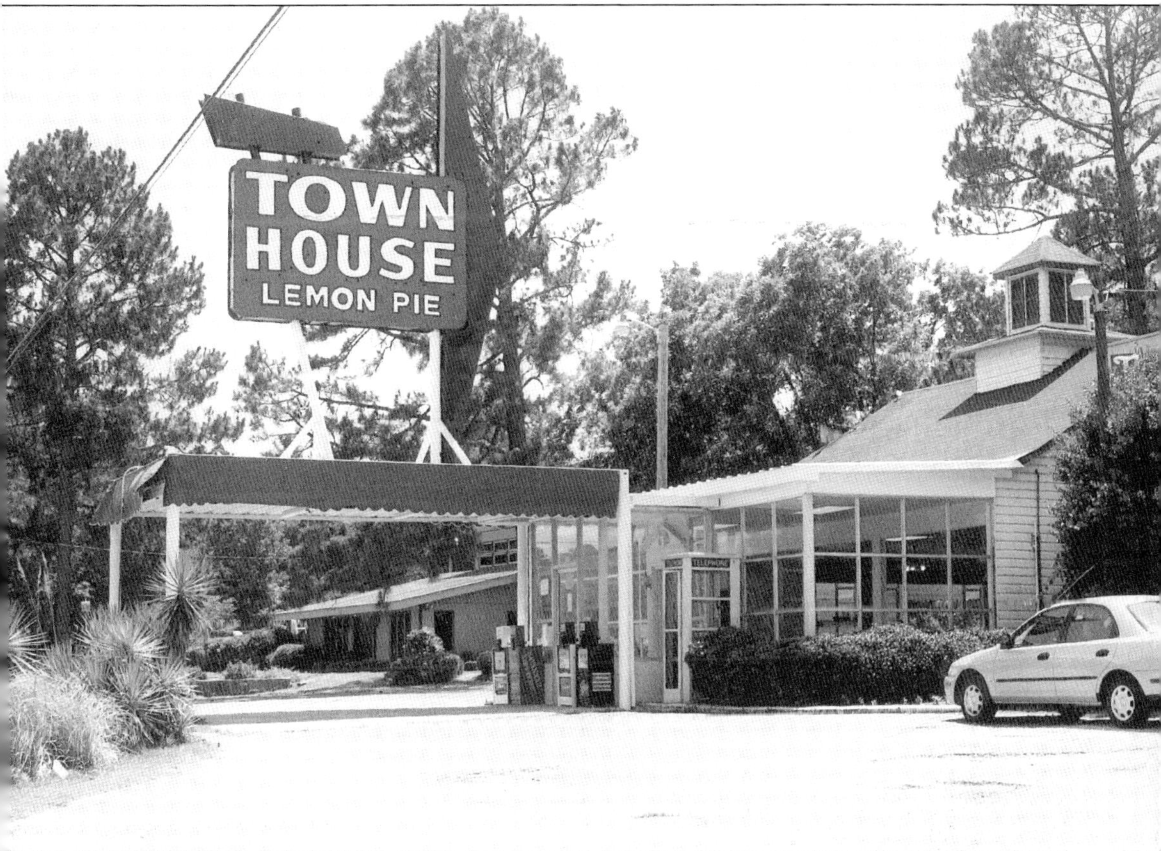

The Town House Restaurant on the edge of town enjoyed a fine reputation from one end of U.S. Highway 301 to the other, and back again. Serving delicious, down-home meals and heavenly desserts, restaurant owner Charles Treado and his staff fed more travelers and stay-at-homes than anyone else in the area.

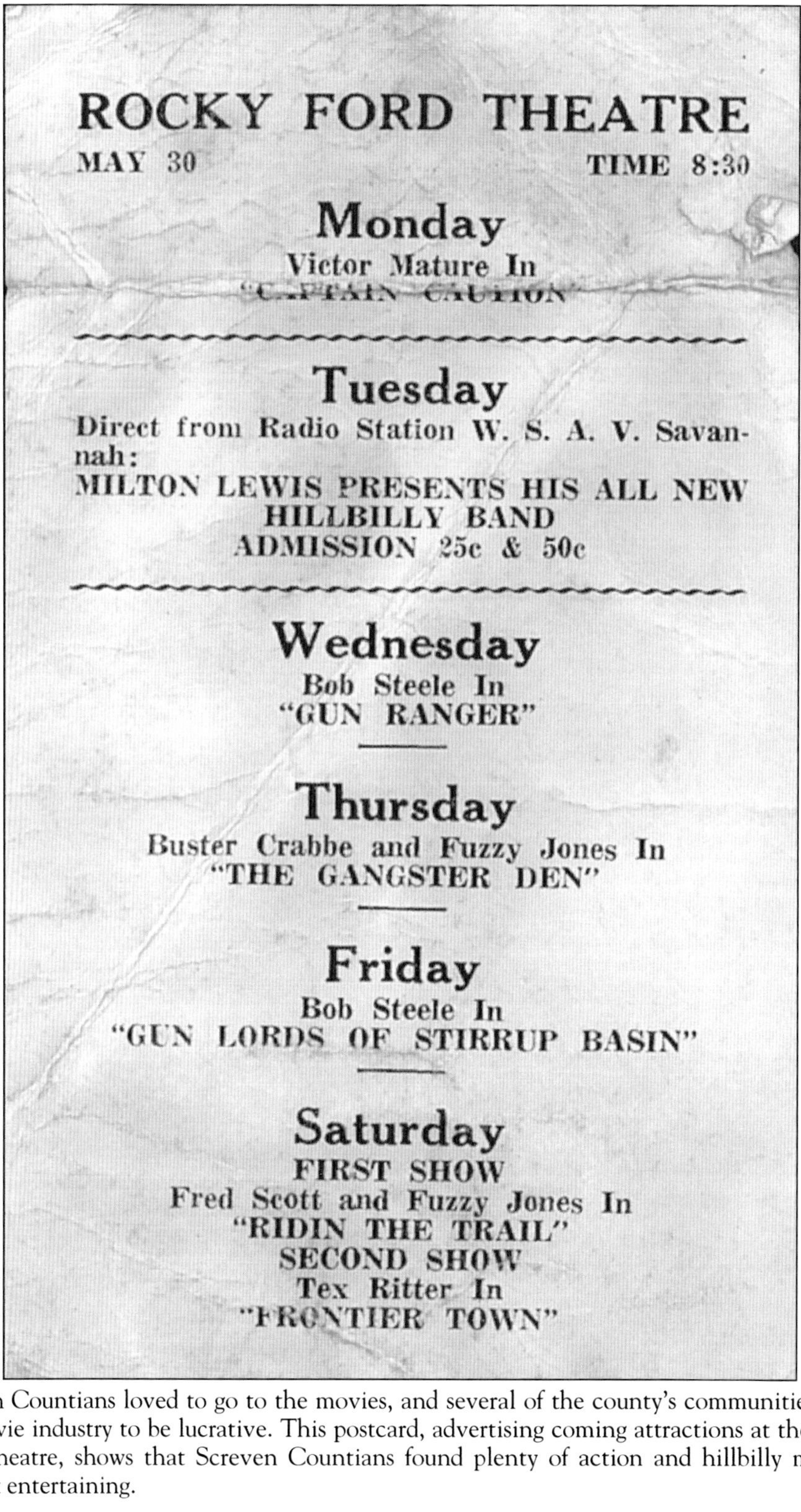

ROCKY FORD THEATRE

MAY 30 TIME 8:30

Monday

Victor Mature In

"CAPTAIN CAUTION"

Tuesday

Direct from Radio Station W. S. A. V. Savannah:

MILTON LEWIS PRESENTS HIS ALL NEW HILLBILLY BAND

ADMISSION 25c & 50c

Wednesday

Bob Steele In

"GUN RANGER"

Thursday

Buster Crabbe and Fuzzy Jones In

"THE GANGSTER DEN"

Friday

Bob Steele In

"GUN LORDS OF STIRRUP BASIN"

Saturday

FIRST SHOW

Fred Scott and Fuzzy Jones In

"RIDIN THE TRAIL"

SECOND SHOW

Tex Ritter In

"FRONTIER TOWN"

Screven Countians loved to go to the movies, and several of the county's communities found the movie industry to be lucrative. This postcard, advertising coming attractions at the Rocky Ford Theatre, shows that Screven Countians found plenty of action and hillbilly music to be most entertaining.

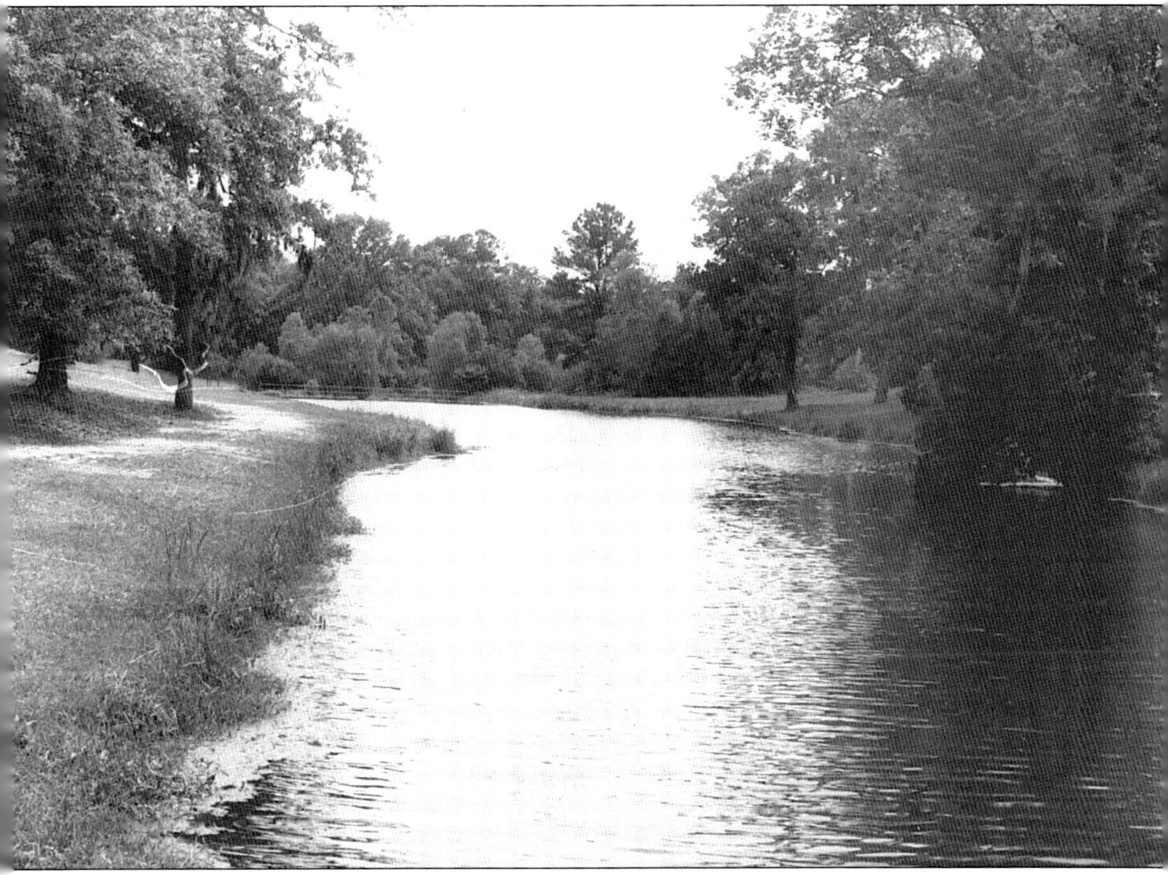

A former prisoner-of-war camp became a playground for area residents when Magnolia Springs, the site of the Confederate prison Camp Lawton in the 1860s, became a state park. Known as a recreation/picnic area since the 1800s, Magnolia opened its gates with swimming facilities, tennis courts, picnic areas, and other features. All that was needed were the people, who came in droves.

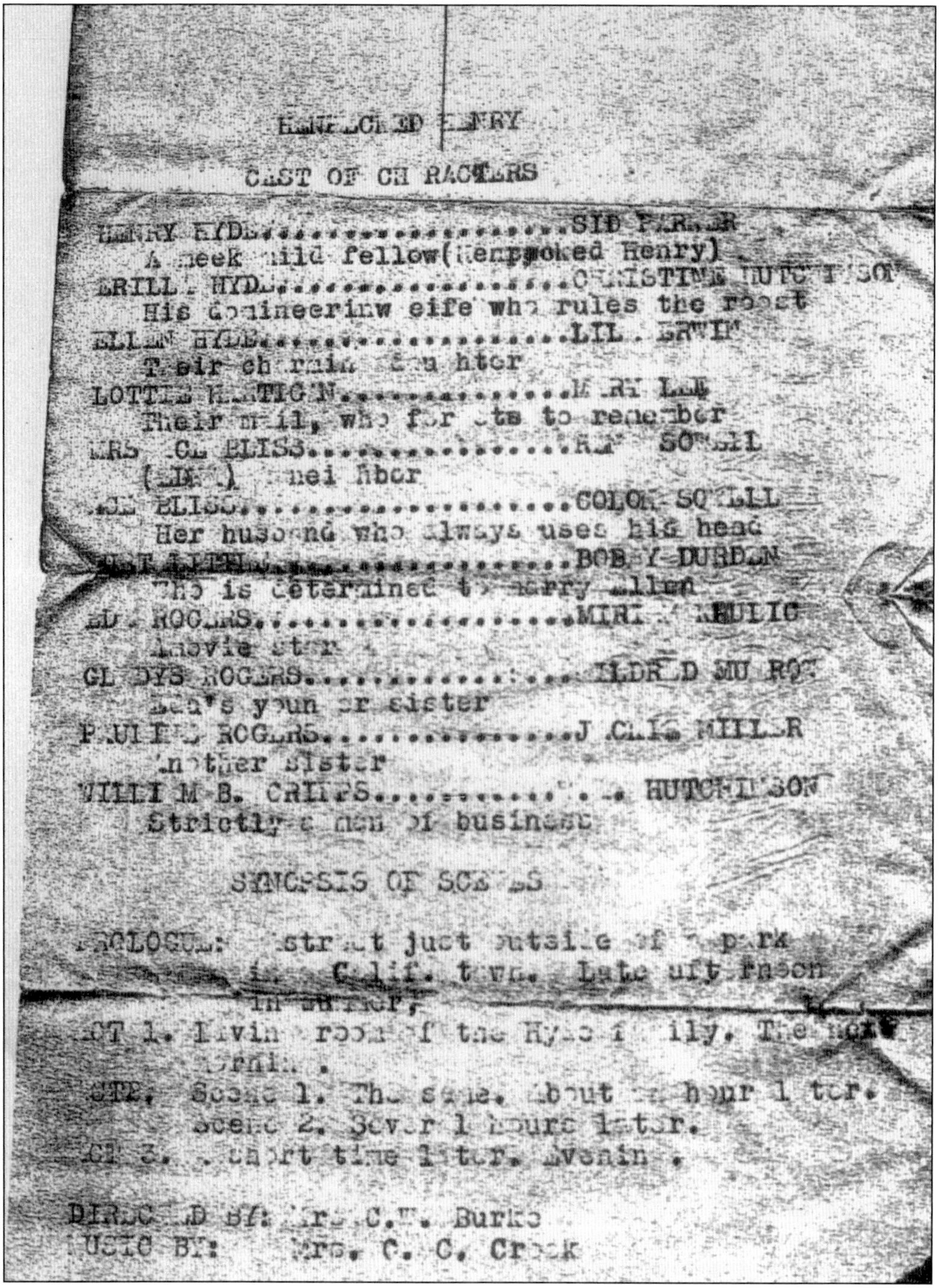

HENPECKED HENRY

CAST OF CHARACTERS

HENRY HYDE.........................SID PARKER
A meek mild fellow(Henpecked Henry)
BRILL HYDE.........................CHRISTINE HUTCHINSON
His domineering wife who rules the roost
ELLEN HYDE.........................LIL ERWIN
Their charming daughter
LOTTIE ....MARY LEE
Their maid, who forgets to remember
MRS. BLISS.........................RENA SOWELL
neighbor
BLISS.........................COLON SOWELL
Her husband who always uses his head
.........................BOBBY DURDEN
Who is determined to marry Ellen
ROGERS.........................MIRIAM KRULIC
A movie star
GLADYS ROGERS.........................MILDRED MURROW
's younger sister
PAULINE ROGERS.........................JACKIE MILLER
Another sister
WILLIAM B. CRIPPS......................HUTCHINSON
Strictly a man of business

SYNOPSIS OF SCENES

PROLOGUE: street just outside of park
in Calif. town. Late afternoon
in summer.
ACT 1. Living room of the Hyde family. The next
morning.
ACT 2. Scene 1. The same. About an hour later.
Scene 2. Several hours later.
ACT 3. A short time later. Evening.

DIRECTED BY: Mrs. C.W. Burke
MUSIC BY: Mrs. C. C. Crook

Entertainment in small towns took on many forms. This cast list for a play called *Henpecked Henry* features several people from as far away as . . . well, Rocky Ford. Playing the lead roles were Sid Parker and Christine Hutchinson. Other cast members were Lil Erwin, Mary Lee, Rena Sowell, Colon Sowell, Bobby Durden, Miriam Krulic, Mildred Murrow, Jackie Miller, and W.A. Hutchinson. Mrs. C.W. Burke was director, and Mrs. C.C. Crook provided musical selections.

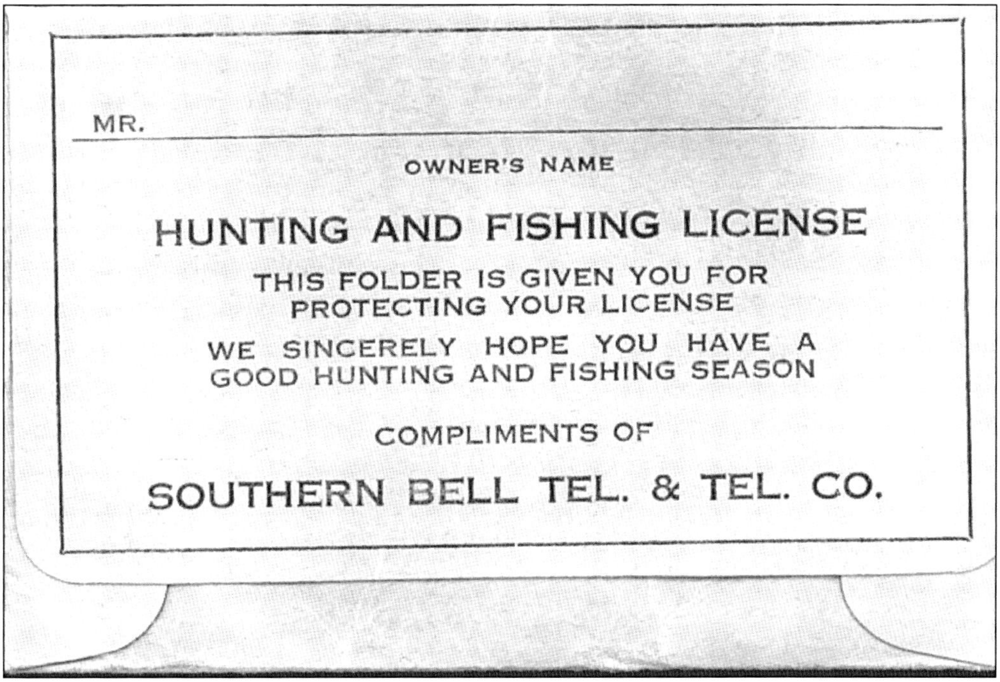

MR.

OWNER'S NAME

HUNTING AND FISHING LICENSE

THIS FOLDER IS GIVEN YOU FOR PROTECTING YOUR LICENSE

WE SINCERELY HOPE YOU HAVE A GOOD HUNTING AND FISHING SEASON

COMPLIMENTS OF

SOUTHERN BELL TEL. & TEL. CO.

Above, we find that Southern Bell Telephone and Telegraph Company encouraged area residents to hunt and fish safely and legally, while area politicians were out to get everybody's vote.

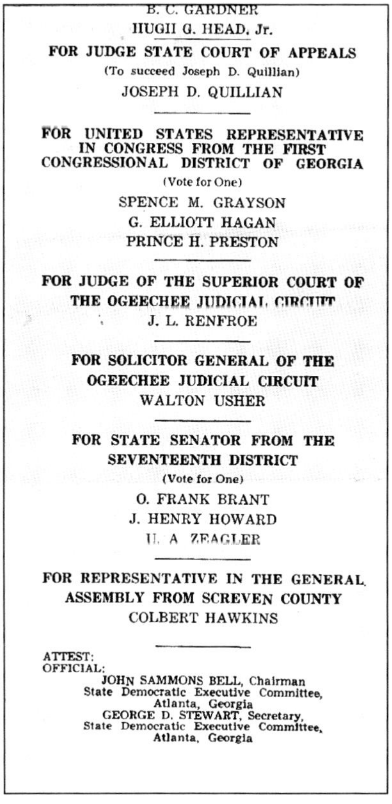

B. C. GARDNER

HUGH G. HEAD, Jr.

FOR JUDGE STATE COURT OF APPEALS

(To succeed Joseph D. Quillian)

JOSEPH D. QUILLIAN

FOR UNITED STATES REPRESENTATIVE IN CONGRESS FROM THE FIRST CONGRESSIONAL DISTRICT OF GEORGIA

(Vote for One)

SPENCE M. GRAYSON

G. ELLIOTT HAGAN

PRINCE H. PRESTON

FOR JUDGE OF THE SUPERIOR COURT OF THE OGEECHEE JUDICIAL CIRCUIT

J. L. RENFROE

FOR SOLICITOR GENERAL OF THE OGEECHEE JUDICIAL CIRCUIT

WALTON USHER

FOR STATE SENATOR FROM THE SEVENTEENTH DISTRICT

(Vote for One)

O. FRANK BRANT

J. HENRY HOWARD

H. A. ZEAGLER

FOR REPRESENTATIVE IN THE GENERAL ASSEMBLY FROM SCREVEN COUNTY

COLBERT HAWKINS

ATTEST:
OFFICIAL:
JOHN SAMMONS BELL, Chairman
State Democratic Executive Committee,
Atlanta, Georgia
GEORGE D. STEWART, Secretary,
State Democratic Executive Committee,
Atlanta, Georgia

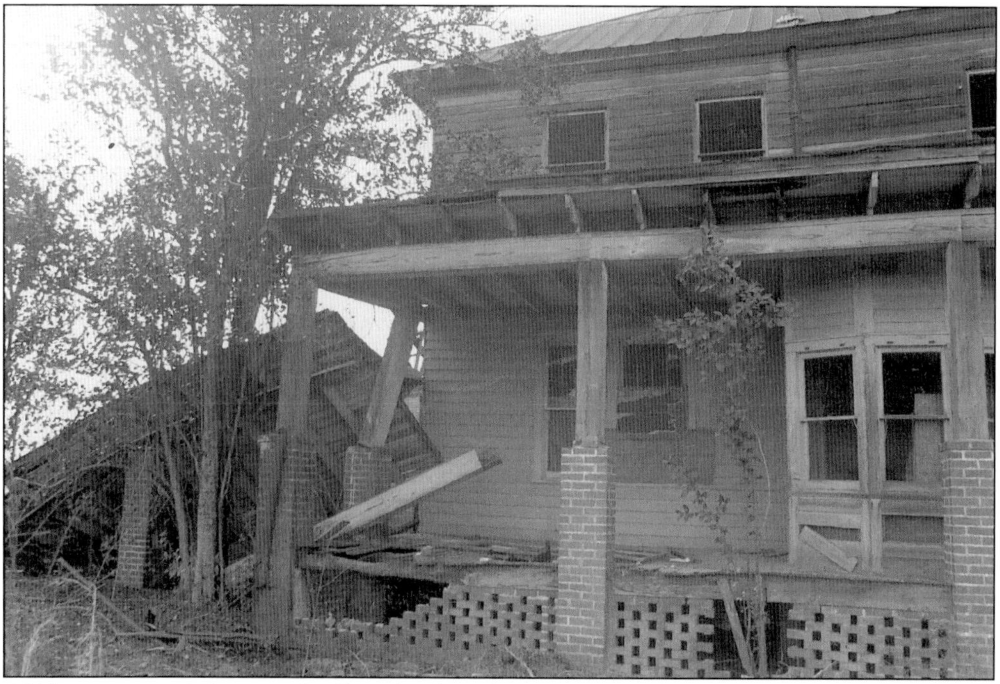

Old houses struggled to stand tall, and girls and cars got better looking.

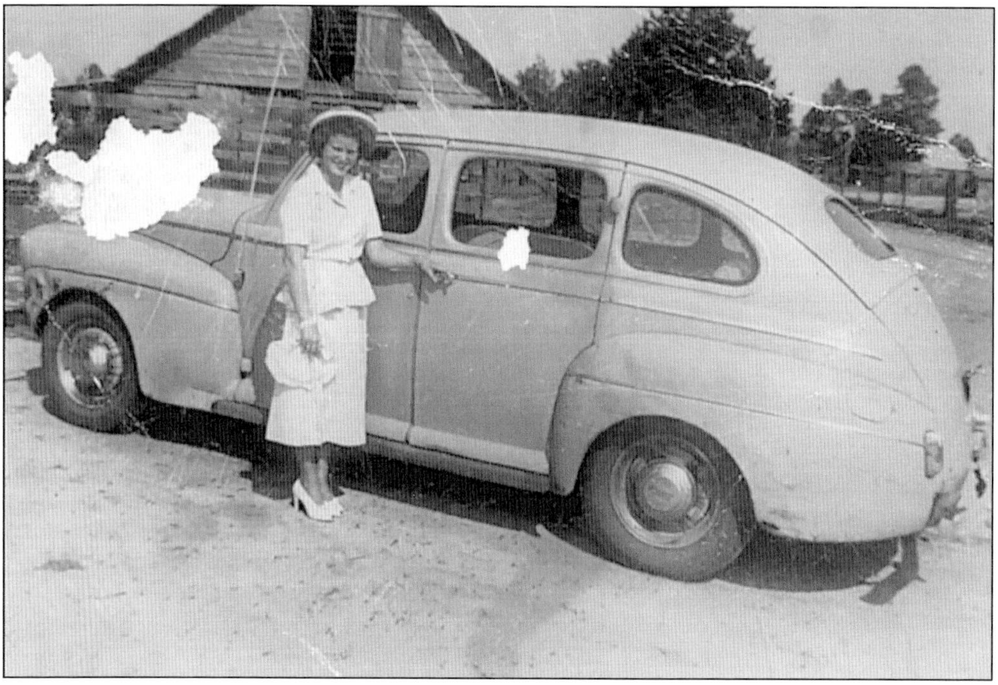

Six

AIN'T LIFE GOOD

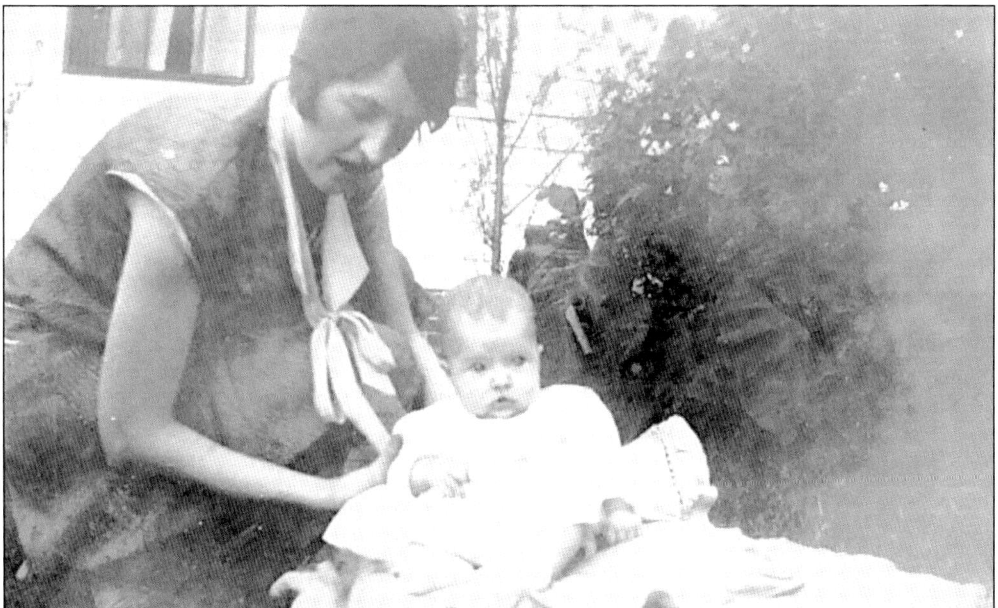

Three-month-old Martha Jeanne Freeman faced life confidently. A pallet, a pillow, and a gentle helping hand provided the moral support needed.

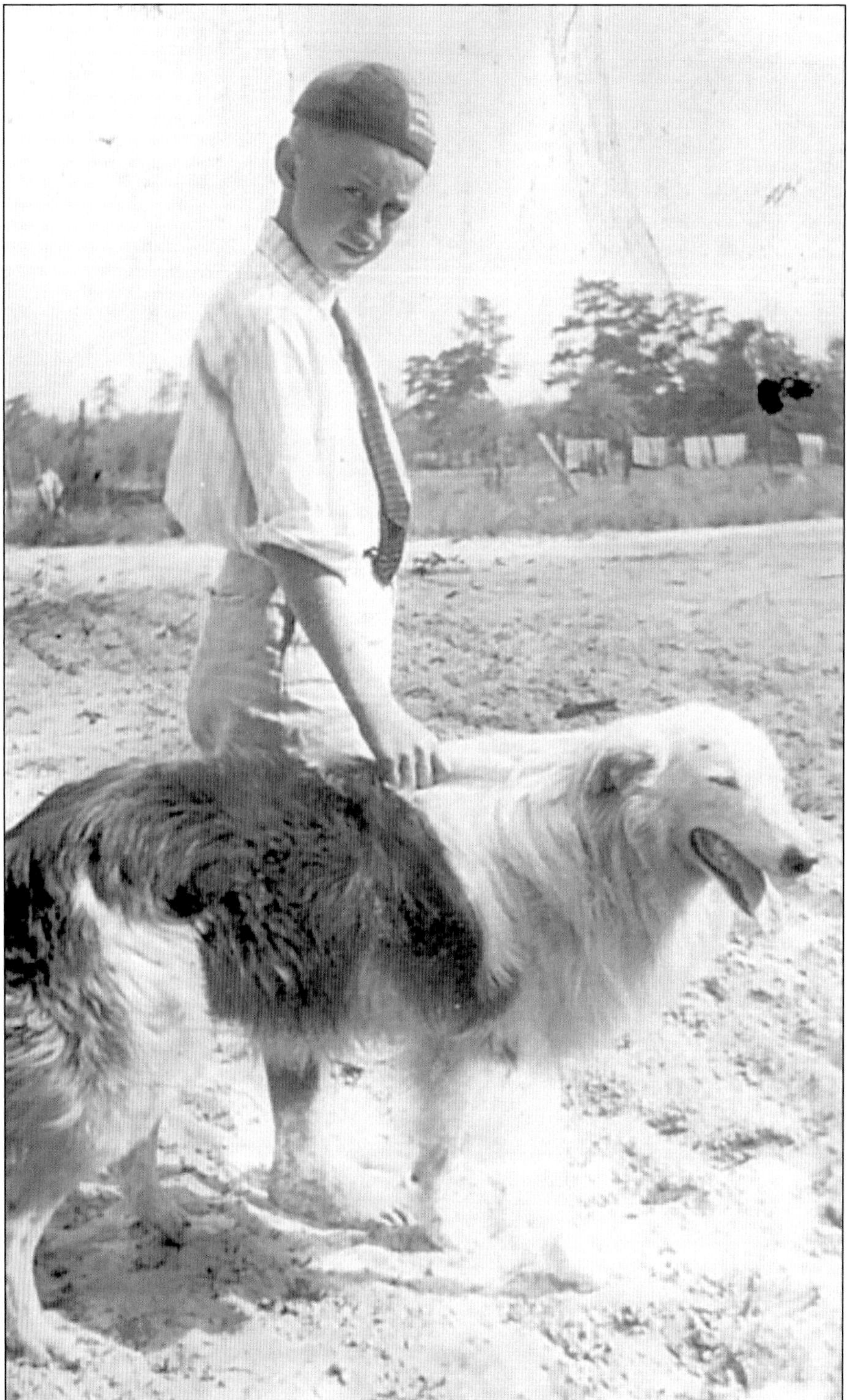

A boy's best friend was gentle, playful, obedient, supportive, and protective. A boy's best friend just might have been his dog.

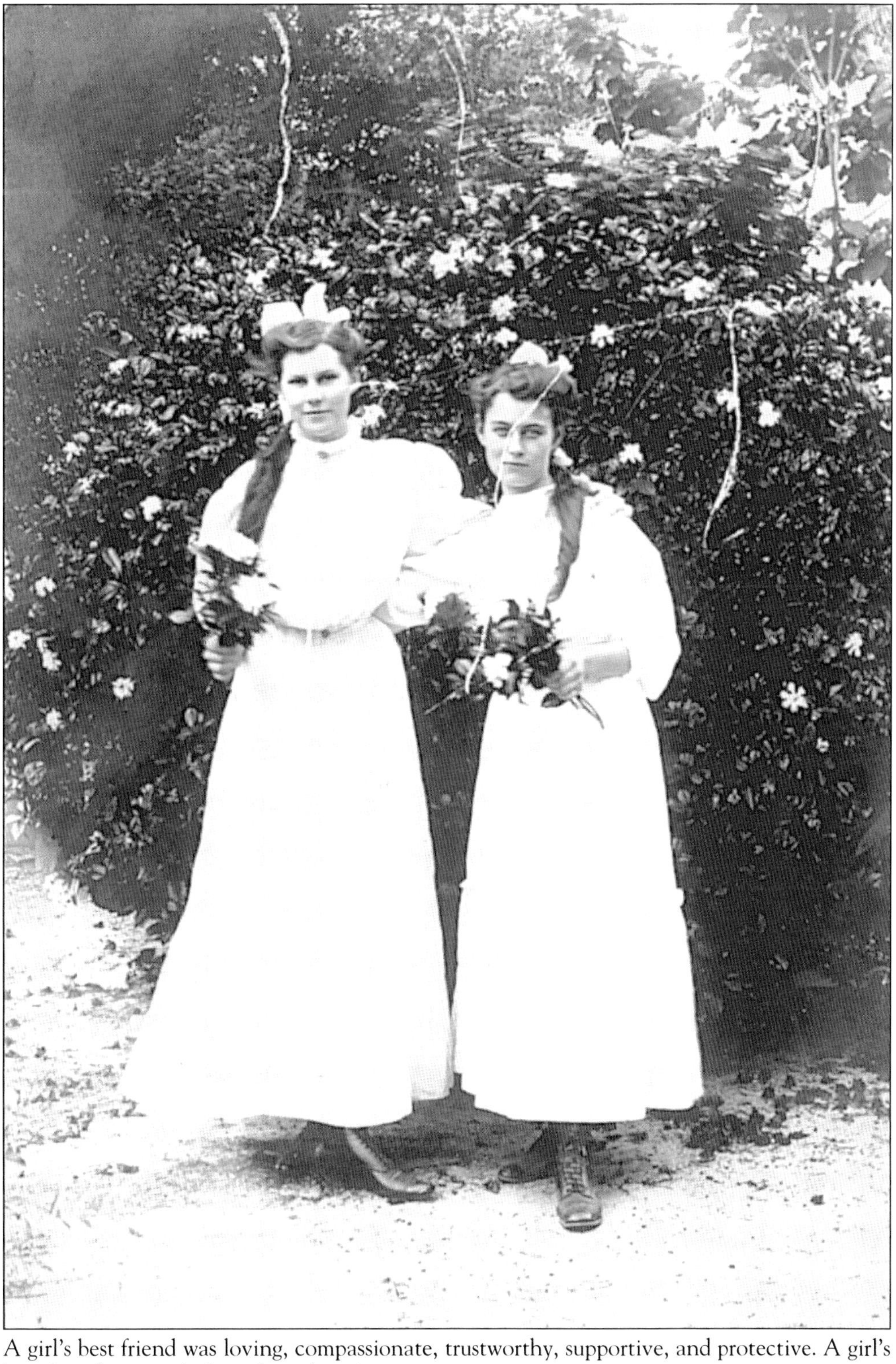

A girl's best friend was loving, compassionate, trustworthy, supportive, and protective. A girl's best friend just might have been her sister.

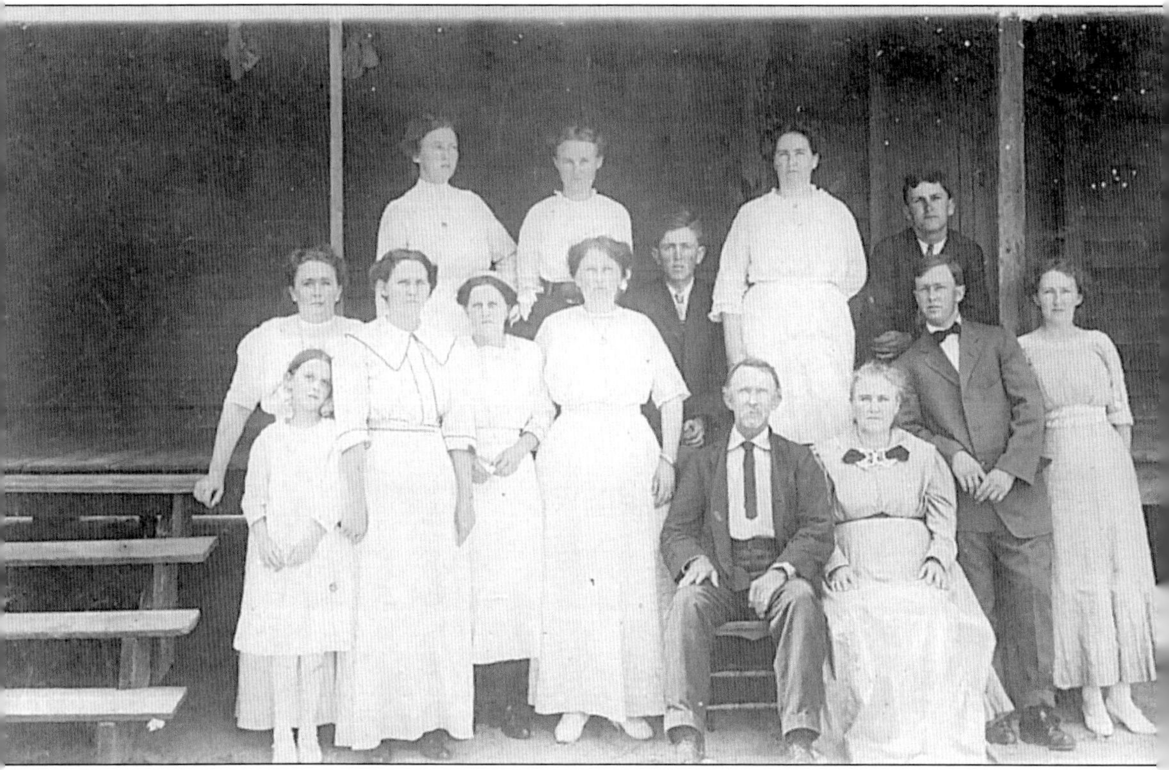

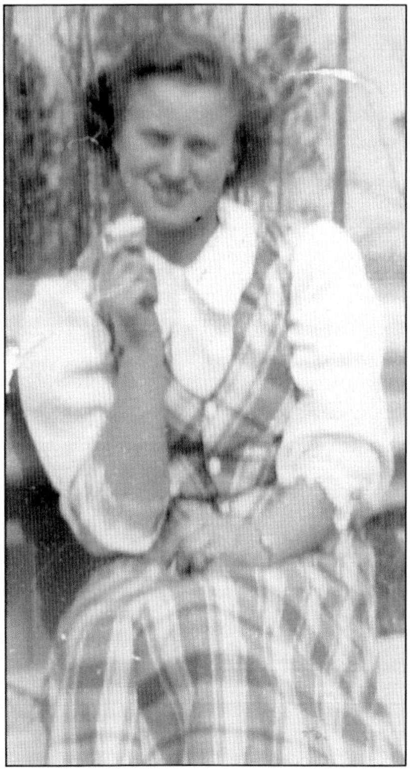

Families were support systems responsible for one another in the sunshine and the rain. In the photo above, the Cates family poses for a group portrait. Family members include the following, from left to right: (front row) Mrs. Mattie Lou Cates Wimberly, Muriel Cates Ashe (the young lady standing in front), Mrs. Mark Cates Stephens, Mrs. Jennie Cates Waters, Mrs. Josie Cates Brinson, Mr. Dock Cates, Mrs. Josephine Cates, Arthur Cates, and Mrs. Laura Cates Godbee; (back row) Mrs. Hamp Cates Godbee, Mrs. Hershel Cates Waters, Henry Judson Cates, Mrs. Beulah Cates Wimberly, and Charlie Cecile Cates.

At left, Screven County teenager Emily Bazemore finds moral support in an ice-cream cone.

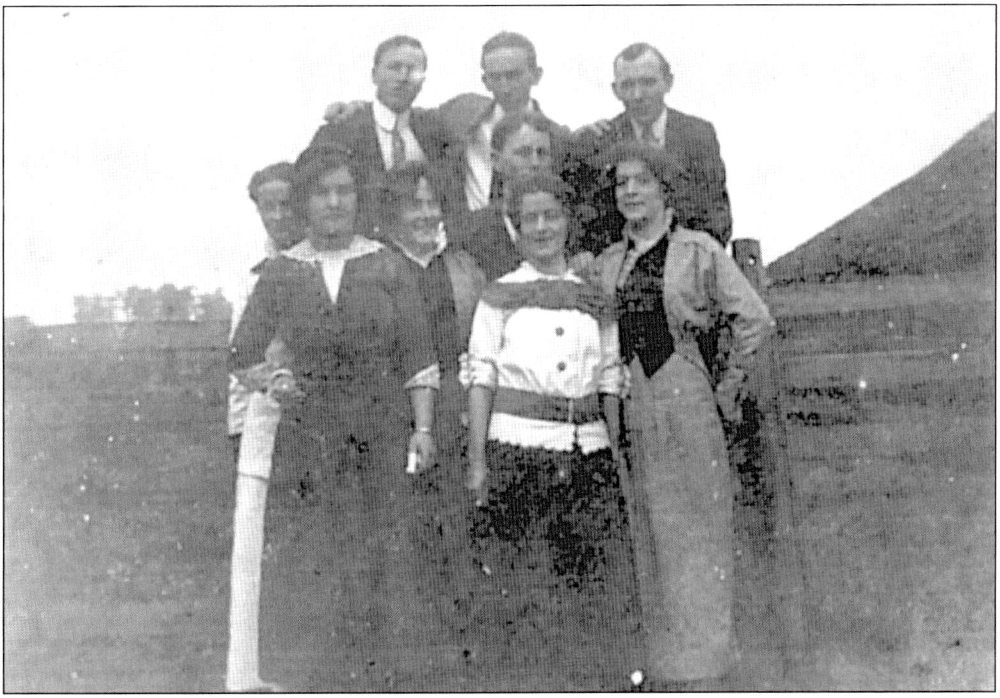

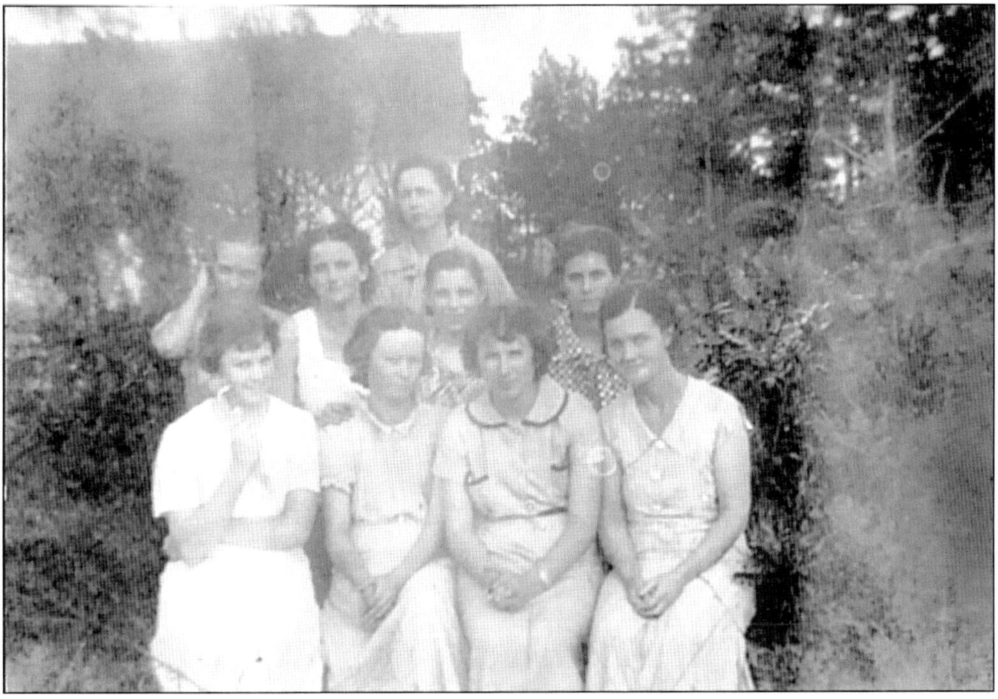

In the early 1900s, area youths became enamored with the more user-friendly cameras that made impromptu snapshots easy accomplishments.

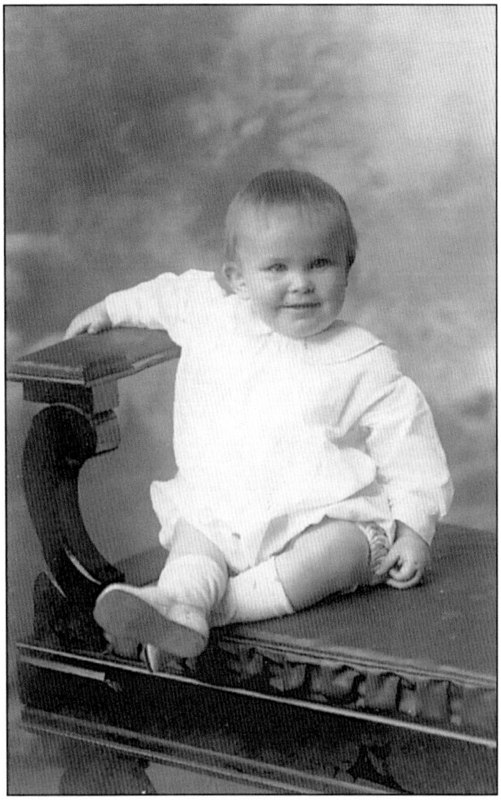

Throughout the years, one thing remained constant. If you pointed a camera at a youngster, he or she suddenly broke out into a full-faced grin. Toddler Sandra Lee, below in the stroller with sister Karen, was no different from her predecessors in the other photos on this page. The times were different, the clothes were different, but the tendency to step out and greet life with a smile was and always will be the same.

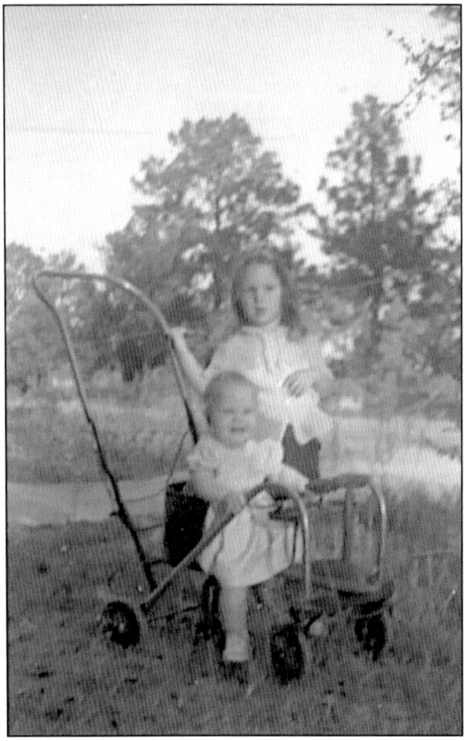

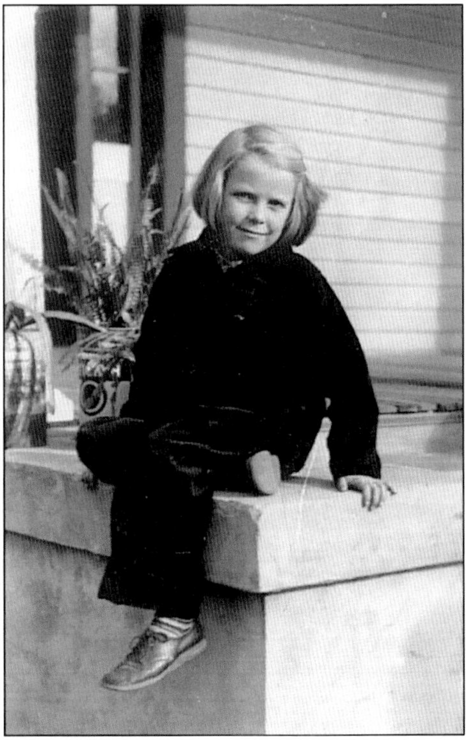

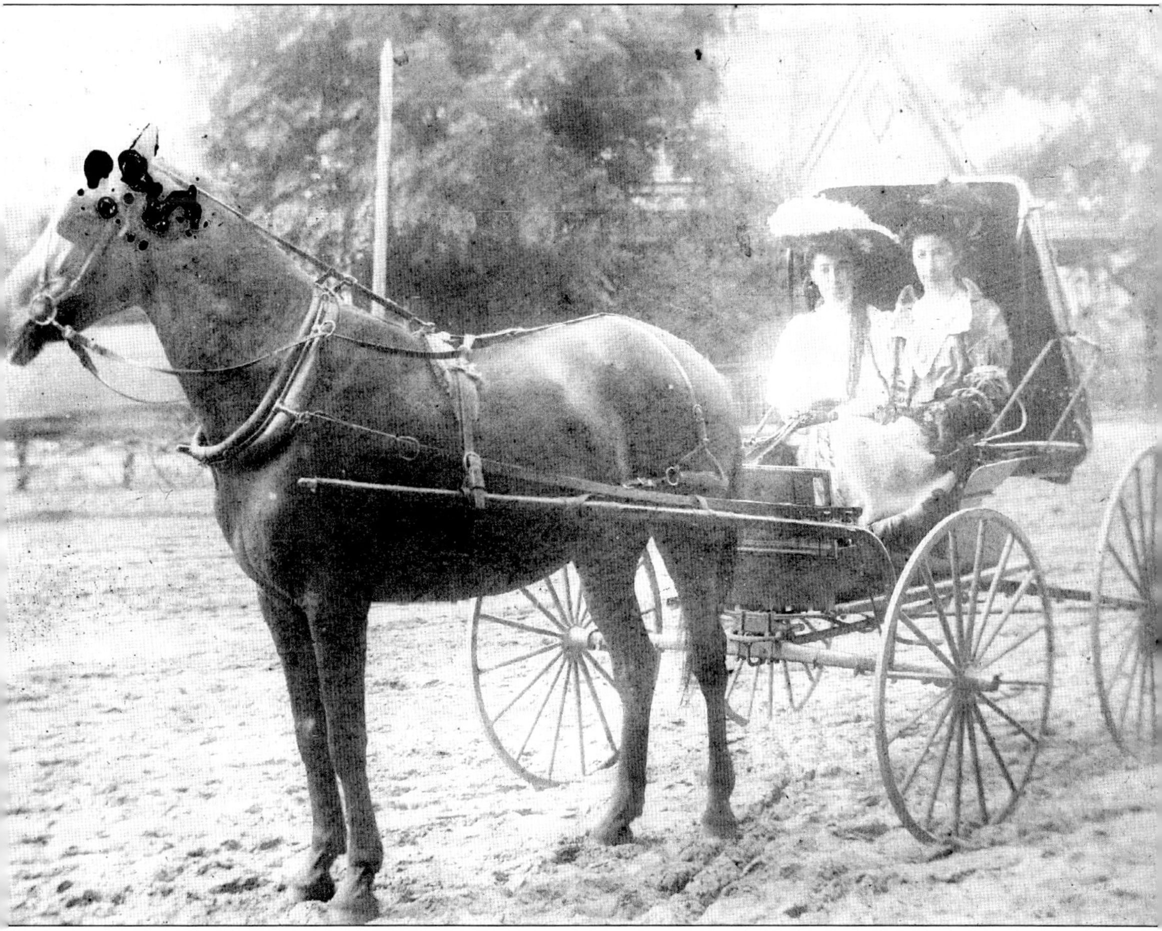

Getting from one place to another was simple. You just harnessed the horse and buggy and went. The journeys were inspirational—with warm sunshine and a cool breeze; bright sunshine shaded by fluffy white clouds that towered toward eternity; gray thunderheads that nudged the horse (and driver) into high gear; smooth stretches of hard-packed sand that made the going so easy; sandy spots in the road where buggy wheels threatened to tip over; a congenial companion bent on making the day pleasant, and a grumpy passenger determined to rain on the other's parade. It was life, pure and simple.

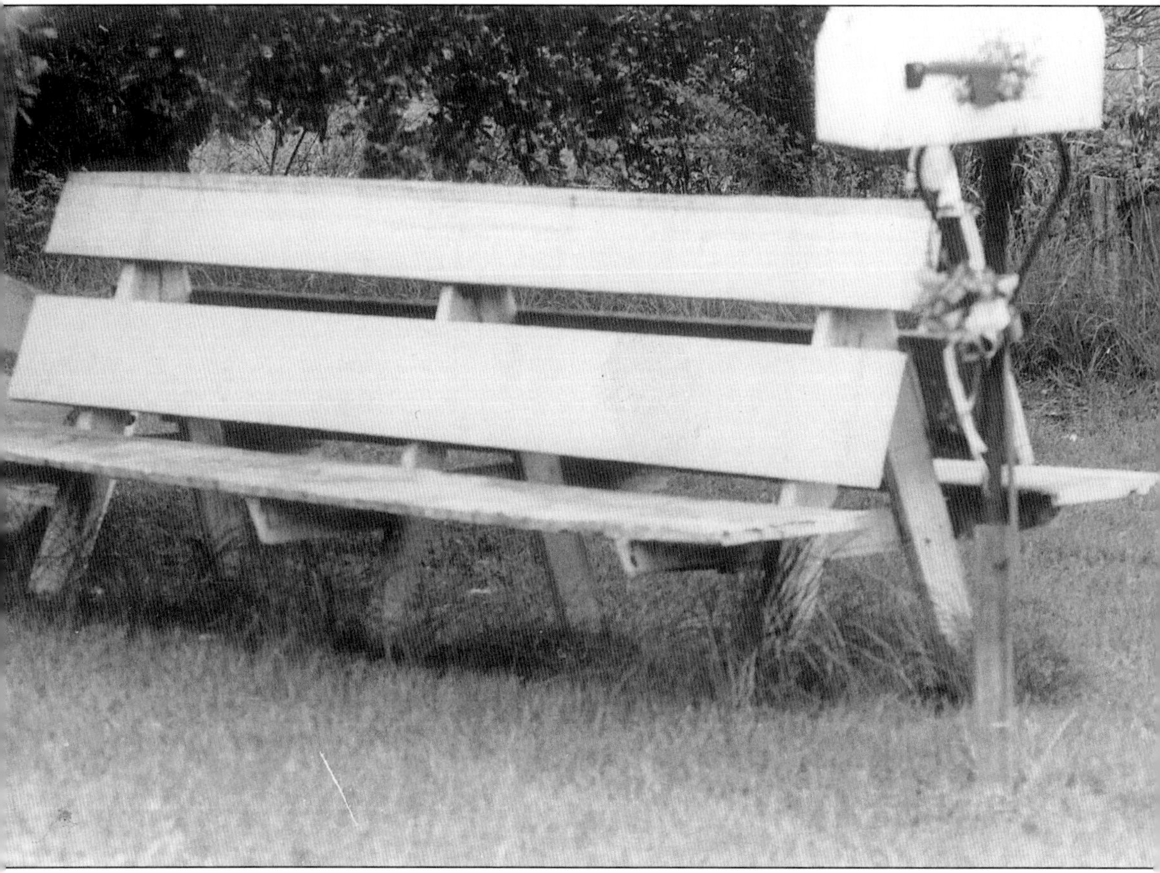

A comfortable park bench like this one in Jenkins County's Herndon awaits any passerby who needs a shady place to sit for a while. Making life a pleasant affair is a priority in Herndon, where visitors are encouraged to sit and watch the train go by or walk down to the Ogeechee River for a refreshing dip. A part of Jenkins County life for as long as anyone can remember, Herndon residents were among those who reluctantly greeted Union General William T. Sherman and his army when the Yankee forces passed through headed for Millen.

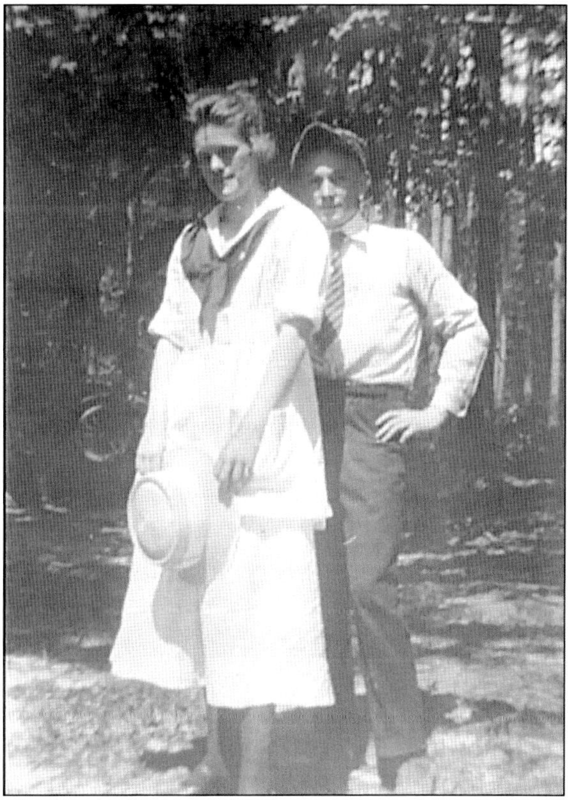

Young folk enjoyed long walks through the countryside, and little girls suffered frills and lace and curls that dangled prettily.

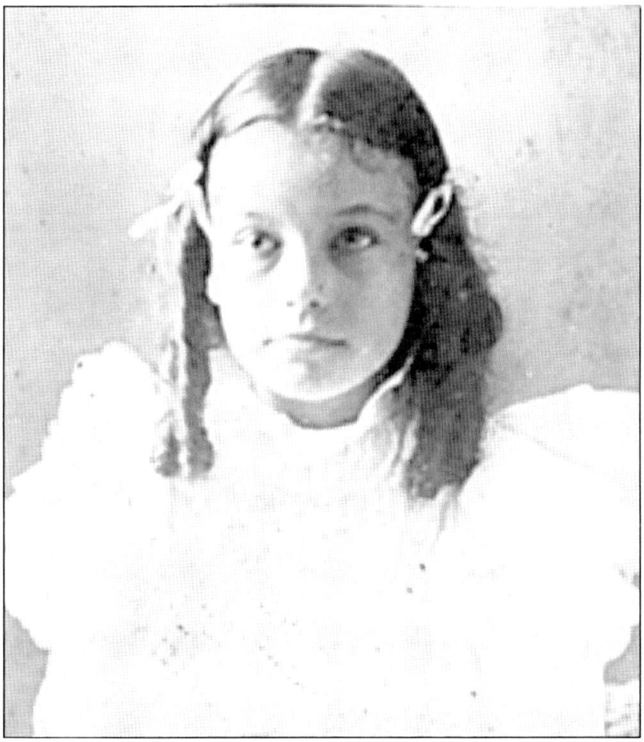

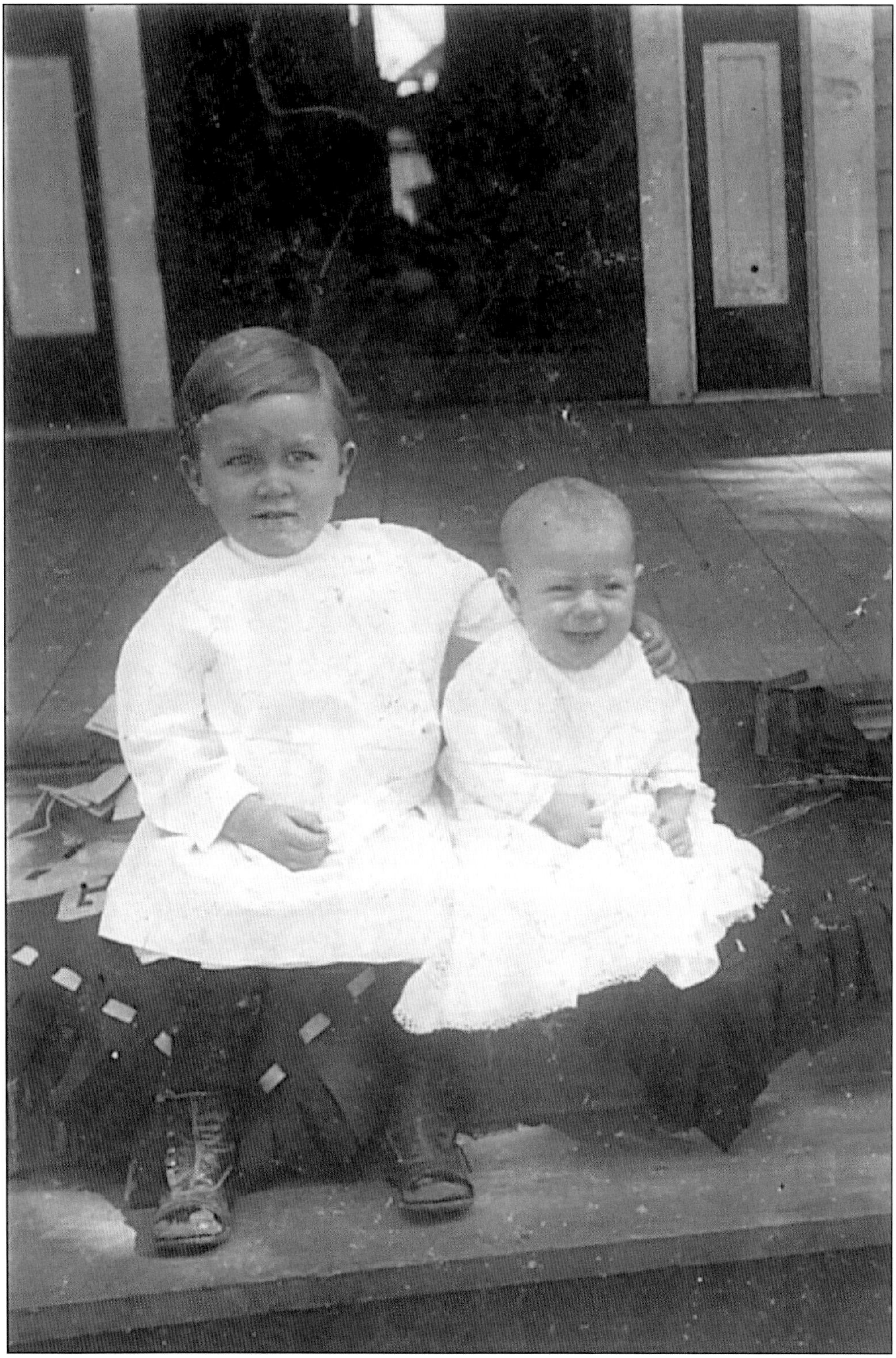

Little boys moved gingerly in white lace and brogans.

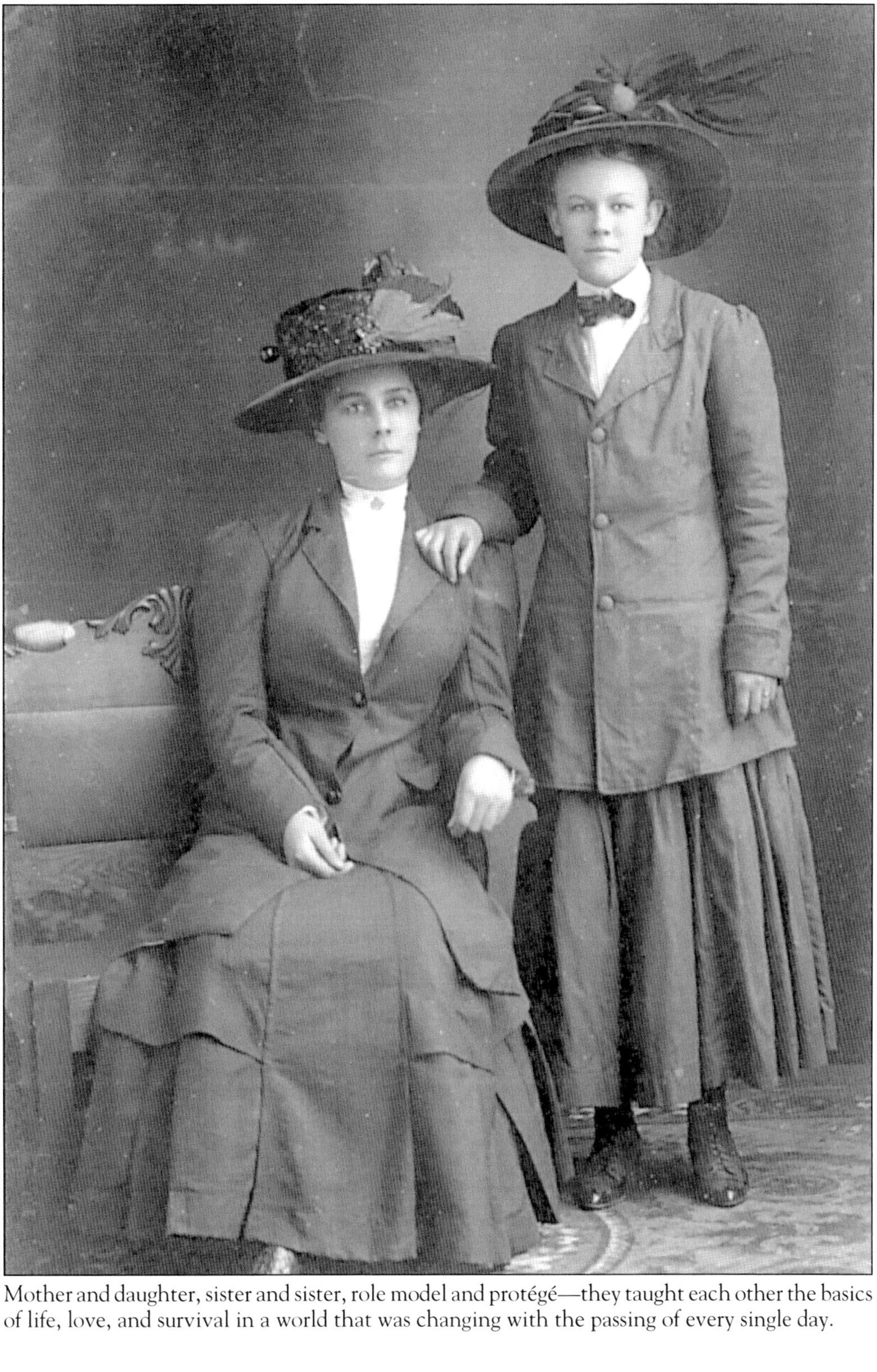

Mother and daughter, sister and sister, role model and protégé—they taught each other the basics of life, love, and survival in a world that was changing with the passing of every single day.

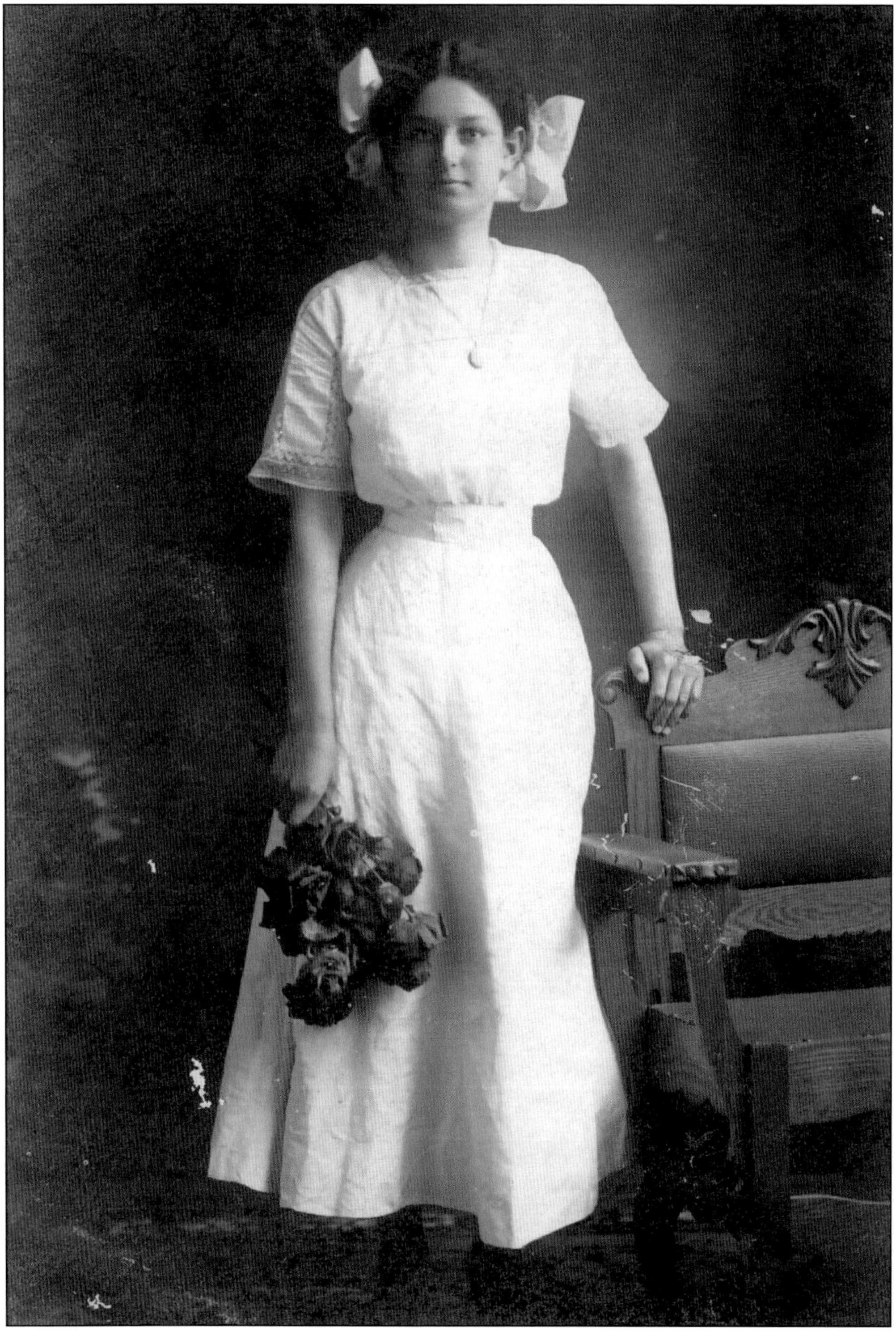

Well-dressed young ladies posed for the camera and mailed the likeness to that very special beau.

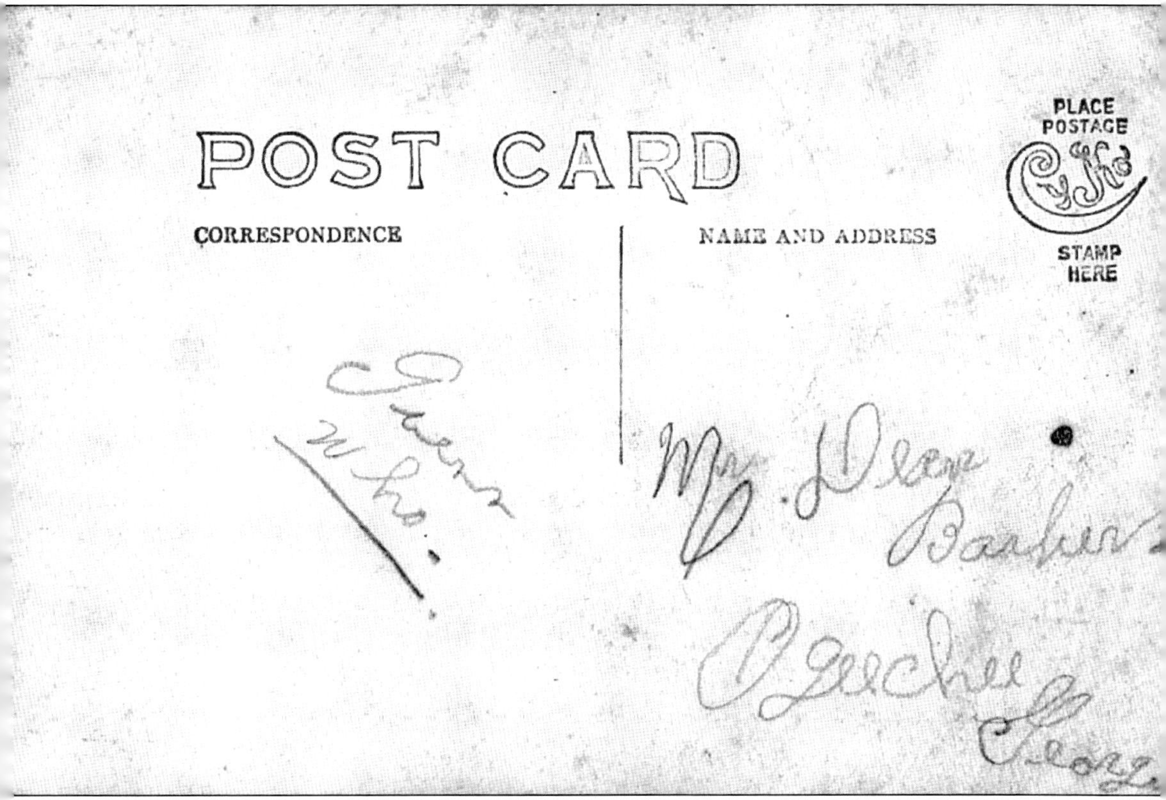

Here is the back of the same postcard that is seen on the previous page.

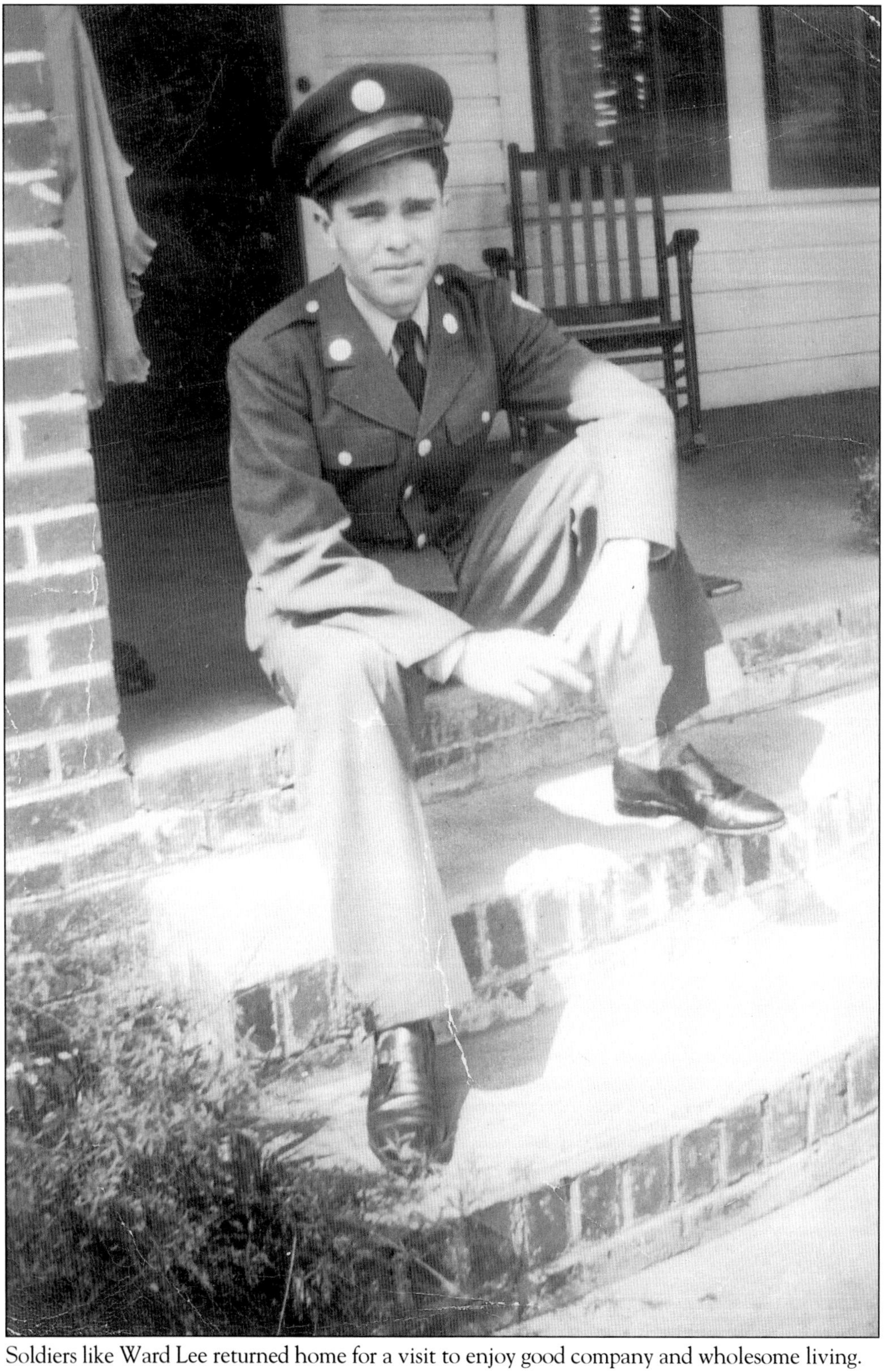

Soldiers like Ward Lee returned home for a visit to enjoy good company and wholesome living.

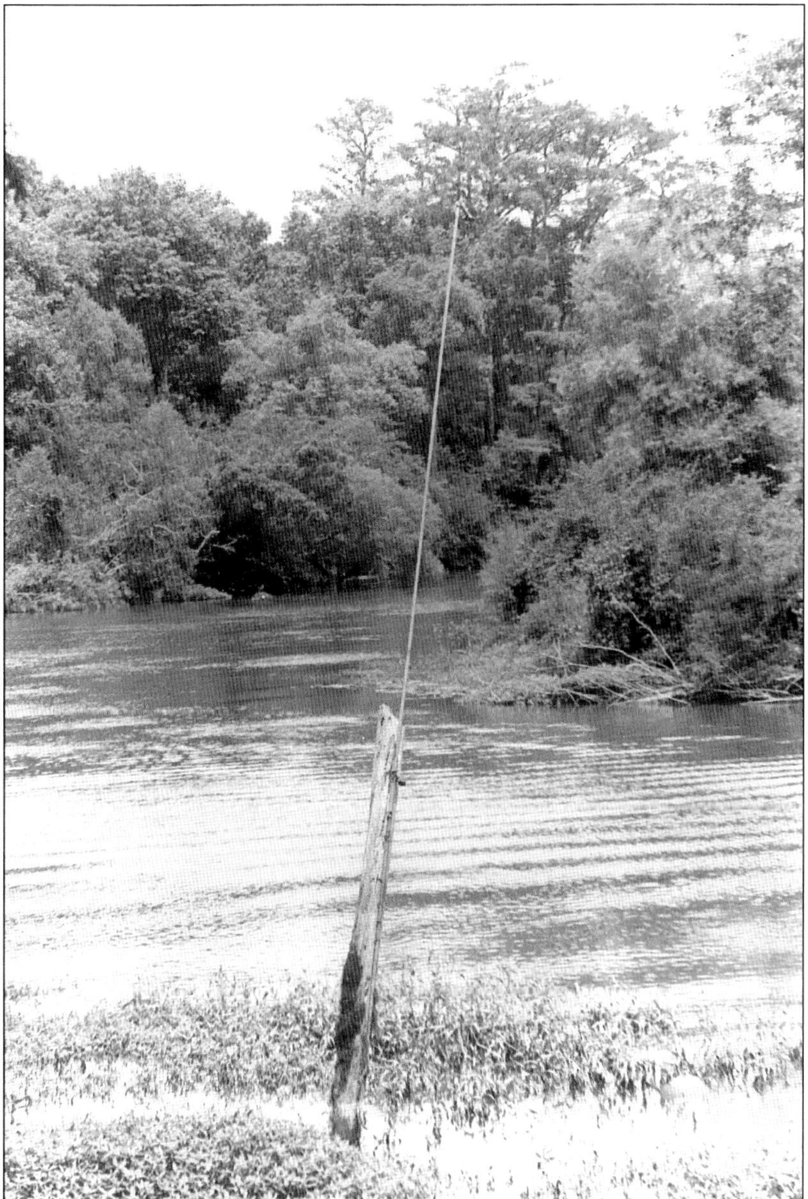

Folks enjoyed pleasant days fishing, swimming, or watching the reeds grow in any of the numerous special places along the Ogeechee River.

A full-fledged river from her headwaters to the sea, the Ogeechee is Georgia's longest waterway with the same name throughout its course. Her name was given by American Indians who roamed her banks and enjoyed her hospitality long before any white man knew she existed. Once he arrived, though, the white man quickly learned to appreciate and respect her. In royal surveys conducted between 1751 and 1771, the king's surveyor-general referred to her as "the Great Ogetchee Stream." In her 250-mile journey from spring-fed streams in Greene County to the Atlantic Ocean, the Ogeechee touches many lives and shares with them her beauty and mystery. Her waters wash the shores of 15 Georgia counties. She is untamed today as she was centuries ago. The Ogeechee is certainly a river that belongs to herself.

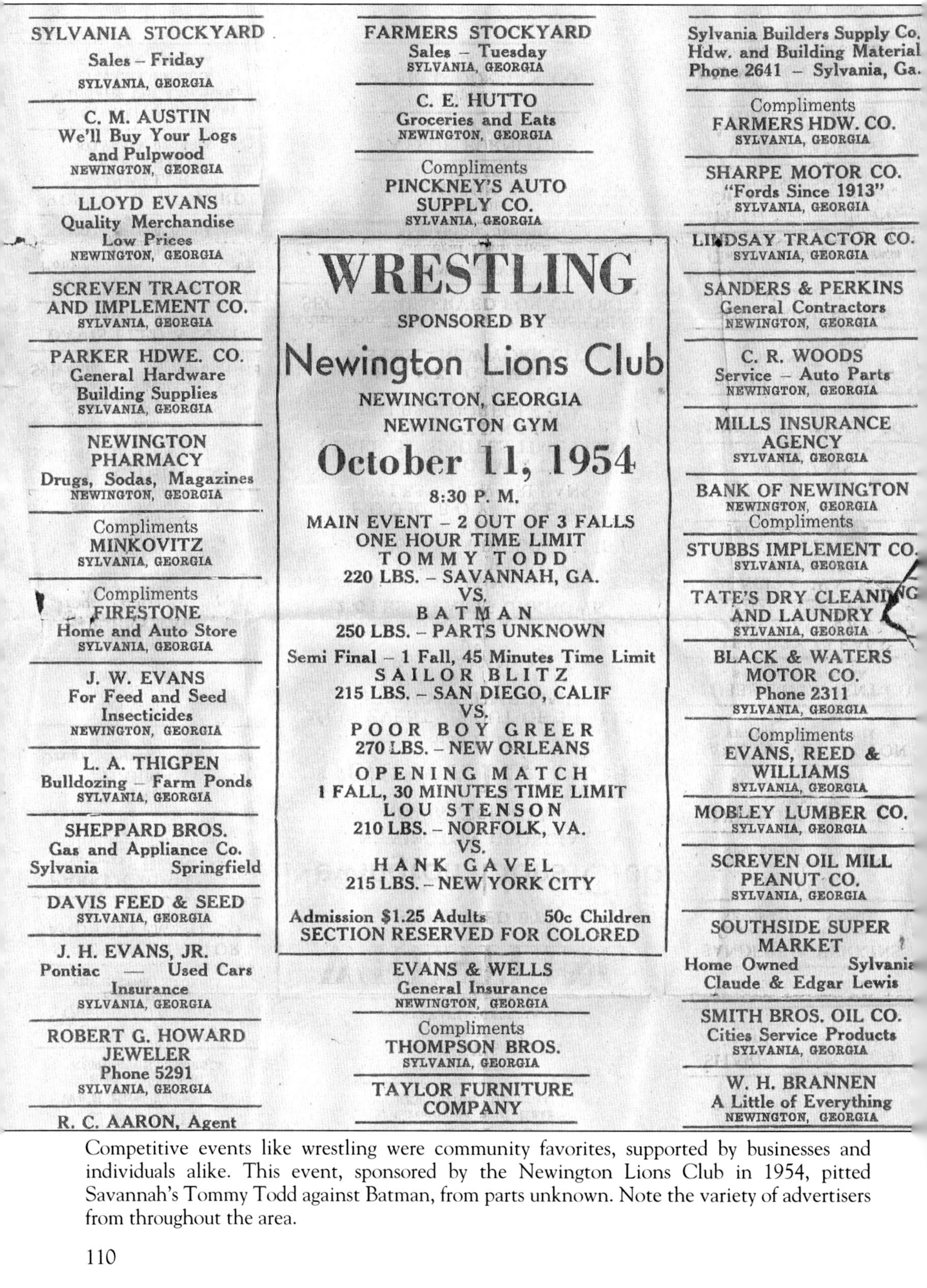

SYLVANIA STOCKYARD
Sales – Friday
SYLVANIA, GEORGIA

C. M. AUSTIN
We'll Buy Your Logs
and Pulpwood
NEWINGTON, GEORGIA

LLOYD EVANS
Quality Merchandise
Low Prices
NEWINGTON, GEORGIA

SCREVEN TRACTOR
AND IMPLEMENT CO.
SYLVANIA, GEORGIA

PARKER HDWE. CO.
General Hardware
Building Supplies
SYLVANIA, GEORGIA

NEWINGTON
PHARMACY
Drugs, Sodas, Magazines
NEWINGTON, GEORGIA

Compliments
MINKOVITZ
SYLVANIA, GEORGIA

Compliments
FIRESTONE
Home and Auto Store
SYLVANIA, GEORGIA

J. W. EVANS
For Feed and Seed
Insecticides
NEWINGTON, GEORGIA

L. A. THIGPEN
Bulldozing – Farm Ponds
SYLVANIA, GEORGIA

SHEPPARD BROS.
Gas and Appliance Co.
Sylvania Springfield

DAVIS FEED & SEED
SYLVANIA, GEORGIA

J. H. EVANS, JR.
Pontiac — Used Cars
Insurance
SYLVANIA, GEORGIA

ROBERT G. HOWARD
JEWELER
Phone 5291
SYLVANIA, GEORGIA

R. C. AARON, Agent

FARMERS STOCKYARD
Sales – Tuesday
SYLVANIA, GEORGIA

C. E. HUTTO
Groceries and Eats
NEWINGTON, GEORGIA

Compliments
PINCKNEY'S AUTO
SUPPLY CO.
SYLVANIA, GEORGIA

WRESTLING

SPONSORED BY

Newington Lions Club

NEWINGTON, GEORGIA
NEWINGTON GYM

October 11, 1954

8:30 P. M.

MAIN EVENT – 2 OUT OF 3 FALLS
ONE HOUR TIME LIMIT
TOMMY TODD
220 LBS. – SAVANNAH, GA.
VS.
BATMAN
250 LBS. – PARTS UNKNOWN

Semi Final – 1 Fall, 45 Minutes Time Limit
SAILOR BLITZ
215 LBS. – SAN DIEGO, CALIF
VS.
POOR BOY GREER
270 LBS. – NEW ORLEANS

OPENING MATCH
1 FALL, 30 MINUTES TIME LIMIT
LOU STENSON
210 LBS. – NORFOLK, VA.
VS.
HANK GAVEL
215 LBS. – NEW YORK CITY

Admission $1.25 Adults 50c Children
SECTION RESERVED FOR COLORED

EVANS & WELLS
General Insurance
NEWINGTON, GEORGIA

Compliments
THOMPSON BROS.
SYLVANIA, GEORGIA

TAYLOR FURNITURE
COMPANY

Sylvania Builders Supply Co.
Hdw. and Building Material
Phone 2641 – Sylvania, Ga.

Compliments
FARMERS HDW. CO.
SYLVANIA, GEORGIA

SHARPE MOTOR CO.
"Fords Since 1913"
SYLVANIA, GEORGIA

LINDSAY TRACTOR CO.
SYLVANIA, GEORGIA

SANDERS & PERKINS
General Contractors
NEWINGTON, GEORGIA

C. R. WOODS
Service – Auto Parts
NEWINGTON, GEORGIA

MILLS INSURANCE
AGENCY
SYLVANIA, GEORGIA

BANK OF NEWINGTON
NEWINGTON, GEORGIA

Compliments
STUBBS IMPLEMENT CO.
SYLVANIA, GEORGIA

TATE'S DRY CLEANING
AND LAUNDRY
SYLVANIA, GEORGIA

BLACK & WATERS
MOTOR CO.
Phone 2311
SYLVANIA, GEORGIA

Compliments
EVANS, REED &
WILLIAMS
SYLVANIA, GEORGIA

MOBLEY LUMBER CO.
SYLVANIA, GEORGIA

SCREVEN OIL MILL
PEANUT CO.
SYLVANIA, GEORGIA

SOUTHSIDE SUPER
MARKET
Home Owned Sylvania
Claude & Edgar Lewis

SMITH BROS. OIL CO.
Cities Service Products
SYLVANIA, GEORGIA

W. H. BRANNEN
A Little of Everything
NEWINGTON, GEORGIA

Competitive events like wrestling were community favorites, supported by businesses and individuals alike. This event, sponsored by the Newington Lions Club in 1954, pitted Savannah's Tommy Todd against Batman, from parts unknown. Note the variety of advertisers from throughout the area.

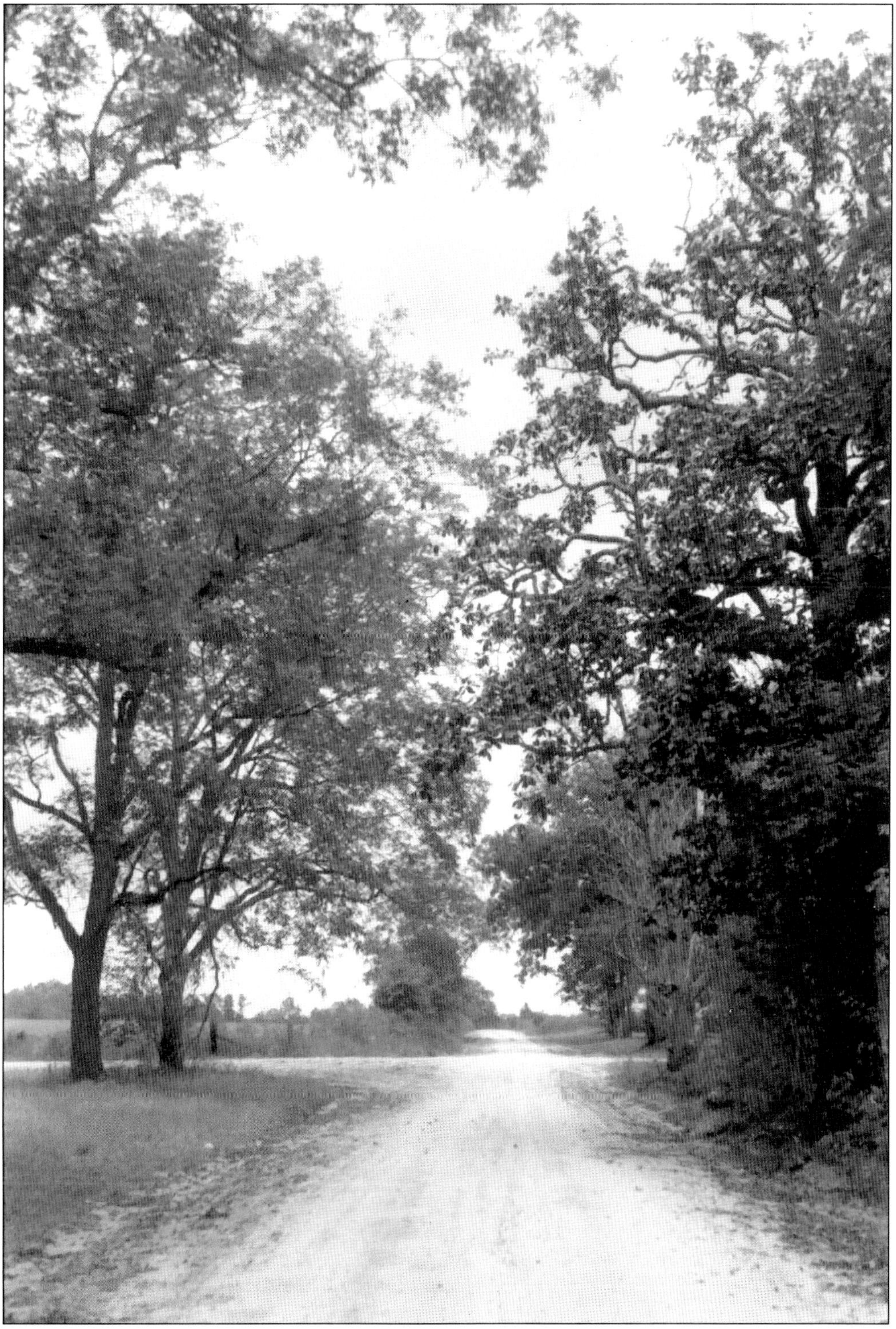

Relaxing activities like a walk down a sandy country road brought meditation, environmental appreciation, and a love of life.

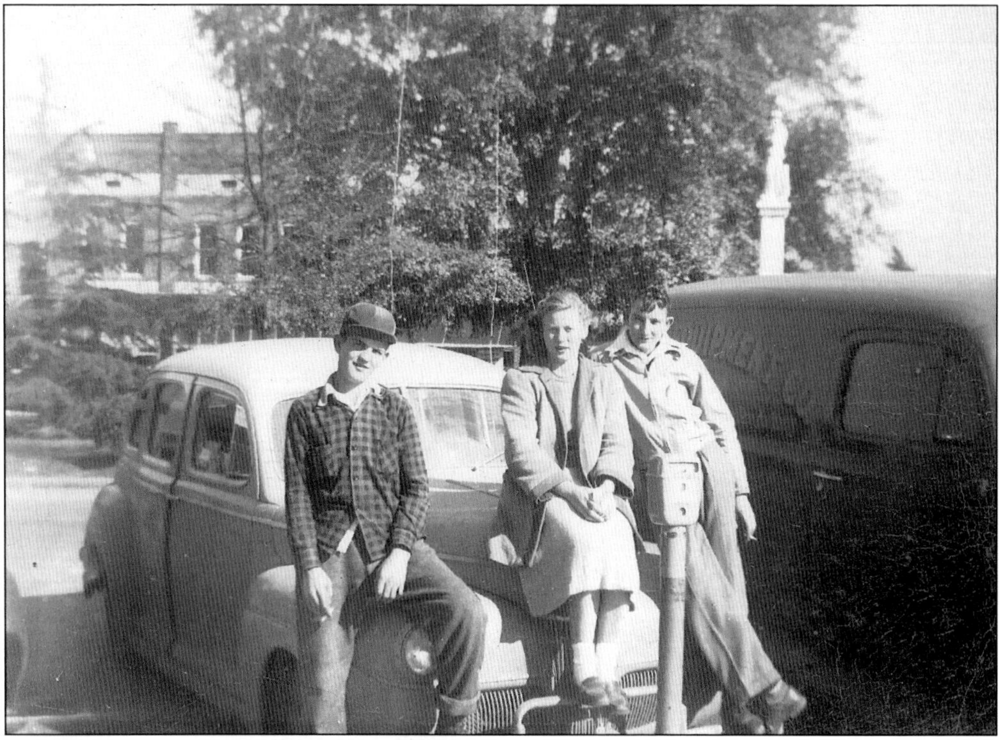

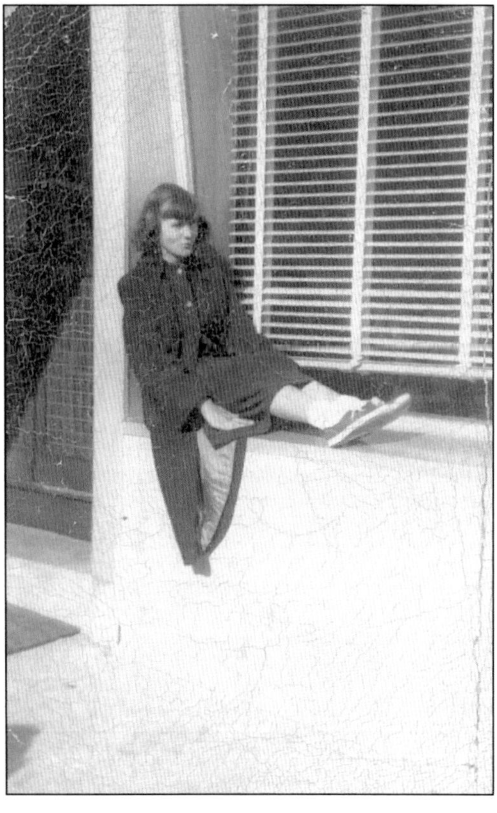

In the early 1950s, young people like Bobby Waters, Emily Bazemore, and Waylon Sheley, pictured above, gathered in downtown Sylvania (note the turn-of-the-century store buildings and the park monument in the background) to swap notes on local events and occurrences. A few years later, teenagers like Tina Bazemore, pictured at left, perched themselves in prominent places to spot the news as it happened.

Families like the children of Annie Taylor, pictured at the bottom of the facing page, continued to gather for special occasions like a mother's birthday. Pictured from left to right are as follows: (standing) daughters Minnie Taylor Bazemore, Sadie Taylor Brower, Johnnie Taylor Nunnally, and Myra Taylor Scott; (squatting) sons Albert and Sidney Taylor (on either side of Mrs. Taylor); (sitting, in front) son Archie Taylor. The infant in Mrs. Taylor's lap is her great-granddaughter, Angela Lee.

Shown on the top of the facing page, soldiers like Lester Bazemore, Bobby Waters, and Waylon Sheley, back from the military world, gathered to catch up on the news.

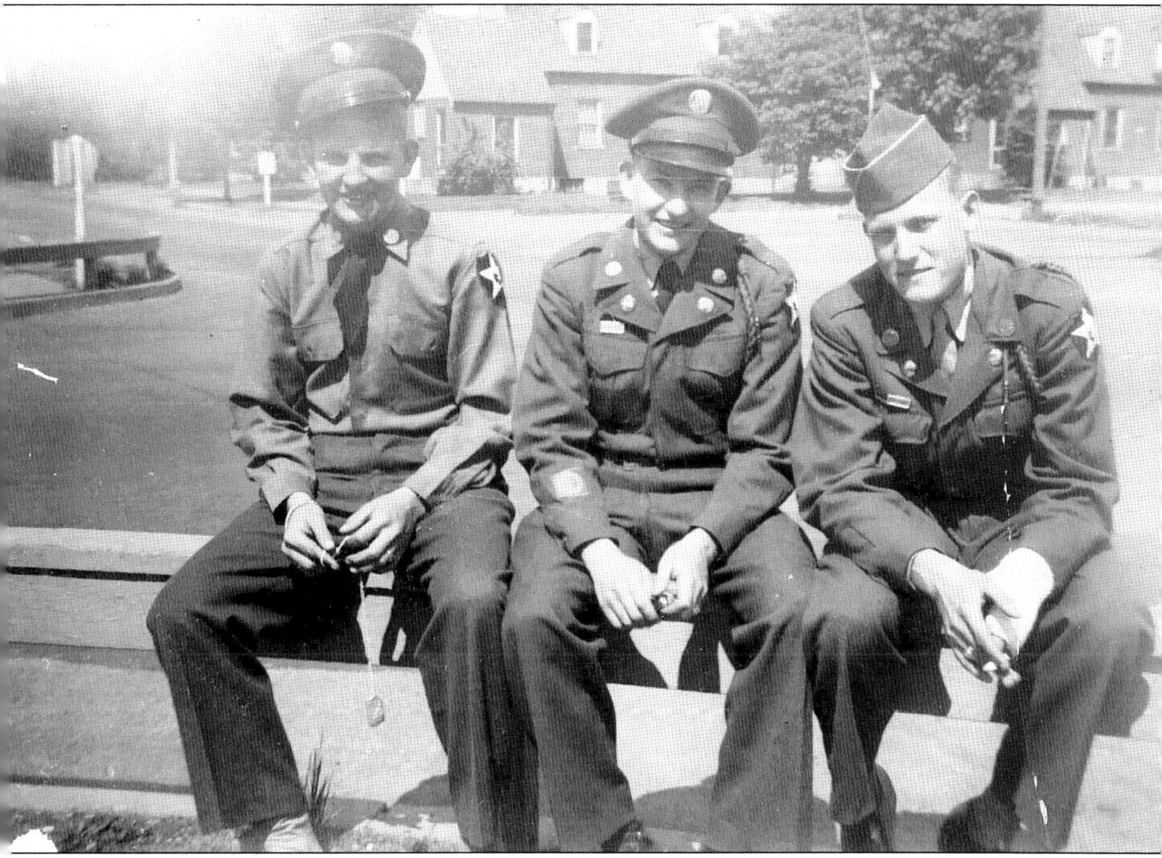

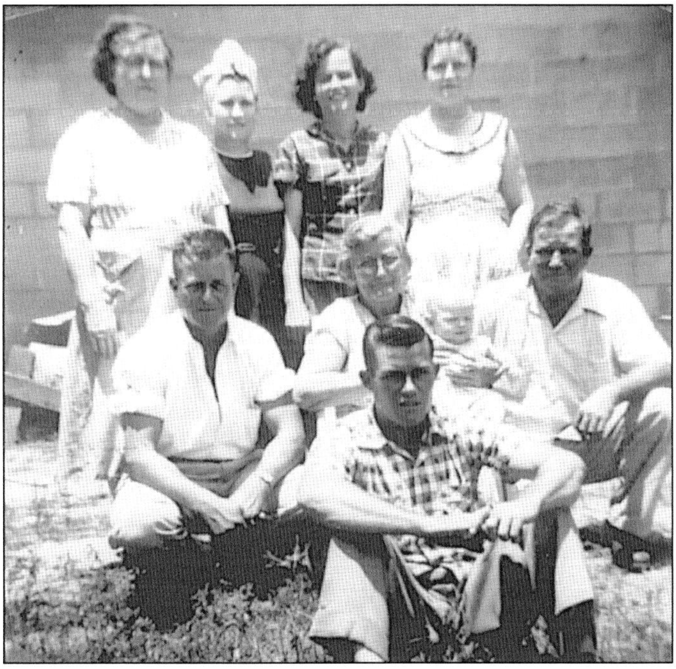

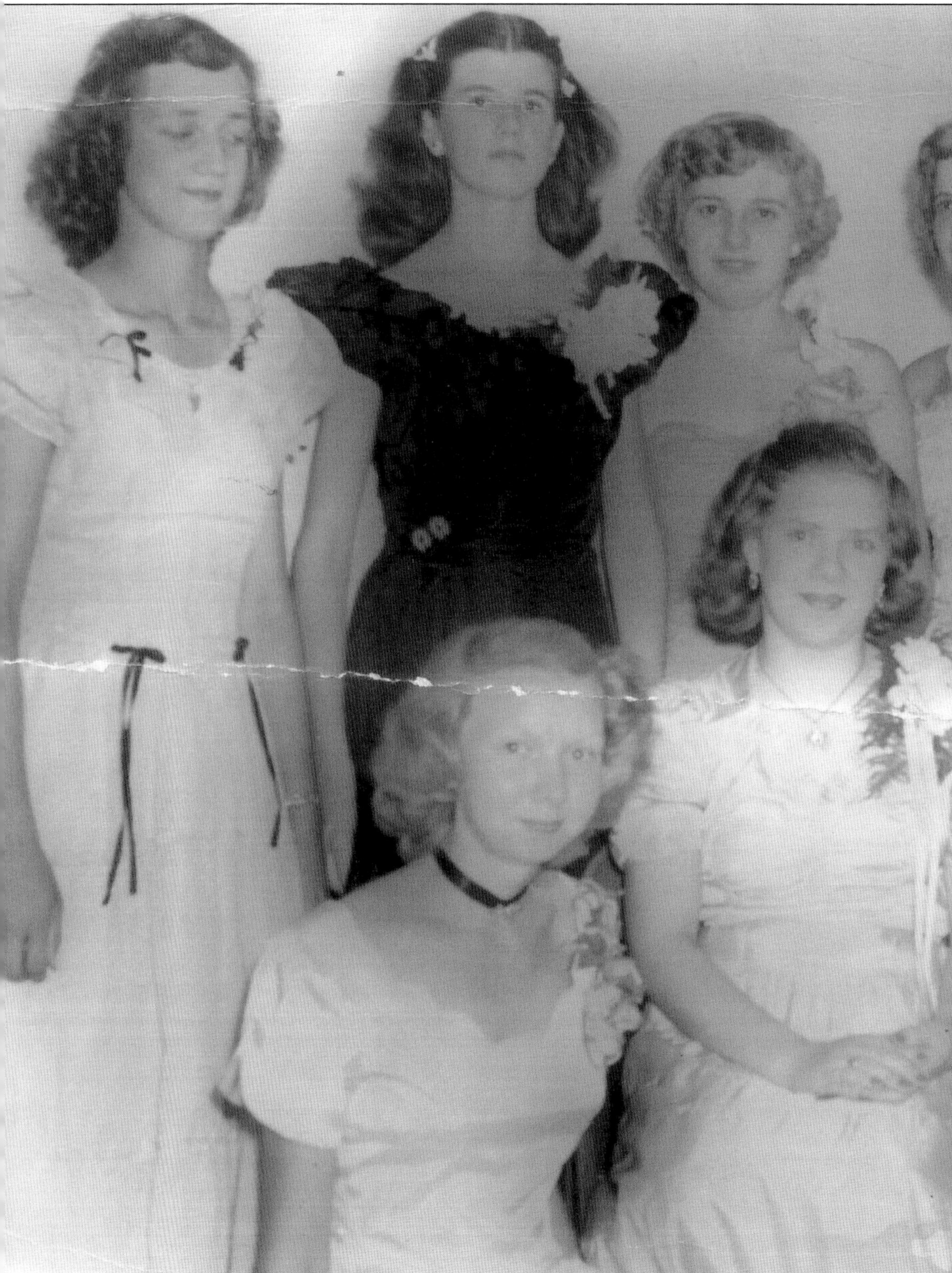

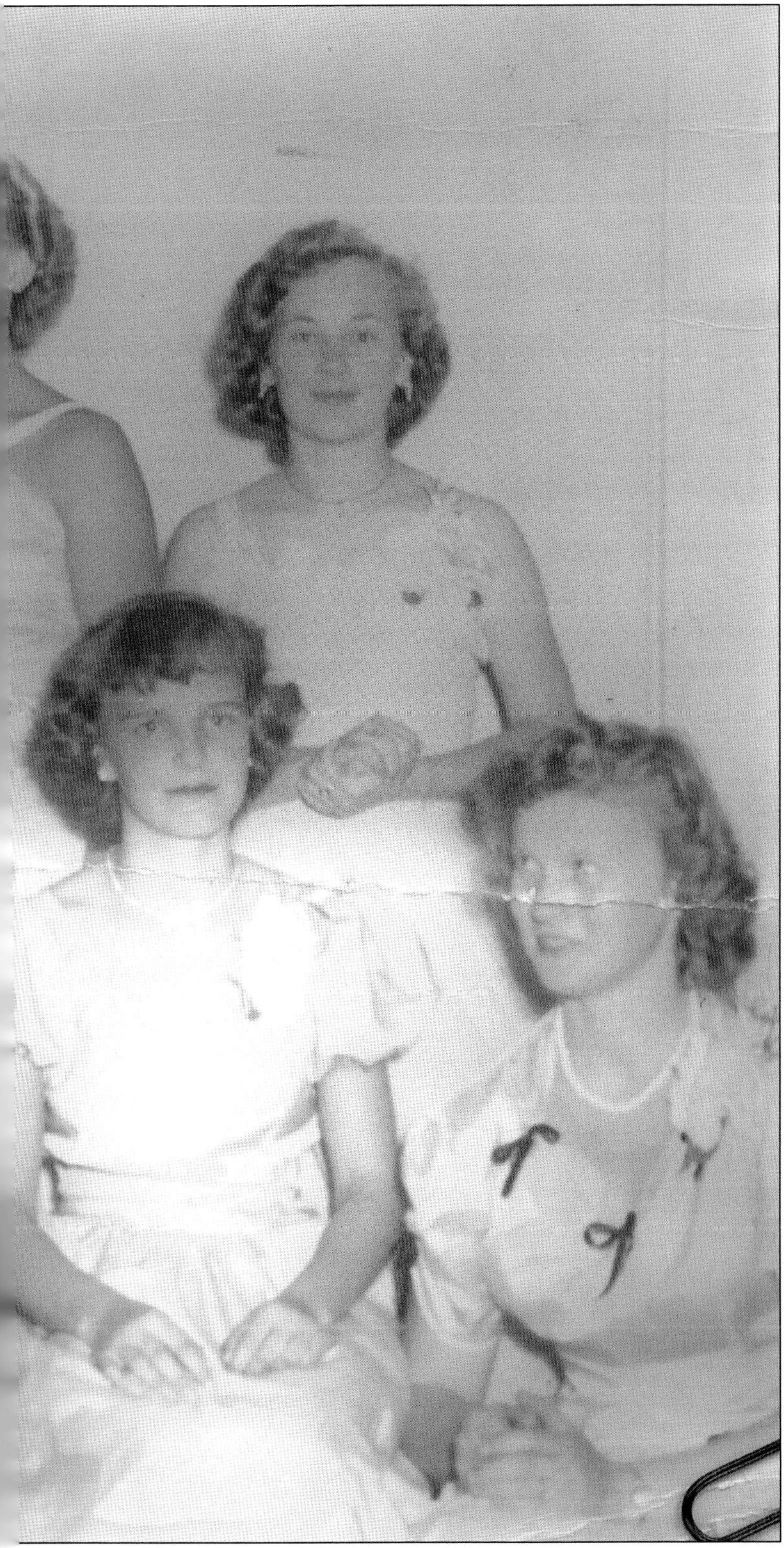

Young ladies got all gussied up for beauty pageants, like the 1948 event sponsored by the Screven County Farm Bureau. Contestants included the following, from left to right: (seated) Bessie Blakely, unknown, Margie Whitehead, and Emily Bazemore; (standing) Ophelia Reddick, Dorothy McDowell, unknown, and Jane Cochran. Who was the winner? No one can remember.

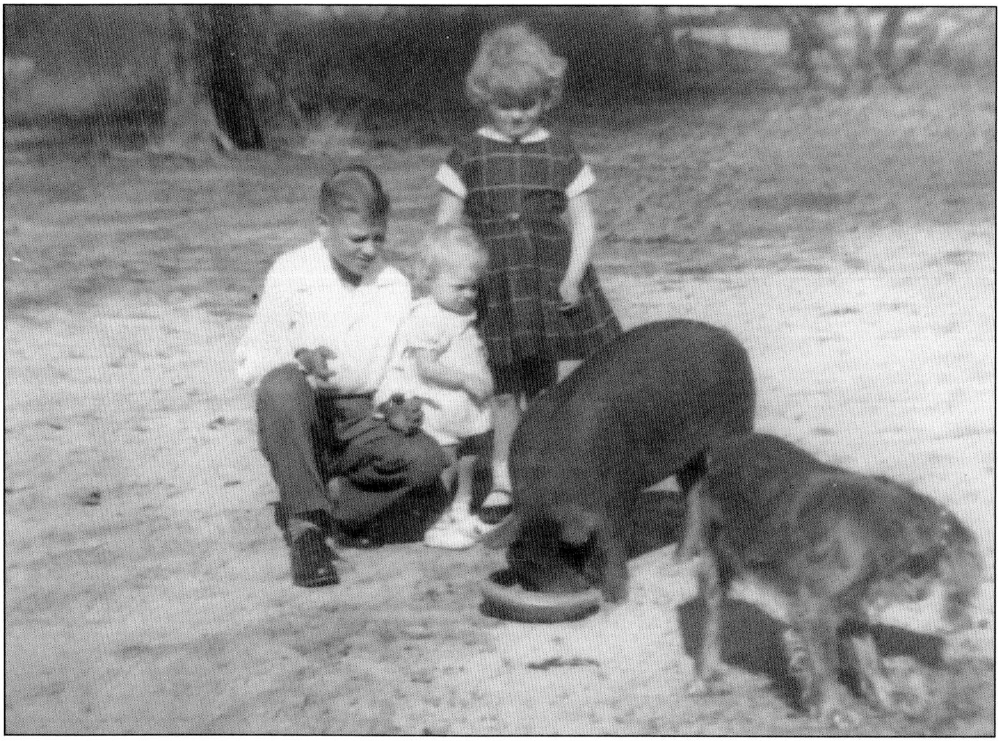

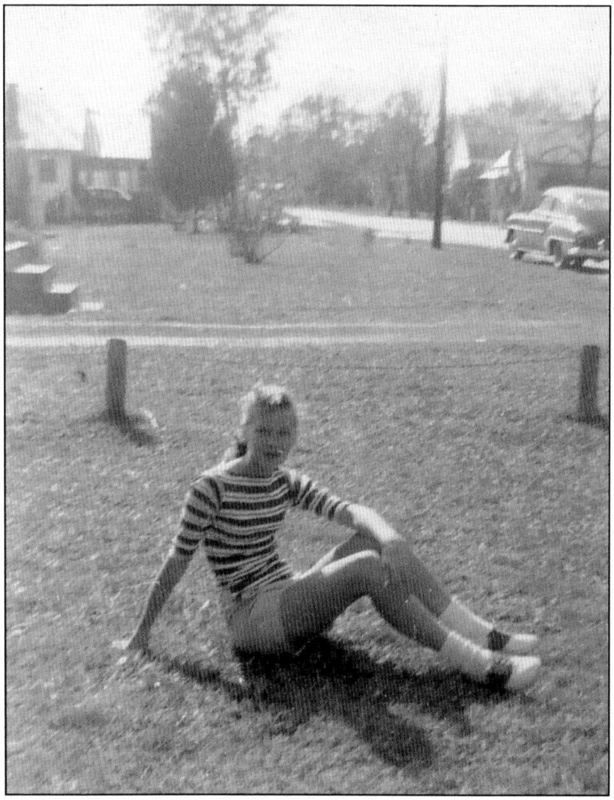

Life on the farm in the 1950s continued to be as exciting as ever. Animals needed food on a regular basis, and youngsters needed to learn some responsibility. Pets were part of the scenery—usually a dog, sometimes a pig, and, every now and then, one of each. In the photo above, Charles Lee, Angela Lee, and Wanda Evans, all of Rocky Ford, are in training. At left, Anne Simmons, of Rocky Ford, appears to be recovering from an unidentified training session of some kind.

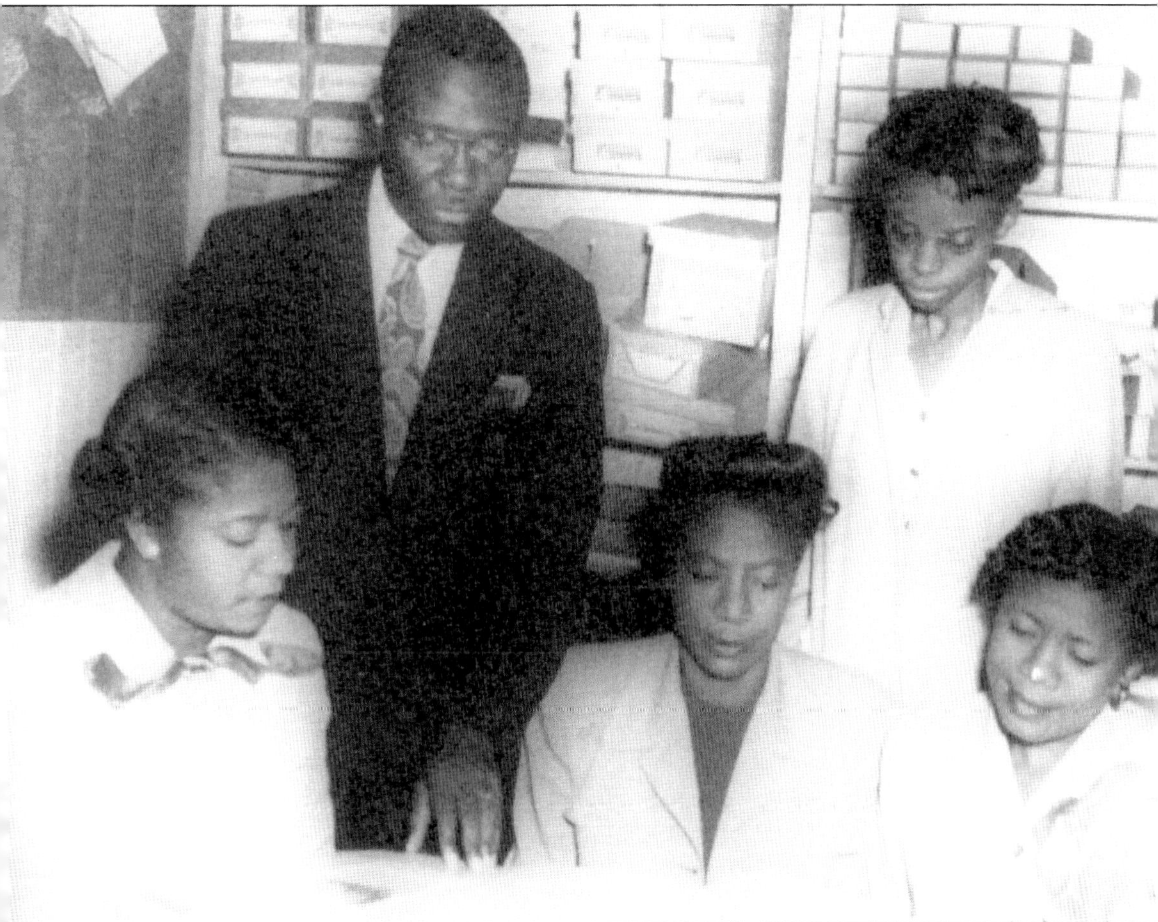

Also in the 1950s, Screven County's African-American citizens stepped prominently into the community improvement arena. One of the several committees they formed, pictured above, was responsible for numerous beneficial projects in the area. Committee members included the following, from left to right: (seated) Callie M. Lewis, Janie B. Mungin, and Eloise Flaff; (standing) J.T. Lacy and Essie Simmons.

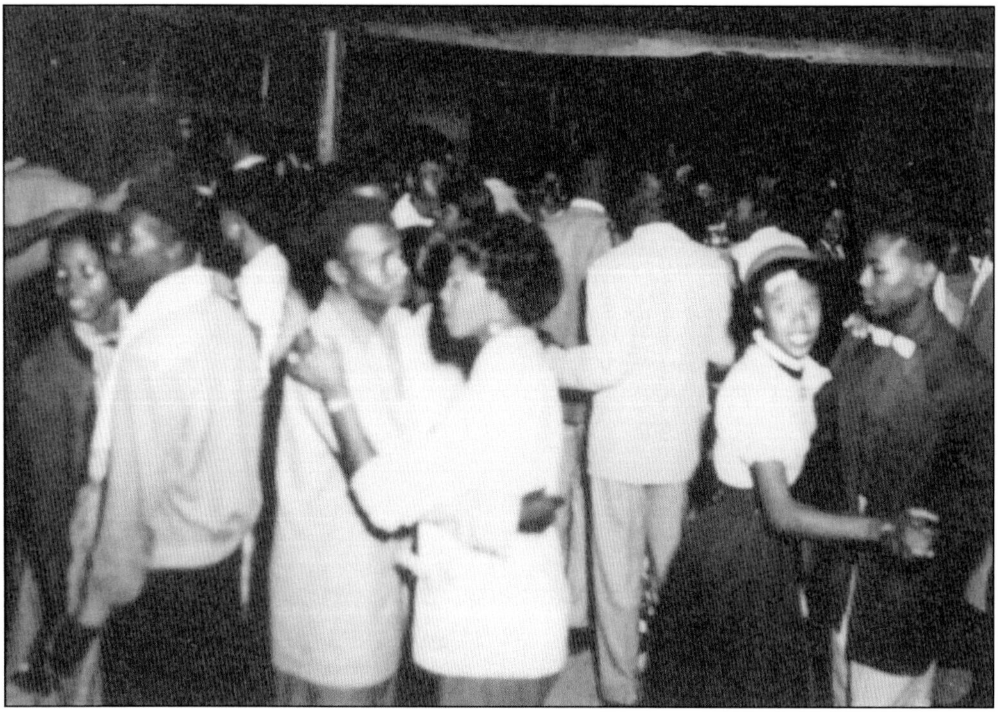

The 1950s saw Screven County's young people enjoying themselves thoroughly at dances and other community-sponsored events. Above, youngsters learns something about the finer points of square dancing. Below, another group gets serious about having a little fun at a weekly dance session.

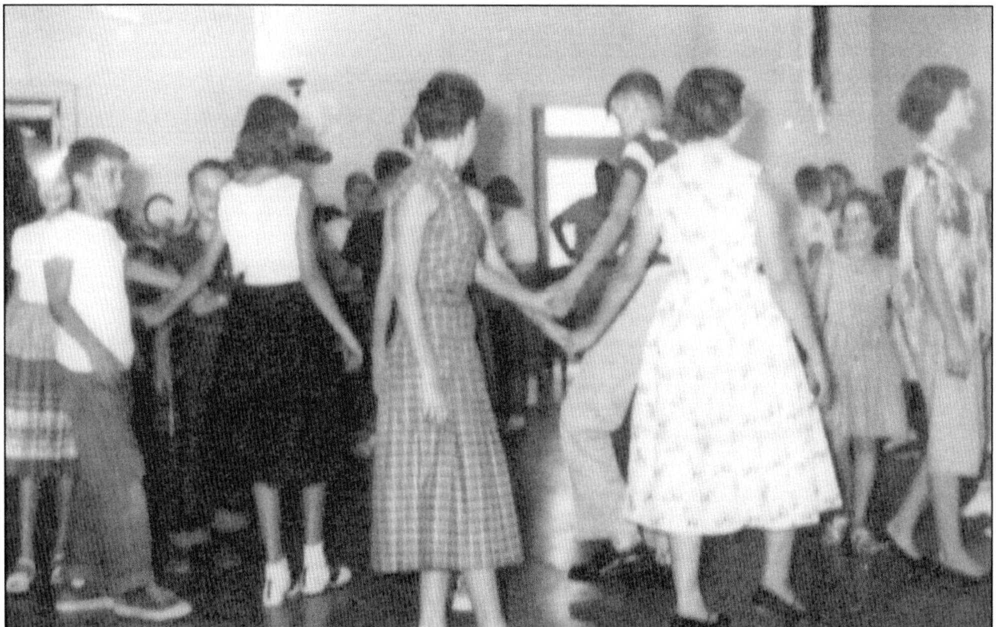

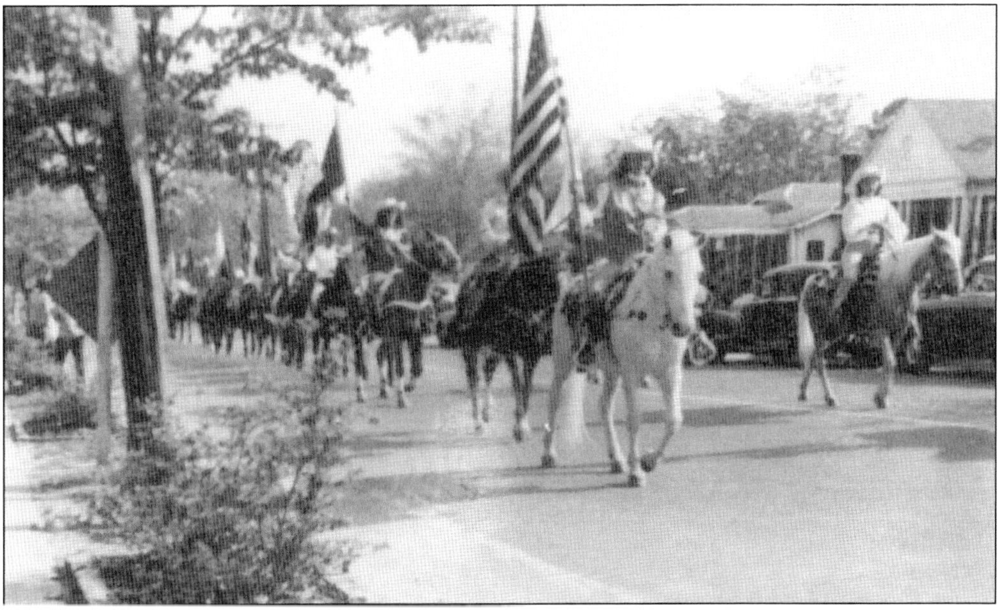

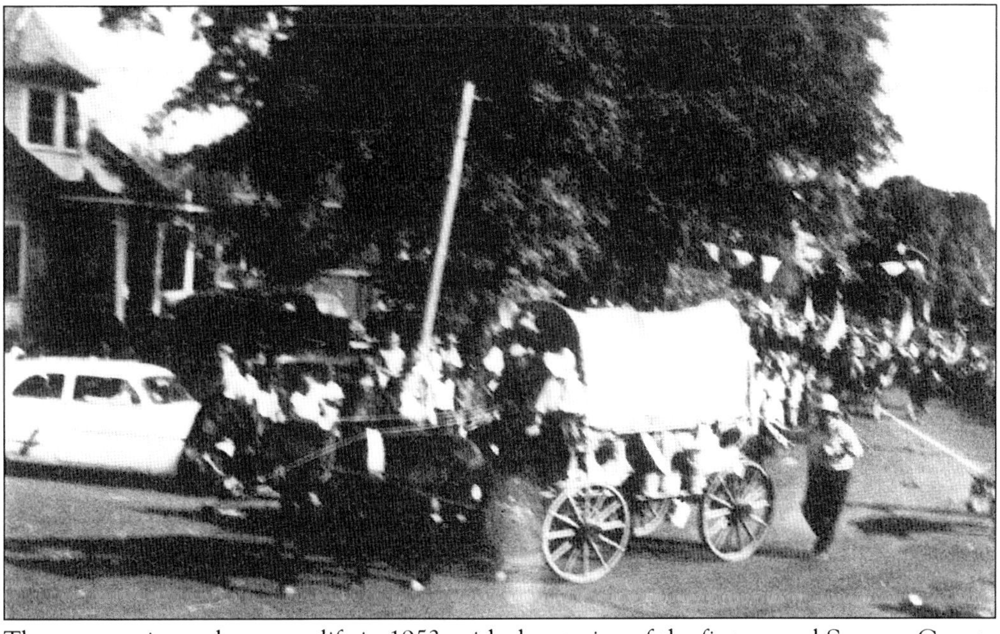

The community took on new life in 1953, with the staging of the first annual Screven County Livestock Festival. The day-long event featured steer and hog shows, a parade, a rodeo, and plenty of county-wide fellowship.

Reigning over the festivities was the county's first livestock queen, Miss Jerry Gentrie. Sammie Doyle showed the grand champion steer. Linda Anderson was the owner of the grand champion market hog.

The event was sponsored by the Screven County Livestock Association, with C.L. Miller as its president. The festival grew out of the association's annual cattle and hog shows, which dated back to 1935. The association succeeded the former Screven County Livestock Association, established around 1919, with John C. Hollingsworth as president.

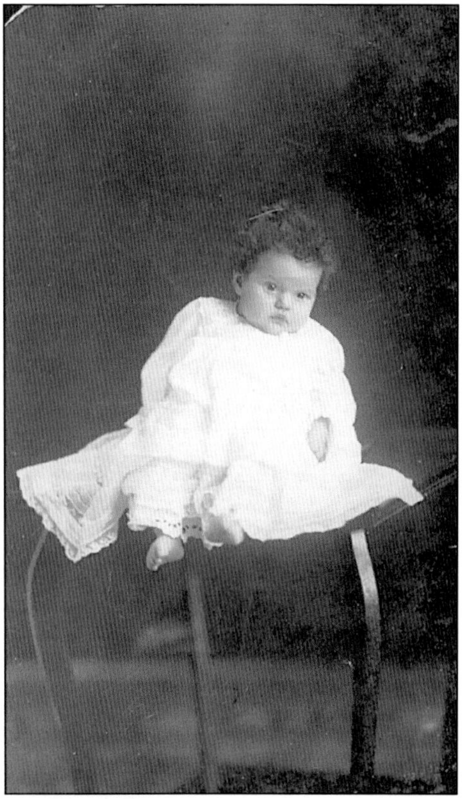

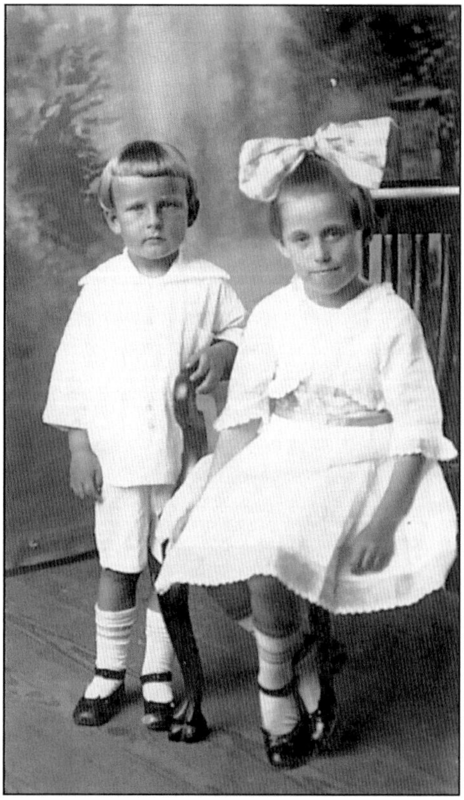

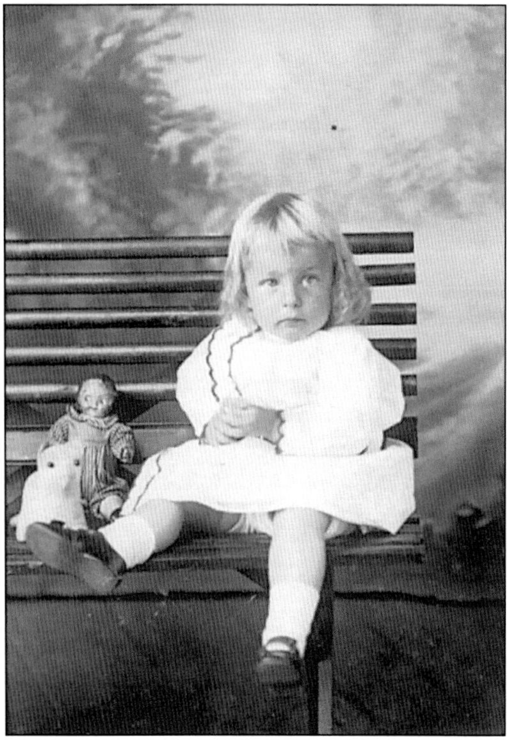

Children were the hope for the future, and they were coddled and guided and disciplined accordingly. Baby boys wore fancy dresses. Little boys in short pants posed distinctively for the camera alongside big sisters, who wore gigantic bows in their hair. And as long as a little girl had her dolly, she and the world were safe for another day.

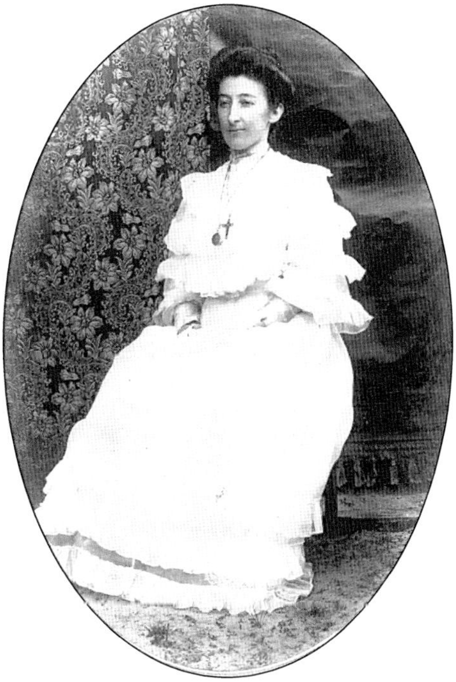

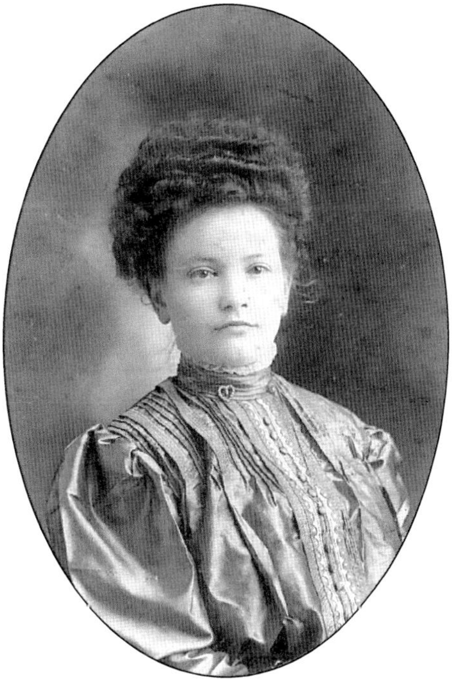

A woman's life was less than easy, with a husband to care for and children to raise and a house to maintain. Chores started at sun-up and continued until bedtime. But, somehow, she still found the time to frock up real nicely, neat dress pressed ever so carefully and hair coifed with care so that her appearance reflected her attitude in general: Yes, life is a busy affair, but one must always take time to appreciate its roses.

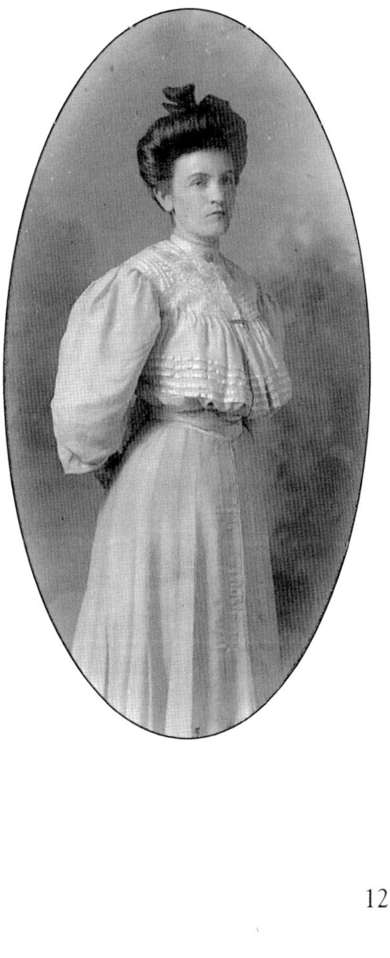

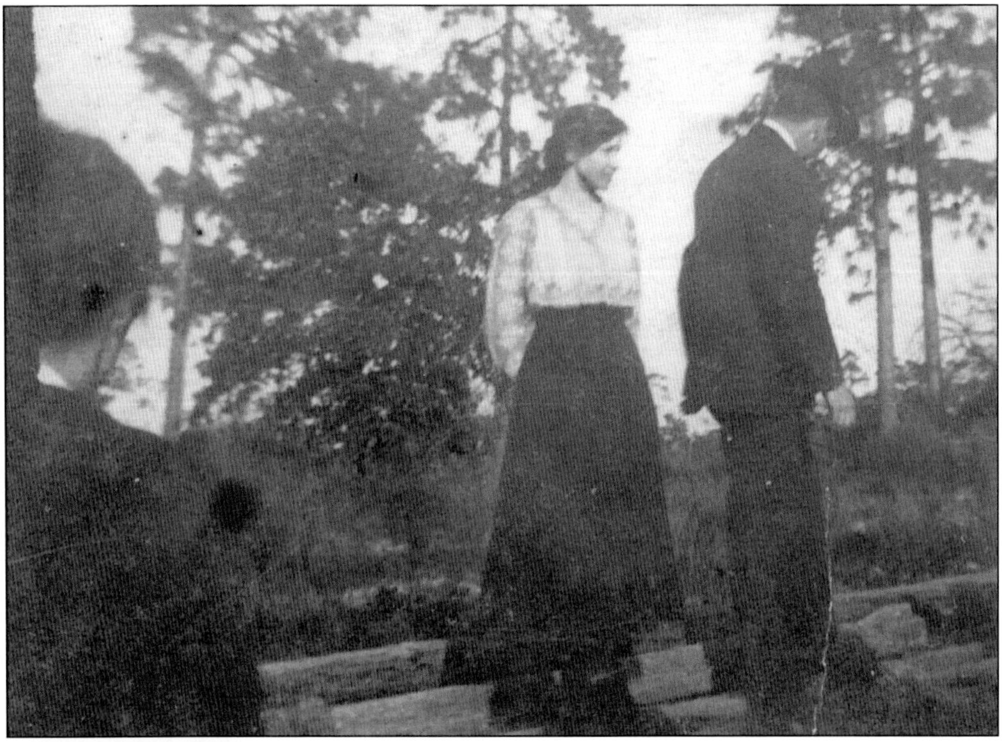

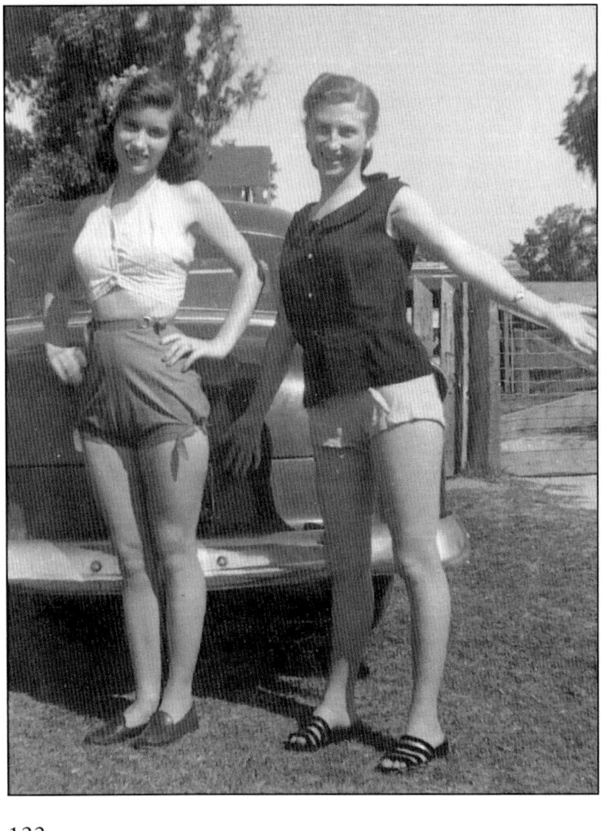

Young couples paused for heart-to-heart talks, above, and teenage girls, like the two at left, worked diligently to be all they could, and more.

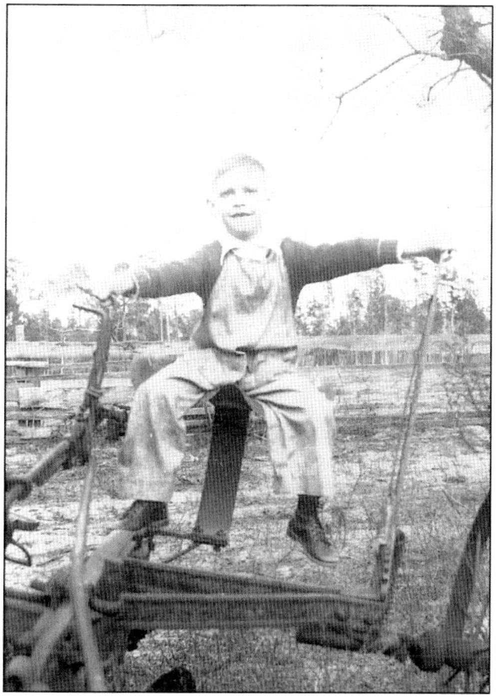

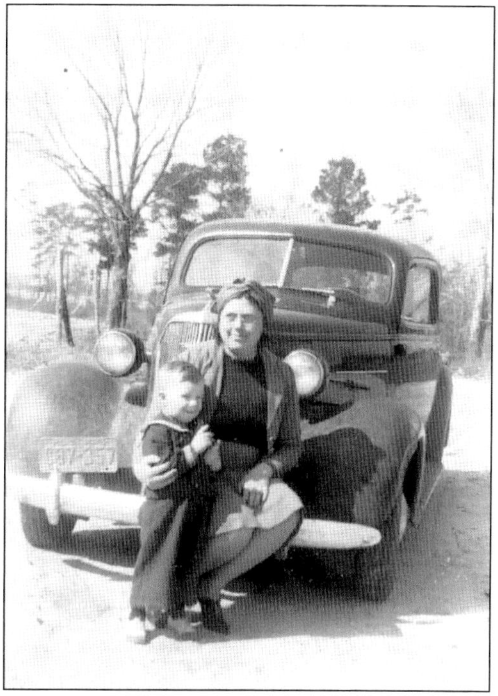

Little boys played with whatever was available (above left) and discovered the world with mother (above right). Gentlemen farmers and businessmen dressed to the nines, then went out into the world to make a living (right).

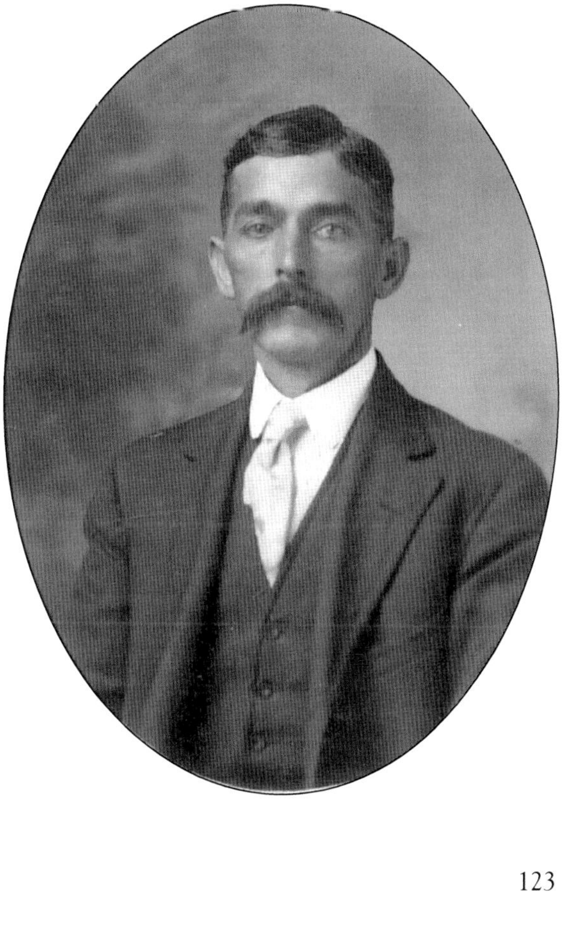

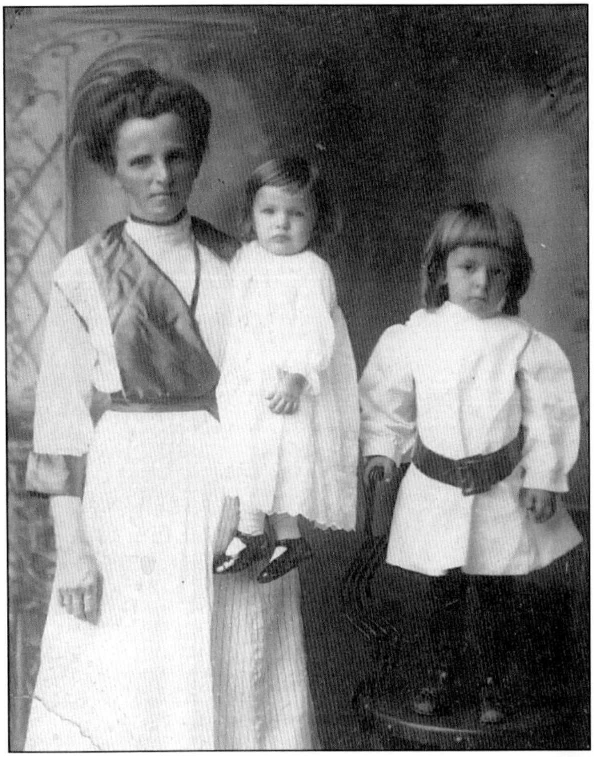

By the early 1900s, having one's picture taken was a fairly common occurrence. Screven Countians frequently traveled as far as Savannah, expressly for that purpose. As a result, a child's development could be savored more dearly from the cradle, to the schoolhouse, to manhood, and beyond. In the photos at left and on the facing page, several different stages of several different lives can be easily traced thanks to a miraculous invention called the camera. Though many, like Mary and David Burke (bottom left), seemed a little timid, they kept going back for more so that likenesses would be available to strengthen the memories.

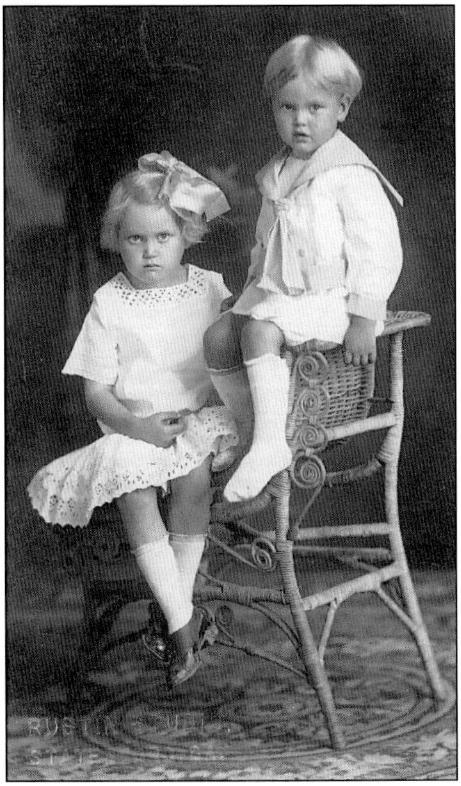

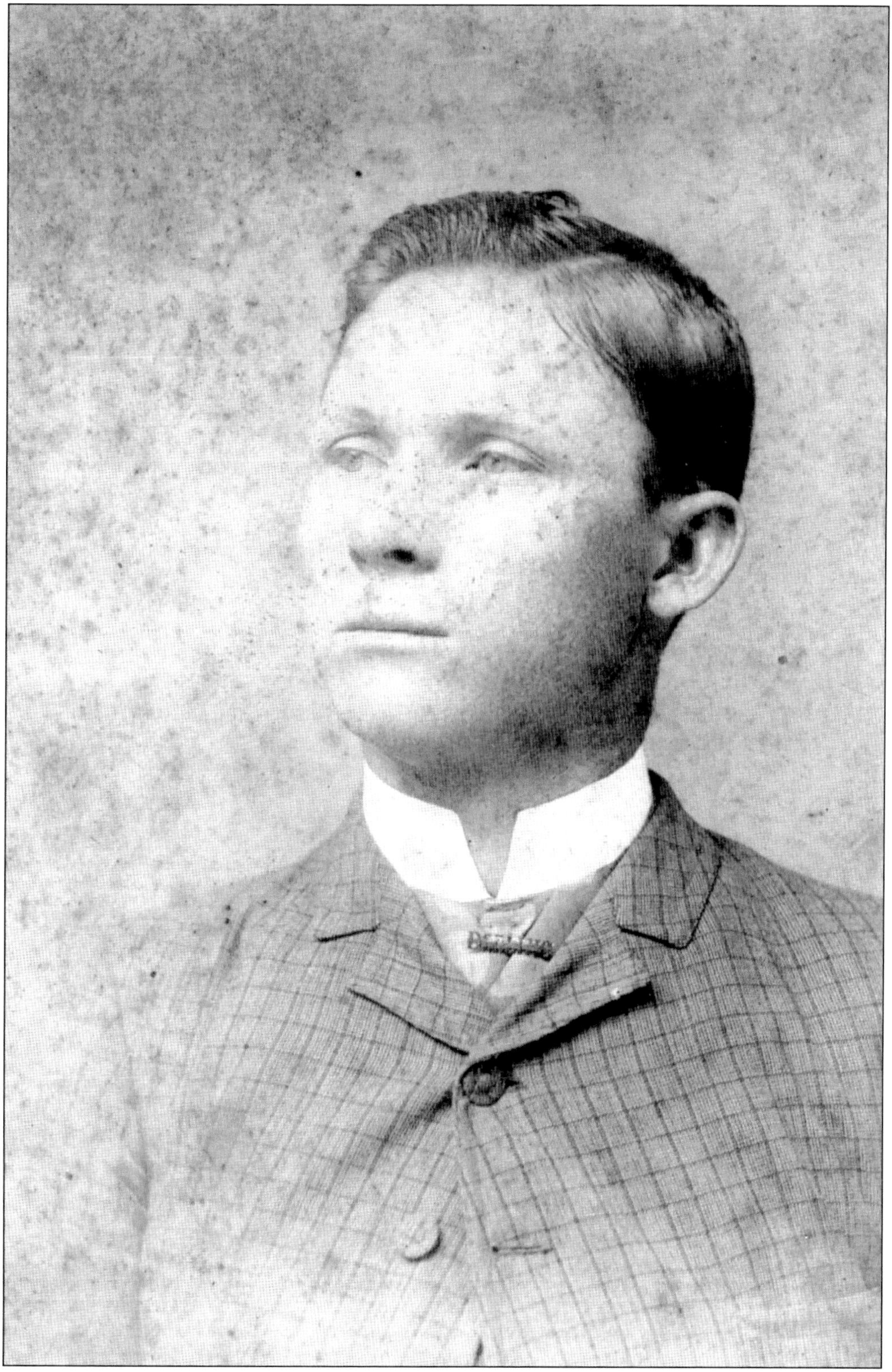

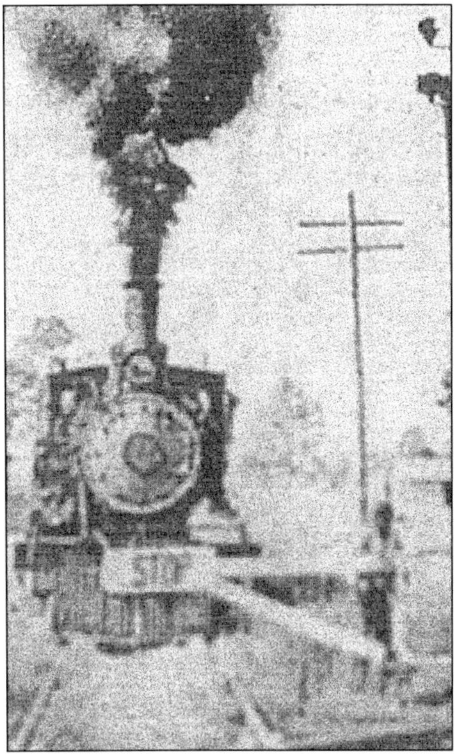

And the old locomotive continued to make tracks through Screven and Jenkins Counties. Among them was a popular train engine known as "Old Peavine," a daily traveler on the tracks between Sylvania and Rocky Ford.

"Old Peavine" was what was known as a mixed train, hauling a few freight cars and a passenger coach. You might call her a Rocky Ford resident, since that's where she generally spent her nights, on a siding not far from the depot. Mornings saw her leaving Rocky Ford at about 9 a.m., when her lonesome whistle began its intermittent wail, that was repeated every so often all the way to Sylvania. She traveled about 35 miles per hour. Her schedule was loose. She stopped here, and she stopped there. Passengers got on, and passengers got off. Freight moved on the train, and it moved off.

Less than 20 miles and several hours later, she arrived in Sylvania, always. But no one could be certain when that would happen. She got there when she got there, and that was all. But by mid-afternoon, at about 2:30 or 3 p.m., "Old Peavine" was back in action, chugging toward Rocky Ford and a good evening's rest.

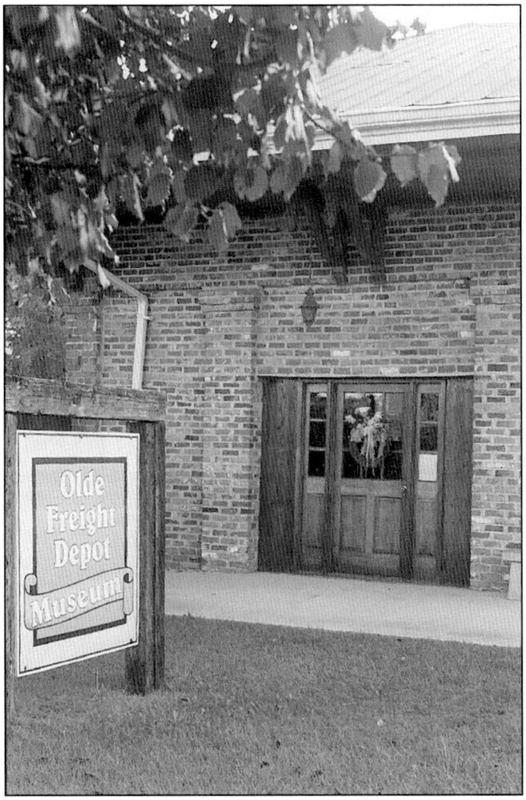

Today, there is a railroad museum where the old train depot used to be.

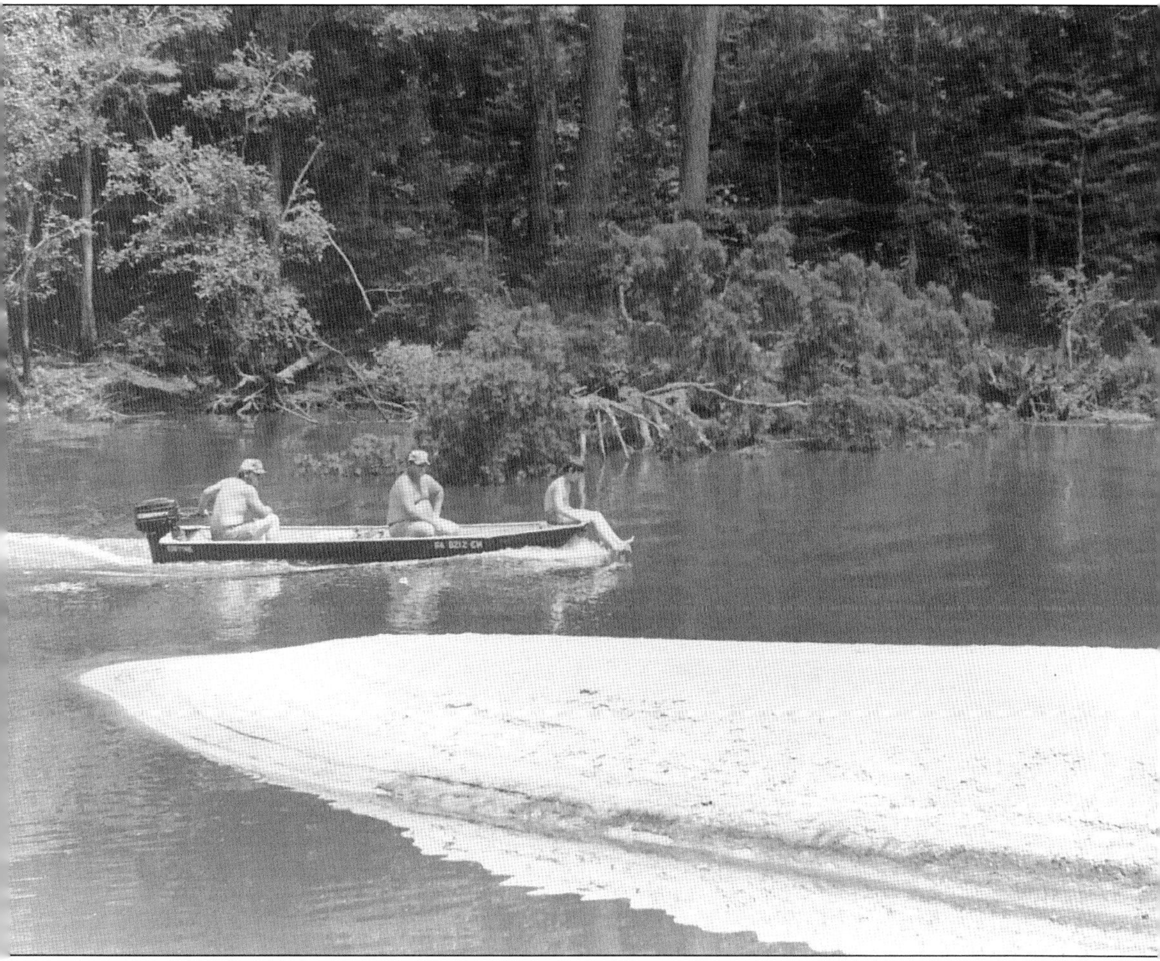

And, like the great Ogeechee, people took life as it flowed.